THE WOMEN IN SHAKESPEARE'S LIFE

THE WOMEN IN
SHAKESPEARE'S LIFE

IVOR BROWN

THE BODLEY HEAD
LONDON SYDNEY
TORONTO

To *my wife in gratitude*
for our Stratford
journeys

© Ivor Brown 1968
SBN 370 00463 9
Printed and bound in Great Britain for
The Bodley Head Ltd
9, Bow Street, London WC2
by William Clowes & Sons Ltd
London and Beccles
Set in Monotype Garamond
First published 1968

CONTENTS

❧

Shakespeare and His Women

THE STREAM of books about Shakespeare naturally reached flood-level at the quatercentenary of his birth which was celebrated in 1964. Having waited for the waters to run down I am adding another trickle. Though it is not a large one it requires some excuse since the complaint that everything on this subject has been said before seems reasonable and must be met.

I can claim no discovery. I have none of the specialist's qualifications or the unquenchable energy needed for documentary research. To delve into the records of royal households and minor legal proceedings of the Shakespearian epoch is a task demanding the industry of the weevil and ability to read the illegible. The investigator must have peculiar gifts and unwearying application. Dr Hotson has made this his life-work and turned up treasure with the acumen which tells him where to look and with devoted application to the digging. While I use the fruits of the labourer without joining in the spade-work among the great store of rolls and records decipherable only by a few, I express my gratitude to and admiration for the zealots of research named at the end of this book.

The commentaries on every aspect of Shakespeare's knowledge, attainments, opinions, vocabulary, and imagery are countless and it would be absurd to add to them. But there is one side of his career which seems to me to be inadequately covered in the academic studies and biographies. I refer to the working conditions and the personal life of a man deeply engaged in the administration and finance of his theatrical company while brilliantly serving it as a playwright and constantly as a player. On that subject I put forward some ideas in my book 'How Shakespeare Spent the Day' which drifted in with the quatercentenary flood.

There remains the private life of the public figure and to that I now turn.

About Shakespeare as 'passion's slave' there have been abundant theories in the editions of the Sonnets. The efforts to illumine the mystery of the Dark Lady cannot be left out of a book which carries the title which I have chosen. But there is much more to be said of the women to whom he returned, once a year according to tradition, and with whom he ended his days. He was a lover, a husband and a father; it can hardly be thought that when engrossed in his theatrical work he forgot that he had a family. He was in fact soon earning enough to house them in style and to invest for their future. They were certainly not forgotten. He had a son who died in boyhood. He had two daughters who, like his wife, survived him. They married during his lifetime two quite different types of man, one eminent and respectable and the other proving to be no credit to his father-in-law who took pride in the status of a gentleman. During some hectic years in London he had a deep affection for a patron and a devastating involvement with a woman. But he ended, as he had begun, as a family man.

The separate facts of Shakespeare's domesticity appear sporadically in the biographies, but they have rarely been assembled to present a family portrait. This seems to me a task worth attempting. Conjecture there must be since the documentary data are few. But there is much ascertainable fact about the Stratford families of whom the Shakespeares were one. The Warwickshire life has always been treated as that of a masculine society. Much has been written about the Grammar Schools and the education of the boys. The old idea, which some who should have known better supported, was of a barbarous town whose councillors kept the accounts without being able to count, went to law without being able to spell out an indictment, and put their mark on documents which only the town clerk could read. This picture of an oafish borough has now been effectively discredited. Yet there is still a silence about the wives and daughters of the tradesmen, so often litigants, and of the local law-givers. Almost total feminine illiteracy has been assumed and there are grounds for challenging that.

The position of women in Shakespeare's epoch has been considered by few of those who have written about the age. That is strange since women readers are at least as numerous as men. Elizabethan women had no votes and did not dream of having them. That does not mean that they had no voice. To be an alderman's wife, as was Shakespeare's mother, was not to have no influence. I have found sufficient evidence that the daughters of the middle class had their schooling, less indeed than that of the boys, but enough to provide a literate grounding. Shakespeare himself has made it plain that a shepherdess could be an eager customer when printed ballads were on sale.

He was doubly a citizen, paying (or tardy in paying) his rates in the capital as well as in the country town. I have found the status of women in London as fascinating as it is in Stratford. Shakespeare's England was a queendom with its powerful Gloriana at the summit of power. Round the unique Queen Bess were a number of queen bees. They had learning as well as wealth and influence. Their feminine monarch had received an education of astonishing scope and intensity in languages, in the arts, and in what sciences there were. Not the senior scholar of Somerville or Girton in our time had received wider or better equipped instruction.

The daughters of the great houses shared the tutors carefully picked from the universities to teach their sons. Some of them became the Tudor Paragons with enough Greek and Latin to satisfy the requirements even of Ben Jonson. They befriended and assisted the poets. Denied appearance on the professional stage the ladies of the court mimed and danced in the sumptuous masques for which the leading poets wrote the texts and the leading artists, notably in Jacobean times Inigo Jones, designed the elaborate and often exquisite décor. Shakespeare knew that swarming-ground of ambitious, cultured, elegant and fashionable ladies. It is extremely likely that he was the guest at Wilton of the Countess of Pembroke, that gifted and well-graced hostess to whom so many dedications were deservedly made in response to her discerning patronage.

In Shakespeare's London women of all classes enjoyed a

freedom which greatly surprised foreign visitors. They went to the plays and were important members of the paying public whose favour he won and kept. They drank in the taverns and beer-gardens. They were not officially in the political world dominated by their queen but who will suppose that their bright eyes had no power to urge a policy?

Shakespeare and his company were particularly favoured by Queen Elizabeth and her successor. As a Groom of the Bed-chamber to King James he was on the fringe of court life and none had a keener vision for the comedy as well as the tragedies of the hazardous careers at Whitehall and of the part that women played in them. Even the fashions and fripperies of feminine London were immediately under his eye since for some years he lodged with a maker of the jewelled head-dresses called tires, a leader in his craft with whom King James's gay Danish Queen Anne ran large bills to be paid later.

He came back to his family; he had lost his son and his fatherly interest had to be centred on the daughters. Some think that they gave him models for the charming young women of his later romantic comedies. One thing they could not do was to give him what, as his will indicates, he most desired, a grandson. In his life-time he had one grand-daughter by Mistress Susanna Hall. She was her only child. He did not live to see Judith Quiney's sons and was spared mourning for their death. He must have been contented enough with the company of his elderly wife since he stayed in Stratford when he might have gone back to join the King's Men in London.

This book has not been written for Shakespearian specialists who may deem all the facts familiar and some of the suppositions fanciful. I have had in mind those who feel so much fascinated by Shakespeare as to create a constant public for his plays and to make the journey to Stratford where the theatre is packed from April to November and there is continual visitation of the 'Shake-speare Properties' so well looked after by the Shakespeare Birthplace Trust. In the year ending March 31, 1967 the atten-dances in the small Midland town were

Shakespeare's birthplace   302,033

Anne Hathaway's cottage   222,572
New Place Museum   46,836
Mary Arden's house   36,780
Hall's Croft   35,239

Many also go to the parish church.

Theatrical audiences in Britain usually contain a majority of women and it is likely that there is a similar proportion among the Avonside tourists. When they have ceased to be Shakespearian conscripts in the schools women may read Shakespeare less than men do. But their voluntary playhouse attendance and their sight-seeing show them to be 'under the influence'. As they pass through the homes where Shakespeare's mother, wife, and daughters suffered the then unrelieved pains and enjoyed the pride of motherhood do they wonder what sort of lives these women led and what were their feelings as their William went and came back, soon with money in hand, from his mysterious triumphs in London? For the tourists and playgoers who are not content to be doing a cultural drill and whose curiosity and imagination are stirred by the personality and affections of one who was a mortal family man as well as the Immortal Bard I hope this book may be of use. Since it is intended for the general public I have not loaded the text with notes in small print and numbers leading to a mass of items at the end. These are necessary in academic studies but they do not make for easy reading. They would not be helpful to those without special facilities since some of the volumes mentioned are old and rare and others are unlikely to be on the bookshelves of a normal home. Frequent detailed reference to their pages would cause more distraction than assistance. Their authors I have named and thanked. So let us go in search of Shakespeare's women in Warwickshire first and in London later.

CHAPTER I

The Mother

THE MOTHERS of illustrious sons are often figures hardly discernible through the curtain of the years. Among those thus obscured is Mary Arden, who married John Shakespeare and had a third child named William. Of her family and its background a fair amount is known; of the family which she bore there is little information except in the case of the boy who became world-famous. She helped in the creation of a genius and lived to see him take a gambler's chance with his career and win beyond all expectation. Her man was much away but returned. After a long life she died a widow in her husband's home. There is no grave-stone epitaph to praise her qualities. Such tributes are of a routine kind but, if over-statement of virtues is allowed for, we may get from them some understanding of a character. Nothing that was said of her remains even in the form of anecdote.

Because everything about Shakespeare is fascinating the indulgence of some speculation about his mother is irresistible. The face cannot be visualised. The Elizabethans who were below the rank of grandee could not afford the portrait-painters who were so constantly employed at and around the royal court. If we try to fashion our own picture, we cannot get beyond the likeness of a hard-worked, faithful, and often-bereaved wife; a well-bred, well-conducted lady of the gentleman-farmer class with some relations rather above that position. The word lady is chosen with a purpose. The Ardens had for a long time been somebodies. The Shakespeares were not to be regarded as nobodies, and they were eager to make that known. But during most of Mary Arden's lifetime they had to work their way up. This her John managed to do in his country town while his son was reaching a different kind of summit in London before he came back to be a gentleman of Stratford.

The dates of Mary's birth and marriage are uncertain. The year of her wedding can be roughly guessed from an entry in the register of Stratford's parish church. On September 15, 1558, there was christened 'Jone, daughter to John Shakspere'. If Jone's mother wedded at twenty or thereabouts she lived to be seventy or more, since on September 9, 1608, there was recorded the burial of 'Mayry Shakspere, wydowe'. For over a decade she had known that her eldest son was a man of renown in London and of means in Stratford. He had bought the best house in the town, where his wife and children were established in comfort. It was a large home with plenty of room into which she could move after the death of her husband, whose burial had been recorded in the parish register on September 8, 1601, 'B. Mr. Johannis Shakspeare'.

She chose to stay on at his home and business premises in Henley Street instead of going down the road to 'the grete house' of New Place. She was not risking strained relations with her daughter-in-law, pleasant though it would have been to watch her two grand-daughters growing up in their new and spacious surroundings. If we are justified in making any surmise about her personality the possession of tact and good sense is a fair conjecture.

If she had married beneath her in the reckoning of Warwick-shire's rural society the ranking had been levelled in 1596. A coat of arms and title of Gentleman had been applied for by John Shakespeare nearly twenty years earlier. The religious and financial troubles in which he then became involved will be explained later. It is enough to say here that he withdrew his claim for the time being. It was pressed again after nineteen years and was successful. His plea was then backed by the list of offices which he had held, justice of the peace, bailiff and mayor, and 'queen's chief officer of the town'. Also urged on his behalf was his compliance with other conditions necessary for an application. He must be able to employ servants and own land and property to the value of five hundred pounds. Another argument put forward to impress the Garter King-at-Arms was that he had married 'the daughter and heir of Arden, a gentleman of worship'. Mary was a social asset as well as a helpmate in the home.

She was not a wealthy heiress but with her modest share of her family's lands she was a good match for one who was the son of an Arden tenant. Soon after his wedding John was on his way up in his own business as a dealer and craftsman in leather goods, especially gloves; he was also assiduous in his work for the Town Council. When the honours were finally granted the Shakespeares reached the Arden level. John had reason to be proud of his climb and Mary to be well satisfied with his satisfaction.

She had borne him a balanced brood, four children of each sex. First came Jone in 1558, then Margaret in 1562. We do not know how long the former lived except that it was not long. The latter survived for only five months after her christening on December 2, 1562. William followed in April 1564. A girl was born in 1569. Since she was the second to be called Jone or Joan it is naturally supposed that the first daughter of that name was dead. The second Joan did more than survive; she lived to be seventy-nine. Eventually it was only through her marriage to William Hart, a hatter, that there were any direct descendants of John and Mary Shakespeare.

Another girl, Anne, was born in 1571 and died at eight and a half. Of her four daughters the mother had lost three before they reached the age of nine. The boys were either more hardy or more fortunate, but there was no longevity for them. Only William lived to be over fifty. Gilbert and Richard, born in 1566 and 1574, died at forty and thirty-nine. There is no record of either having married. Edmund, the youngest, followed William's example and went to London to seek a theatrical career. He was born in 1580 and died, without surviving issue, in 1607. From this it is seen that Mary was bearing children over a period of twenty-two years.

Considering her fertility it is strange and tragic that there was so little survival of this branch of the Shakespeare family. When she died a widow her grandson, Hamnet Shakespeare, had been lost at the age of eleven. She had been a mourner at many funerals

and was one 'for whom the bell tolls' with a cruel repetition. The
solemn, melancholy peals were constantly heard when and where-
ever the plague struck, as it did in Stratford four months after the
birth of William. It was a lethal epidemic. The death-rate soared
there. Between January and July 20 there were twenty-two burials;
between July 30 and the end of the year there were two hundred
and thirty-seven. Fortunately Mary could take refuge with her
baby in her family home three miles away. Had she not done so
there might have been no 'Works of William Shakespeare'.

The home was at Wilmcote, which lies to the north-west of
Stratford. It was locally known as Wincot. In her father's will it
was spelled Wyllemecote; perhaps that was preferred by a
lawyer who thought that a higher fee might be justified by a
splashing of letters on the village's name. As Wincot Shakespeare knew it and wrote of it in *The Taming of the Shrew*. 'Ask
Marian Hacket, the fat ale wife of Wincot, if she knows me not',
says Christopher Sly the bibulous tinker. That the induction to
the play sets the scene in Warwickshire is shown by Sly's statement that he is 'Old Sly's son of Burton-heath' which is some
twenty miles from Wincot. Burton had also an Arden connection.
Mary's brother-in-law, Edmund Lambert, to whom some of
her property was mortgaged by John with her consent in 1578,
lived there. The Ardens had deep and wide roots in this part of
the Midlands. If any boasted that their ancestors had come over
with the Conqueror they could reply that they were before him
and had also done some conquering since they managed to retain
their land when many others were being robbed of it.

The family name was originally a Saxon one, Turchill, and
this had to be changed. G. K. Chesterton in his admirable poem
'The Secret People', a potted history of the English commoners,
wrote:

> *The fine French kings came over with a flutter of flags and dames,*
> *We liked their smiles and battles, but we never could say their*
> *names.*

The Turchills did not pretend to be Normans. One of them took
the title of the adjacent forest, as did Mary's son when he chose a

timbered setting for a comedy of French-sounding gentry, the
sons of Sir Rowland de Boys, and of extremely English yokels. It
was a happy choice, simple, easy, and pleasing. Mary Arden's
name comes naturally to the ear as the mother of a poet who could
paint a woodland scene with his matchless sense of words and
music. There is no reason to be sentimental about the Arden
county and climate. Shakespeare was never that. The banished
Duke in *As You Like It* was as ready to deplore winter, rough
weather, and the icy fang of the wind as he was to draw sermons
out of stones in the way of an emotional pantheist.

It is possible to be as cold on the banks of the Avon and on the
slopes around even in 'proud-pied April' as anywhere else in
the southern half of England. As the author of *As You Like It*
knew by experience, Arden could be gaunt as well as gay in the
changing seasons. An exquisitely directed production of that play
by Glen Byam Shaw at the Shakespeare Memorial (now Royal
Shakespeare) Theatre in 1952 has glittered in my memory
because the settings began so rightly without the greenwood look.
The trees were naked in the freezing wind until the action moved
on to the sunlit greenery proper to the cluster of courtships and
somewhat incredible weddings of the finish. Shakespeare had
something shiversome to say of the forest before he bestowed
upon two of his 'little eyases' that most charming of spring songs
for boyish trebles, 'It was a lover and a lass'. I do not visualise
Mary Arden, however equable by nature, going about her work
with 'a hey and a ho and hey nonino' when frost was biting the
Wilmcote fields and an icy fog cloaked the view over her father's
lands which, though she was the youngest daughter, she was soon
to inherit.

My fancy is that Shakespeare was thinking of his mother's
home when he wrote the lyric, superb in its simplicity, which is
the cadenza of *Love's Labour's Lost*, a play which is set in France
and is often as English as bacon and eggs for breakfast. Sings the
actor or boy-player who is Winter:

> *When icicles hang by the wall,*
> *And Dick the shepherd blows his nail,*

And Tom bears logs into the hall,
And milk comes frozen home in pail,
When blood is nipt and ways be foul,
Then nightly sings the staring owl,
> *Tu-whit;*
Tu-who, a merry note,
While greasy Joan doth keel the pot.

When all aloud the wind doth blow,
And coughing drowns the parson's saw,
And birds sit brooding in the snow,
And Marian's nose looks red and raw,
When roasted crabs hiss in the bowl,
Then nightly sings the staring owl,
> *Tu-whit;*
Tu-who, a merry note,
While greasy Joan doth keel the pot.

Whenever I am reading or hearing these lines again they always create a picture for me of the poet's young experience. I see not a park in Navarre but a steading near Stratford. It is not wildly imaginative to suppose that Shakespeare is recollecting a boyhood Sunday at his mother's home. He has been dragged off to Wilmcote's old parish church of Aston Cantlow for a cold, wheezy, and catarrhal session with a sermon scarcely audible if it were worth any attention at all. At breakfast maid Marian's face had displayed 'the roseate hues of early dawn'. She started the shiversome day by coaxing with chapped hands some warmth out of Tom's logs. The more fortunate Joan had a blaze in which to perspire before and after mid-day dinner as she skimmed a stew or scoured the pots. (The meaning of keel is uncertain.) The vision created is that of a fair-sized farmhouse with a hall and a cowman to bring in the milk from nature's refrigerator. Shakespeare could not have been thinking of his father's house and shop when he wrote that. Wilmcote is far more likely, and his mother is at the centre of the picture.

Little as we know of Mary Arden's personality we have plenty of documented information about her home. She was the seventh daughter of Robert Arden who, when he died in 1556, owned the farm-house and land at Wilmcote and two farms and houses at Snitterfield, lying to the east. There Richard Shakespeare, father of John, was one of the tenants. She probably married her man in 1557 when he was already settling down in trade as a Stratford townsman. The money left by her father was small, less than seven pounds, but she also inherited a farm of sixty acres, an estate known as Asbies, lying round the house in which she had been brought up. That could be mortgaged for forty pounds when John Shakespeare's time of need came in 1578. She was a woman of property.

Mary had lived in good circumstances. We have the inventory of her father's goods and chattels drawn up at his death. Robert Arden, as well as collecting his rents, had run a mixed farm with eight oxen, two bullocks, seven cows, four weaning calves, pigs, and poultry. If the girls wanted to ride or to be driven into Stratford there were four horses and three colts in the stables. They were not all, and perhaps none of them were, cart-horses since oxen were then used for ploughing and drawing heavy wagons.

The Wilmcote house was acquired by the Stratford Birthplace Trust in 1930 and is well worth a visit. The word museum is sometimes used as a term of contempt, but there is nothing musty and dull about the farm with its old domestic and agricultural equipment. Here one may get as close to the life of a well-placed Elizabethan and his family as in the various museums of Stratford itself. It is a handsome, richly timbered building which has been capably restored. In Mary's time it was well furnished and decorated as Robert Arden's inventory shows. The details are given in full in Oliver Baker's book 'Shakespeare in Warwickshire', the work of an excellent antiquary who made constant and rewarding research into the history, economy, and crafts of the district.

As mentioned in Shakespeare's Winter Song there was 'the hall' into which Tom carried the logs. The two tables were of the trestle kind whose tops could be lifted when space was wanted for a social occasion after the meal had been eaten. There was nothing common about that. The wealthy Capulet in *Romeo and Juliet* cries to his servants when a dance is going forward 'Come, musicians, play. A hall, a hall. Give room and foot it, girls. More light, you knaves, and turn the tables up.' Along with the cushions, cupboards, and shelves there were two painted cloths in the hall and others elsewhere in the house. In the main bed-room known as 'the chamber' the linen-chest was kept with its sheets and towels. There were also five table-cloths which counters the idea that the people of that time fed in squalor and were slovenly at their meals.

The best bed was a feather one; the girls slept on truckle beds, several times mentioned by Shakespeare. That article was a little bed kept under the main bed and pulled out for use. Mercutio was jesting when he spoke of going home to sleep on one. They had the rush mattresses which were in general use. Lying soft was a luxury which could be enjoyed with a coverlet of quality by the parents at Wilmcote. In the inventory of Arden's widow, Agnes, made fifteen years later, the bedding and bedspreads were 'Apreeware'. That was a woven textile imported from or imitated and named after Ypres in the Low Countries whose weavers were famous for their skill. Also in this 'chamber' there were either displayed, or stored when the inventory was made, five painted cloths.

The kitchen was amply equipped for ample feeding. There were two cauldrons, two brass pans, and three skillets which were large saucepans for boiling and stewing. In one of these would be the hissing crab-apples of the Song. There were grid-iron, frying-pan, and spit, a kneading trough, a quern or grinding-mill, a vat, and barrels. 'Greasy Joan' and Marian of the red and raw nose had plenty to do with all this to 'keel'.

The number of painted cloths is of particular interest. They indicated some prosperity and were a regular feature of a good home. It has been stated that the fashion came from Italy, but Oliver Baker showed that they had long been a product of English craftsmanship, serving a double purpose. They were hung on a wall for decoration or served to conceal unwanted things and to protect from draughts.

There is no mention of framed pictures in the Arden home. Ownership of these was a luxury limited to milords. They were usually hung on the wall and were family portraits and were sometimes known as tables. That was a shortened form of tableaux and evidence of a French fashion brought in by travelled and wealthy persons. They had cloth coverlets to protect them from becoming dusty or faded. Olivia in *Twelfth Night* is in the table-owning class. When she removes her veil to reveal her face she says, 'We will undraw the curtain and show you the picture.'

Olivia lived in an elegance unknown to English farmers even of the prosperous Arden type. The inventory does not include pictures, but makes it certain that Mary was brought up surrounded by painted cloths. If John Shakespeare did not have them when he took her as his wife to Henley Street she brought some of them with her or acquired others. It is an obvious fact, often proved in his plays, that his son William was closely acquainted with the themes, mainly classical or biblical, which they presented. They served as a picture-book and as a form of elementary schooling which brought history and mythology into vivid life for the young while they were decorative amenities for their elders.

The cloths and the characters shown on them are not only alluded to by Shakespeare; they are made the subject of speeches and incidents in his plays. There are many inventories of the sixteenth century which catalogue the painted cloths and give the nature of the scenes depicted. In one list of a property which had passed into the tenacious hands of Henry VIII the Seven Ages of Man were displayed. The cloths had a well-known set of characters. The Ages with their various representatives of the decades would not be known only in royal and lordly mansions. On a view or memory of this cloth seen at home or in a neighbour's house could have been based the famous observations of Jaques who significantly was at large in Mary's own Arden. It is curious how often the scenery and atmosphere of Wilmcote come into the early comedies.

A frequent topic for the cloths was 'The Nine Worthies'; these ancient heroes appear in the bungled mummery or the drollery, as it was then often called, performed at the end of *Love's Labour's Lost*. These antics were followed by the Winter Song already quoted with its named farm-house characters and the facial detail of the maids. In *The Taming of the Shrew*, whose induction is set beyond question in the Wilmcote or Winton district, Christopher Sly, sodden with Marian Hacket's ale, is brought to the house of a lord. When he is recovering from the effects he is shown painted scenes for his bewildered entertainment. He is offered cloths presenting ancient lovers, gods, and nymphs. One of them reappears in Shakespeare's early narrative poem of 'Venus and Adonis'. It is described and explained for Sly with emphasis on its realism.

> *Adonis painted by a running brook*
> *And Cytherea all in sedges hid,*
> *Which seem to move and wanton with her breath*
> *Even as the waving sedges play with wind.*

Another specimen of convincing naturalism was:

> *Daphne roaming through a thorny wood*
> *Scratching her legs that one shall swear she bleeds;*
> *And at that sight will sad Apollo weep,*
> *So workmanly the blood and tears are drawn.*

The detail is so exactly mentioned that Shakespeare must have been recollecting an artistry of realism which had particularly attracted his young fancy. Another of the well-known cloths presented 'The Rape of Lucrece'. Both of Shakespeare's long poems, written early in his career, had their source in the graphic arts.

Not long ago the substantial home at Wilmcote was called 'Mary Arden's Cottage'. The Hathaway farm at Shottery is still thus spoken of. The word cottage appears to have a specially alluring sound for the sightseers in search of Olde England. It was a nonsensical term in the case of the Ardens. Theirs was a manor. That was proved by the ownership of a pigeon-house of which there are good remaining specimens. The buildings were large and the pigeons were not pets. They were there to be eaten after the New Year when beef and mutton were scarce owing to the big autumn slaughter necessitated by lack of winter feeding in the limited resources of Elizabethan stock-breeding. One surviving pigeon-house has six hundred nesting-holes.

Farmers naturally detest pigeons when they come swarming in to feed on all kinds of crops. In Shakespeare's time there was a ban on general building of special accommodation for the birds because of their powers of consumption. But it was not an 'Age of Fair Shares'. Only privileged people could build specially for the keeping of pigeons. The parson could have a pigeon-house at his vicarage and probably needed it as much as any since his stipend was so small. Those who owned a manor house and not a mere farm were also exempt from the veto. The presence of a pigeon-house is evidence that Mary Arden was no cottager. When she married she went to the workshop from the manor. Her aristocratic relatives, the Ardens of Park Hall, may have thought poorly of this.

There is nothing to show that she resented her downward move and that it was not a happy marriage on the whole. She had a wearing life with eight pregnancies: in addition to the births and deaths in the church register there may have been miscarriages. The fact that Shakespeare's wife Anne had no more children after her twins may have been due to misfortunes of that kind. So may the inability of her daughter Susanna to have more than one child, Elizabeth, who in her turn was twice married and had no children at all.

Mary had the frequent pain of creating young lives as well as the distress of losing them. There was none of our modern expertness in the use of anaesthetics. Her grand-daughter's husband, Dr Hall, was an eminent medico but he only came to Stratford when she was in her sixties. We know nothing of the midwifery available in the town and can only charitably assume that it was above the early Victorian level suggested, perhaps with more humour than accuracy, by Dickens when he created Mrs Gamp. But hygienic conditions are hard to achieve without clean water.

Fouling by seepage was likely and the purity of the water in some of the Stratford wells is questionable. It was common for the townsfolk to keep pigs, poultry, and other stock which wandered about on the grass verges of the town's road. Dung was heaped up before it was carted away to manure the fields. Delay in removal was dangerous. Stratford's council was aware of the risk to health and tried to prevent it. It was indeed remarkably strict. One householder was fined for shelling peas in the street and leaving the pods for his pigs to eat. John Shakespeare was fined a shilling, then by no means a trivial sum, for something less pardonable. He allowed a pile of this kind, honoured with the Latin name of *sterquinarium*, to collect outside his premises in Henley Street. He was not the only offender: several citizens of some standing were also charged for this offence and paid their penalties. Absurd stress has been laid on this incident by those who strangely insist that William could not have been a poet and dramatist in London because his father was neglectful about garbage in Stratford. In any case the date must be noted. The breach of the town's mild sanitary rules occurred in 1552, twelve years before William's birth and when John was a young, unmarried man. There is no news of his carelessness occurring again.

It is a reasonable guess that after Mary Arden had arrived as Mrs Shakespeare she let her husband know that her folk of the manor-house class did not do that kind of thing and that, if he was ambitious to be a gentleman, he must mend his manners and avoid prosecutions for oafish conduct. Since Dickens has been mentioned it is worth noticing that Elizabethan Stratford was ahead of early-Victorian London since it did at least try to enforce a by-law against dung-heaps. In 'Our Mutual Friend' Noddy Boffin became the Golden Dustman because he amassed and profitably sold the contents of his mounds in North London. Their contents were partly derived from the multitude of earth-closets still existing. He does not appear to have been breaking any law in the capital as he would have done if he had amassed and exploited his mounds in Stratford.

That John Shakespeare could keep some domestic staff was shown in the application for his coat of arms; that was sixteen

years after Mary's last son had been born. But he was prospering
in his business soon after they married and could maintain a maid
or two. The housewife who was frequently a mother needed them
since water had to be brought in from a well, even in the comparatively sumptuous premises of New Place.

Mary had a husband who for a while was steadily winning the
confidence and respect of his fellow Stratfordians as well as
developing his business. There was some consternation for her
twenty years after their marriage when he encountered the
mistrust of his colleagues on the town council, probably more
because of religious disputes than through financial failure. That
trouble will be discussed later. Mary was involved because they
had to mortgage her inherited land at Asbies and that led to a
long wrangle with her cousin by marriage, Edward Lambert.
The quarrel and the money involved have been argued over at
length in the major Shakespearian biographies. All that concerns
us here is that Mary stood by her man in his adversity and saw
him emerge in prosperity renewed.

John was charged with recusancy and breaking the law of the
land which made church-going compulsory. It has never been
settled whether his objection to attendance at the Anglican
services was based on a growth of Puritan or Roman Catholic
sympathies. If his loyalty was to the Old Religion his wife could
sympathise with him. The Ardens had been a prominent Catholic
family. Some of them accepted the Reformation, but others did
not. One of the latter faith, Edward Arden, carried his defiance
of the Protestant order so far that he kept a 'massing priest'
disguised as a gardener. In 1583 he was accused of sharing in a
stupid as well as criminal conspiracy to assassinate the queen.
This had been started by a reckless and possibly crazy relative of
his called John Somerville who committed suicide when the plot
was discovered. Edward Arden was arrested and convicted of
treason, perhaps unjustly. After a trial in Warwick he was hanged
in London. The fate of traitors was mutilation after their end
on the gallows and the exposure of the severed head on
London Bridge. Edward was not a close relative of Mary Shakespeare but the outrage and its penalties brought disgrace to

her family. Her husband's troubles were petty compared with this.

There was much confusion of religious beliefs and practices during Mary's lifetime. The Reformation had largely triumphed, but there were rebels on both sides of the Anglican settlement. There were the Puritans who wanted to destroy old rituals and ornaments of the churches. There were the extreme Romanists such as Edward Arden who held treason and violence to be not only pardonable but a duty in a Protestant kingdom. There were far more people who were confused and wavering. By sentiment they were attached to the Old Faith. But as law-abiding persons they conformed to the new establishment.

Mary's father was one of these. When Robert Arden made his will he began with a Catholic dedication bequeathing his soul to 'Allmyghty God and to our bleside Ladye Seint Marye and to all the holye compenye of heven'. That was not the Protestant formula. But he asked to be buried in the parish church of Aston Cantlow whose vicar, if he was not a law-breaker and risking his living and perhaps his life, conducted Protestant services. His daughter Mary was married and buried by the Protestant clergy in Stratford, but it is quite likely that she had a lingering, unspoken loyalty to the catholicism to which most of the Ardens had been strong adherents. But Edward's disastrous folly, coming when she was middle-aged, may have impelled her husband and herself to observe the conformity prescribed by law and vigorously enforced in their diocese of Worcester by Bishop Whitgift. We can fairly visualise the housewife in Henley Street as a broad-minded Christian woman who took the changing world as she found it, practised the accepted virtues as best she could, and did not follow the doctrinal quarrels which appealed to some fanatical men but were over the head of a busy woman with a load of mundane cares.

There are no unmistakable signs that Shakespeare made 'copy' of his family as Dickens, with a somewhat similar middle-class background, was ready to do and brilliantly achieved. He did indeed make all the Victorian world his stage while Shakespeare, except in the bourgeois and small-town setting of *The Merry*

Wives of Windsor, kept to the social extremes with the emperors and kings at one end and the tinkers and toss-pots at the other. He could meet the latter at a sheep-shearing or in a tavern; when well established in London his company was attached to the court. He could see behind the scenes and he had an earl as patron. What he did not note with his eyes he could with his genius imagine. He wrote least of the people whom he knew most. The *Merry Wives* is a useful play for those studying the middle way of Elizabethan life, but it is risky to look into its homes for a series of family portraits.

It will be suggested later that the ghost of Shakespeare's dead son Hamnet haunts some poignant speeches in *King John*. It has been claimed by several that he had one of his daughters in mind when he made the young heroines of his later plays display their knowledge of horticulture as well as their delight in many species of flowers. Perdita could be repeating with enhanced quality some remarks of Susanna or Judith to her father, now in his forties, after a return to the garden of New Place.

> Here's flowers for you;
> Hot lavender, mints, savory, marjoram;
> The marigold, that goes to bed wi' the sun,
> And with him rises weeping: these are flowers
> Of middle summer, and, I think, they are given
> To men of middle age. Y'are very welcome.
>   (*The Winter's Tale*, IV.iii.103–9.)

The further praise of wind-braving daffodils, violets dim, and primroses pale occurs in a speech so well and justly famous as to need no repetition. Less familiar are the echoes of Perdita coming from the lips of other girls. In the exquisite burial lines spoken by Marina in *Pericles* the favourites come back in the flow of the word-music,

> The yellows, blues
> The purple violets and marigolds
> Shall, like a carpet, hang upon thy grave
> While summer days do last.

The marigolds appear again as 'winking mary-buds' with golden eyes in *Cymbeline* in which play Imogen, disguised as the boy Fidele, evokes flower-paintings of the finest when the lad is supposed to be dead. Shakespeare wrote these plays just after his mother's death in 1608 and the funeral could not be forgotten. Twice he repeated the words about the flowers being laid on a grave with some hope of their remaining alive and in hue 'while summer lasts'. Mary was buried in early September while the summer days did last.

A direct portrait of her is not discernible, but in *The Winter's Tale* there is a passage which has the colour and cordiality of a Dutch master at work in a festive kitchen. It is so detailed that it seems to be drawn from the life. The shepherd, at home in his very English Bohemia, rebukes his daughter for being a shy hostess and remembers the jovial, bustling reception which her mother used to provide, not forgetting to replenish herself.

> *Fie, daughter! when my old wife lived, upon*
> *This day she was both pantler, butler, cook;*
> *Both dame and servant; welcomed all; served all;*
> *Would sing her song and dance her turn; now here,*
> *At upper end o' the table, now i' the middle;*
> *On his shoulder, and his; her face o' fire*
> *With labour, and the thing she took to quench it,*
> *She would to each one sip.*
>
> (*The Winter's Tale*, IV.iii.54–62.)

If Mary Shakespeare prompted this picture of a far-from-still life in a home with convivial company she had the nights of gladness which her patient conduct of her long partnership and frequent motherhood had amply earned.

CHAPTER II

Country Girls

THE GIRL Mopsa in *The Winter's Tale* is not a character likely
to be included in a book on 'The Women in Shakespeare's
Plays'. She makes a brief appearance 'Before the Shepherd's
Cottage' when the action of the play has moved from the passionate storms of Sicily to the peace, flowers, rogueries, and festivities
of a sheep-shearing day in Bohemia. Mopsa does not say much
but she provides important information about the life of the
Shakespearian countryside. Autolycus, the songful, swindling
pedlar has been announcing his wares deemed suitable for a
rustic and holiday market, linen, cyprus, gloves, 'masks for faces
and for noses', bracelets, necklets, perfume, quoifs, and
stomachers

> *For my lads to give their dears;*
> *Pins and poking-sticks of steel,*
> *What maids lack from head to heel:*

The youngster marked as clown, the shepherd's son, is there with
Mopsa and Dorcas, two shepherdesses who have just taken their
part in a country dance. He is, in his own words, 'enthralled' by
Mopsa and so is ready to enter on a spending-spree. What then
does she lack and crave? Here is the significant passage which is
worth quoting at length since it indicates an ability to read
possessed by the humblest of farming women and the nature of
the reading-matter available in a pedlar's pack.

Clown. Fear not thou, man, thou shalt lose nothing here.
Autolycus. I hope so, sir; for I have about me many parcels of
   charge.

Clown. What hast here? ballads?

Mopsa. Pray now, buy some: I love a ballet in print a-life, for then we are sure they are true.

Autolycus. Here's one to a very doleful tune. How a usurer's wife was brought to bed of twenty money-bags at a burden, and how she long'd to eat adders' heads and toads carbonadoed.

Mopsa. Is it true, think you?

Autolycus. Very true; and but a month old.

Dorcas. Bless me from marrying a usurer!

Autolycus. Here's the midwife's name to 't, one Mistress Tale-porter, and five or six honest wives that were present. Why should I carry lies abroad?

Mopsa. Pray you now, buy it.

Clown. Come on, lay it by: and let's first see more ballads; we'll buy the other things anon.

Autolycus. Here's another ballad, Of a fish, that appear'd upon the coast on Wednesday the fourscore of April, forty thousand fathom above water, and sung this ballad against the hard hearts of maids: it was thought she was a woman, and was turn'd into a cold fish for she would not exchange flesh with one that loved her: the ballad is very pitiful, and as true.

Dorcas. Is it true too, think you?

Autolycus. Five justices' hands at it, and witnesses more than my packs will hold.

Clown. Lay it by too: another.

Autolycus. This is a merry ballad, but a very pretty one.

Mopsa. Let's have some merry ones.

Autolycus. Why, this is a passing merry one, and goes to the tune of 'Two maids wooing a man': there's scarce a maid westward but she sings it; 'tis in request, I can tell you.

Mopsa. We can both sing it: if thou'lt bear a part, thou shalt hear 'tis in three parts.

Dorcas. We had the tune on't a month ago.

Autolycus. I can bear my part; you must know 'tis my occupation have at it with you!

(*The Winter's Tale,* IV.iii.209–298.

30

The Bohemian interlude in this play is as English as Warwick-shire and the shearing might be happening at Wilmcote itself where Mary Arden's step-mother mentioned a flock of twenty-six sheep in her will. Mopsa and Dorcas might be the out-of-door employees where Marian and Joan were coping with the indoor chores.

It is beyond question that Mopsa can read. Why else should she love 'a ballet in print a-life'? She does not want one ballad-sheet only. She wants and gets at least four. The clown is delighted and is ready also to spend his money, which cannot have been much, on Dorcas, who claims that she has her share of the lad's attention. (One may wonder whether the two girls remained good friends.) At the end of their discussion about ballads the clown says 'Wenches, I'll buy for you both. Pedlar, let's have the first choice.'

Ballad-sheets abounded in the streets of London and were obviously available and coveted in the country. Their authors, who were many, were despised as 'pot-poets' by the literary men. Their market was large because the words used by them were short and simple in contrast with the rich verbosity and long sentences customary in the cultured writing of the time. The subjects were taken from the news of the world, the more fabulous the better. The rhymes and songs ranged from crimes and hangings to the monstrosities of nature on the one side and to the ardours and endurances of lovers on the other. They had a wide circulation. They were written for the apprentices and artisans in the city and also, as we are shown, for the women as well as the men who worked on the farm. Dorcas and Mopsa, with these gifts offered them, never mentioned the other 'fairings' in the pedlar's stock, attractive as these must have seemed to the girls with a taste for adornment and the pleasing of a masculine eye. No bracelets, no necklets, no scent, no gloves until the appetite for 'ballets in print' had been satisfied.

If Mopsa could read it is very hard to believe that Shakespeare's mother in her Manor House, Anne Hathaway, daughter of a yeoman who was not wealthy but above the rank of Tom Whittington, his shepherd, and Shakespeare's two girls, daughters of a man living and prospering with his pen, were illiterate. That could not be said of Susanna Hall because her well-written signature survives. But it has been constantly alleged and not only by those anti-Stratfordians anxious to demean the town and its people in order to argue that it could not have produced the Swan of Avon. The men, even locally important men like John Shakespeare, as well as the women have been regarded as unable to read and write. The mistake has been caused by the unjustified belief that those who made their mark on a document were incapable of signing it.

It has been sufficiently shown by the specialists in Stratford research that people who could and did sign their names sometimes attested a document with their marks. These marks were of two kinds. There was the simple sign of the cross which had something of the value of the oath still spoken in a court of law. If the testifier said that he or she was bearing true witness in the presence of others the mark of the cross on a deed sufficed. To use it was a solemn matter. The other kind of mark was personal: it might be a private invention. Oliver Baker, who made a close examination of the mark-signed documents in Stratford and many other places while he was preparing his book 'In Shakespeare's Warwickshire', includes a convincing proof that the mark did not prove illiteracy. 'Thomas Walker made a printed T and an interlaced double V so cleverly drawn that it seems incredible that he should not have been able to write. Sure enough, lower down the page is his clearly written signature, Thomas Walker.' Also mentioned is the case of Adrian Quiney whose mark was a neat circular flourish. Yet several letters written by him have survived.

John Shakespeare had two different marks. They were based on his craft and membership of the Guild of Glovers. According to Edward Fripp, the supreme authority on Elizabethan life in Stratford, John, when he was one of the affeerors, officials who fixed the fines of delinquents, signed the minutes with a daintily drawn form of glover's 'divider'. At another time he drew a glover's 'clamp' as his sign-manual. There are illustrations of both in Fripp's 'Shakespeare, Man and Artist'. Baker provided many examples of those who signed with their name at one time and with a mark at another. It is absurd to assume that because John Shakespeare's marks and not his signature survive he was incapable of reading a line or putting his name to paper.

How could one who at various times held the posts of affeeror, chamberlain in charge of the borough's financial accounts, bailiff or mayor and justice of the peace have conducted his public duties if he were unable to read or write? It is specifically and several times stated in the Stratford records that he 'made the accounts', not that he passed them when authorised to do so by the town clerk who some think was the only man in charge of affairs able to distinguish a from b and one from two. The town, though its population was then small by our standards, ranked as third in the county. Only Coventry and Warwick were larger. Leland, the antiquary who toured and wrote of England from 1534 to 1542, wrote that there were smiths in Birmingham who made knives and cutting tools. That was a useful but still a very small start on the road to the city's now immense commerce and wealthy population, but it was of no importance in Shakespeare's time. Stratford was then of more consequence and the members of its council had much business to transact.

It is usually assumed that Elizabethan and Jacobean girls were far behind the boys in education and capacity for reading books and writing letters. Of the aristocracy this was often completely untrue and the middle-class girls in London were great readers. There is also proof that domestic servants, at least in the towns, were able to share in this recreation. Sir Thomas Overbury's book of 'Characters' appeared in 1614; among what are now called profiles, there is one of a chamber-maid. In this he said that 'she reads Greene's works over and over and is so carried away with the 'Mirror of Knighthood' that she is many times resolved to remain one herself and become a Lady Errant'. Much earlier Edward Hake had written 'A Touchstone for this time Present' which was dedicated not to a nobleman but to his friend 'Edward Godfrey, Merchaunt'. It laid down rules for 'all parents and scholemaisters in the trayning up of their Schollers and Children in learning'. With 'children' girls were included

3

since he lamented that the young miss is often provided with improper reading matter. 'Eyther shee is altogither kept from exercises of good learning and knowledge of good letters or else she is so nouseled in amorous bookes, vain stories, and fonde trifling fancies that she smelleth of naughtinesse even all hir lyfe after.'

In the latter half of the sixteenth century there was a steady flow of books about famous lovers of history and legend, books for which there was a ready market in the middle-class homes despite a stream of denunciation evoked by their supposedly evil influence on the girls. There was less concern about the effect on young men. They perhaps did not bother with romance in biography and fiction and sought their excitement in a free and lusty way of living which was taken for granted and beyond rebuke in the case of males.

Shakespeare himself contributed fruitfully to the delight of feminine readers when 'Venus and Adonis' was published in 1593. It was constantly reprinted and did not go out of fashion until the puritans came into power and then was secretly treasured in the way of all books banned or frowned upon. There were five editions issued between 1617 and 1640. In the Cambridge play of 1600 *The Return from Parnassus* a character called Gullio leaves Spenser and Chaucer to 'the duncified world' and says 'I'll worship sweet Mr. Shakespeare and to honour him will lay 'Venus and Adonis' under my pillow.' It remained a favourite of the passionate young. In a play of 1640 a man cries 'Oh for the book of 'Venus and Adonis' to court my mistress by!' He would not have said that had his mistress been averse to poetry and there is other evidence that women doted on it. Country girls were less well placed for obtaining books and feeding their desires on the 'vaine stories' which caused them, as Hake had said, to 'smell of naughtinesse' thereafter. But that their appetite for amorous ballads 'in print a-life' was well fed is shown not only by Shakespeare in *The Winter's Tale* but in another book of characters published by John Earle in 1628. The pot-poets, to his indignation, were still at work and when their ballads of hearts aflame were being 'nouseled' by Mopsa and her kind 'the poor country wench melteth like butter'.

One of the scolds who railed at the follies of women attacked their squandering of time on correspondence as well as on excessive attention to music, poetry, coiffure, and the looking-glass. In 'A Dyall for Dainty Darlings', published by William Averell in 1584, the author censured the girl who wastes hours 'in trimming her head, in glaring in the glasse, in fingering her lute, in singing of sonnets, in devising of letters, as well as in dancing with her lovers'. One cannot think of Mopsa as dainty while she melted over the product of a pot-poet or as a frequent writer of letters and it is unlikely that any of Shakespeare's family were much occupied with correspondence. What is to be discovered is how much schooling was available for girls in the country. Somebody must have taught Mopsa to read. If she learned at her mother's knee, who taught the mother?

It is assumed by some that girls coming from ordinary homes in the country-towns and countryside had no regular schooling. But that is easily disproved. There was nothing like the thorough grounding in Latin which the boys got at the Grammar Schools but there was elementary education available which the daughters could for a few years share with their brothers. Dorothy Gardiner in her book 'English Girlhood at School', written after a copious examination of records and founders' statutes, completely dispels the idea of a masculine monopoly. At Banbury, twenty miles from Stratford, the statutes of the Grammar School, drawn up in 1594, ordered the admission of a certain number of girls; this facility was limited in its range and scope. They were not to stay on after they were nine and were to leave before that if they were thought to be sufficiently proficient in the reading and writing of English.

When a school at Uffington was opened by Thomas Saunders thirty years later it did exclude girls. The founder was apprehensive about mixing the sexes but he made an important admission. In his statement of purpose he stated that 'whereas it is the most common and usual course for many to send their daughters to the common schools to be taught together with and amongst all sorts of youths, which course is by many conceived very uncomely and not decent, therefore the said schoolmaster may not

35

admit any of that sex to be taught in the said school'. The 'common schools' were thus admitted to be common in both senses of the word and they practised co-education.

The common school was sometimes called a petty school. There was one at Stratford which fed the Grammar School with boys suitably prepared. The earliest age at which a boy could be admitted to the Grammar School was seven. By that time he had to be able to read and write English and be properly fitted for coping with the Latin which would henceforward be a large part of his curriculum.

Towards the end of Shakespeare's life Thomas Parker, a teacher licensed by the Bishop of Worcester, was in charge of it. Some of the town's boys may have been well enough taught at home by their parents to need no attendance at the common school. Whether John and Mary Shakespeare had the time and capability to carry their William through the rudiments of English and save him from going to the common school is unknown. What is known, with Shakespeare's own words for evidence, is that a country schoolmaster was accustomed to teaching girls along with the boys.

In *Love's Labour's Lost,* whose comedy scenes in France are as native to Shakespeare's England as are the Bohemian episodes in *The Winter's Tale,* Sir Nathaniel, the curate of the parish, talks with Holofernes, the absurdly pedantic pedagogue who likes to show off his superfluity of Latin. But the conversation leaves us in no doubt that his school was petty and co-educational.

Sir Nathaniel. Sir, I praise the Lord for you: and so may my parishioners; for their sons are well tutor'd by you, and their daughters profit very greatly under you: you are a good member of the commonwealth.

Holofernes. Mehercle, if their sons be ingenious, they shall want no instruction; if their daughters be capable, I will put it to them:

(*Love's Labour's Lost,* IV.ii.82–87.)

Nathaniel, though he is called Sir, is described in charming detail, 'a foolish mild man, look you, and soon dash'd. He is a marvellous good neighbour'. That is said by the yokel Costard who also pays a compliment to the curate's skill on the bowling-green. This is village talk and the school kept by Holofernes is not an aristocratic academy for the high-spirited young lords of Navarre who, in the manner of the time, would have had their own tutors. In any case if they had attended the class-room of Holofernes they would have ragged the poor man to death. It is a parish school that Shakespeare had in mind and also had under his eyes in Stratford. To such a one as Thomas Parker kept later his mother could have been brought or sent in from Wilmcote, whose means of transport, as was noted, were copious, and his wife from the Hathaway farm at Shottery, only a mile away among the fields and orchards.

Holofernes is said to conduct 'a charge-house' which some interpret as a boarding-school. (A worse housemaster would be hard to imagine.) It is much more likely that he kept a petty school with petty fees to which the children brought their pennies since there was no endowment of the teacher.

There are several allusions to school-girls and their habits in Shakespeare's plays. Bianca in *The Taming of the Shrew* is a member of a wealthy family in the tutor-keeping class. Her father Baptista says:

> *She taketh most delight*
> *In music, instruments, and poetry,*
> *School-masters will I keep within my house*
> *Fit to instruct her youth.*

The plural is to be noted. Baptista was a lavish employer. What the tutors confronted with her sister Katharina the Shrew must have endured is shown in the play as a grim experience.

There was no going out to classes for Baptista's girls, but Helena and Hermia in *A Midsummer Night's Dream* have been fellow-pupils at a school. Says Helena, when attempting to stop their quarrel in Act III scene ii,

> *Oh, and is all forgot?*
> *All school-days' friendships, childish innocence?*

What they chiefly learned together was apparently needle-work, but there is mention of fellowship of mind which suggests some reading and discussion of books. In *Measure for Measure* Isabella makes a curious remark about school-maids who

> *change their names*
> *By vain though apt affection.*

Why should that irrelevance be introduced? There is a probable memory here of some games with nick-naming played by Shakespeare's daughters and their friends when they went to their petty school.

The lessons of the common school were limited to quite early years and it seems that there was little or no further teaching for girls except in large towns unless their parents could privately arrange it. There had been a sad decline in the educational provision for girls since the Reformation which harassed and often abolished the old Nunnery Schools. The training provided by these had once been limited to the children of 'good family' but the daughters of tradesmen and yeoman farmers began to be more and more admitted. Their teaching was not merely religious; it encouraged reading of secular books and composition in Latin as well as English. In Skelton's 'Boke of Phylyp Sparowe' little Jane Scrope, pupil at an Abbey, has read Chaucer and tales of classical and romantic heroes. As a writer she charmingly confesses:

> I cannot in effect
> My stile as yet direct,

but she adds that:

> My wit I shall assay
> An epytaphe to wryghte
> In latyne plaine and bright.

The schoolmistress nuns were erudite and their contributions to the general culture were varied as well as large. Shakespeare may not have known it but the first Christian practitioner of his profession was a woman, the Abbess Hroswitha, who in Saxony during the tenth century wrote plays in Latin based on the history and legends of her faith. The model was classical but the morals were Christian.

The Reformation destroyed much but it encouraged the reading of the Bible in English. Protestant mothers were expected to read the Bible to their children and they could not do that if they had not themselves been taught to read. Shakespeare's knowledge of the Scriptures was large and frequently appears in his writing. Much of that acquaintance could have been made at school but some of it may have been acquired from his mother. It is very difficult to believe that a man as widely read as he would be content to leave, or let his wife leave, his two daughters completely uninstructed when they were too old for the common or petty school.

That the elder, married to the learned Dr Hall, was a good writer we know from her signature. There is no existing proof of Judith's penmanship. She made her mark with the plain cross signifying the solemnity of the occasion when witnessing a deed. But it has been convincingly shown that mark-making was a custom of literate and even scholarly men. There is no reason why that could not be the practice of literate women. Judith is not to be dismissed as a dunce if she sometimes used a sign-manual instead of her signature. She was socially superior to the Mopsas on the farms and in high company as an addict of the mark.

In *The Merry Wives of Windsor* Shakespeare has left us his only picture of the middle-class way of life in a country town. We can study it to find domestic conditions and personal accomplishments similar to those in his own Stratford. The Wives, Mistress Ford and Mistress Page, have husbands on the social level of Shakespeare's father. They are not aristocrats and we do not know the source and size of their incomes. They have their field-sports. In the cast-list they are styled gentlemen. There is no sign of illiteracy in their wives whose status was that of Shakespeare's mother and his wife.

When we first meet them Mistress Page is reading an amorous and would-be seductive letter from Falstaff, the legibility of whose writing, after drink taken, might be vexatious. The letter is handed to Mistress Ford with the order that she too must read it. There is no idea of any difficulty on the part of either. The Pages have a boy William who, like any pupil at Stratford Grammar School, is struggling with his Latin.

Both women are jovial and live comfortably. Mistress Ford mentions one maid-servant and there may have been others. She calls more than one man-servant to carry out Falstaff when he is hidden under the dirty linen in the big basket. If either of them wanted additional domestic help they could find the kind of person who is sometimes called 'a treasure'. There was near to the Fords and Pages one who fully deserved that complimentary title. She was Mistress Quickly who in the play is described as 'Servant to Dr. Caius'. 'I keep his house', says she. 'I wash, wring, brew, bake, scour, dress meat and drink, make the beds, and do all myself.'

Housekeeping set no problems for those who could employ staff and for this the housewife would have to pay very little. The cost of living was low beyond any modern imagining.

In her book 'Gossip from a Muniment Room' Lady Newdigate-Newdegate published in 1897 some extremely interesting letters written by two sisters who come from Gawsworth in Cheshire. One was Mary Fitton who went to be a maid of honour to Queen Elizabeth, misbehaved, and was disgraced. She was seduced by or seduced the Earl of Pembroke who refused to marry her and was sent to cool his ardour in the Fleet Prison. Of both more will be said later. The other girl, Anne Fitton, married well, became Lady Newdigate, and stayed mainly in the country. Mary, known as Moll or Mall, after her affair with Pembroke married twice. When she was Mrs Polwhele Anne came to stay with her at Perton in Warwickshire. Found among many letters was a record of her expenses. She may have been doing some of her sister's housekeeping. Here is a list of payments which reveal the cost of living and scale of tips at the beginning of the seventeenth century when the Shakespeares were living at New Place.

Item chickens 14	o	2	4
It: 6 chickens	o	1	2
It: clarett wine	o	2	o
It: a dozen & halfe of pigeons	o	2	3

It:	for rosmarye flowers	o	o	4
It:	halfe an elle of lace for lettice	o	2	o
It:	to Mr Mathyas	o	10	o
It:	broumes	o	o	4
It:	to goodwife gardener for her halfe yeare's wages ending at 1607 our La: daye	o	15	o
It:	12 ducklings	o	2	6
It:	aquavita	o	1	6
It:	5 couple of rabets	o	3	o
It:	to Will: Walker the Joyner	o	o	9
It:	tow pans more then the ould	o	5	1
It:	Wooden ware for the dogs house	o	1	o
Item	a pore man	o	o	4
It:	a girdle for dicke	o	2	6
It:	peirceing 50 pearls	o	1	6
It:	makeing Malls ringe	o	1	o
It:	a paire of shooes for Jacke	o	1	o
	virginall wiers	o	o	4
It:	a paire of shoes for myself	o	2	6
It:	a paire for lettice	o	1	o
It:	the shoemaker's man	o	o	4
	12 elles of cloeth weaving & tow dossen of napkins	o	1	o
It:	nursse on her goeinge	o	10	o
It:	12 yeards of cobbweb lawn	o	8	o
It:	6 thread laceses	o	o	6

At my being at perton

It:	the keeper at Brude parke	o	10	o
It:	the keeper's men	o	2	o
It:	in the house at perton	o	8	o
It:	to my sister for silver chamlett	1	o	o
It:	Doctor Cherriboode	2	o	o
It:	at Sr Walter Leuseon	o	4	6
It:	mending the Coatch	o	2	6
It:	my sisters nursse	o	2	o
	etc. etc.			

41

Anne Newdigate was a lady of title, living in a big house, and would not be going round the shops looking for poultry at bargain prices. 'Goodwife gardener' presumably got her keep. What duties she had to perform is not stated. Fifteen shillings for twenty-six weeks does not suggest excessive remuneration. If the Perton goodwife's reward was at standard rates the nurse's ten shillings on leaving was her pay for four months. The charitable distribution was slender, but the 'pore man', if he liked his ale, could swallow a lot of it for fourpence. The keeper Brude appears to have done comparatively well in the way of tips and much better than his assistants. Dr Cherriboode came nicely out of it, but we are not told the number of his visits or the nature of his services. After reading Lady Newdigate's domestic budget and wage-list we may wonder what Dr Caius paid Mistress Quickly for her manifold exertions with 'one pair of hands'. The staff employed at New Place would not have been a serious burden to the Shakespeares' purse.

So it was easy going for the Stratford housewives in many respects. They had consolations unknown to the women of today. There were no crowds, no queues, no pushing and shoving to get a place in a train or a bus. But they had their perils to face. The shadow of the recurrent plague hung darkly over them. There was the further hazard of fires sweeping through the town on a dry and windy day. For the spreading conflagrations there was plenty of inflammable material supplied by the thatched roofs. While food was cheap and plentiful there was nothing like the variety we know and in hot weather there was no ice to keep it fresh and safe. A life without imported canned fruit, refrigeration, and a safe water-supply piped into the house would be much resented by a modern housewife. The Elizabethans did their baking at home and doubtless the families got much tastier and more nourishing bread than the insipid and spongy stuff which we get without trouble from our mass-producing bakeries. In the poorer homes with no hired help for the mother the woman's work was continual as well as exacting.

A particular hardship was the absence of easily available lighting. After four o'clock on a winter afternoon the people settled down to darkness in the home as they were facing it in the street. Good candles were a luxury costing a shilling for three pounds; the crude kind had wicks drawn from rushes which were plentiful by the river-side and busily gathered. The rushes could be doubly used when well dried. As substitutes for carpets they were strewn on the floor. They also provided the inner part of a rush-light whose chief ingredient was kitchen fats. Whale-oil for lamps was imported but probably did not reach the Midlands owing to difficulties of transport. Mentions of indoor lighting in Shakespeare's plays are frequently accompanied with a groan. He hated 'the smoky light that's fed on stinking tallow' and the flickering lamp 'whose wasting oil is spent.' In the rich houses torches were set in brackets on the wall and candles of quality were plentifully used. But an Elizabethan farm in and after the dull droop of a December day must have owed its illumination more to a log fire than to oil and tallow. One of the most frightening lines in Shakespeare runs simply

To a dark house and a detested wife.

There is no need to rip that out of its context and bring it in as evidence of a marriage which dismally failed. But for Shakespeare in his boyhood and much later, if he was at home in the winter, the gloom of dark streets and houses was familiar; to the women who did not get away from home the absence of light was a prolonged deprivation. There was little encouragement to use that ability to read which they acquired when, along with the boys, they were equipped with an Absey (ABC) Book at the common school. This alphabetical primer, which had a handle for a child to hold, was a sheet mounted on wood and protected with horn. It made entry to elementary writing and reading as easy as might be. But further reading when it was too dark or too wet for out-door games needed the convenience of a well-lit room and that was difficult to secure.

Mistress Page in her indignation at Falstaff's impudence said that she 'would exhibit a bill in the Parliament for the putting down of fat men'. She knew about London and its legislation. But the men, whether obese or skinny, were most unlikely to be suppressed. Emancipation was a word unknown to the women of Stratford who were living in a masculine world despite the presence of a popular and powerful woman on the throne. Mary Arden became the wife of the town's bailiff or mayor but she did not have the ranking or the responsibilities possessed by a mayoress today. She was not regarded as the town's first citizeness. This provided no grievance since she had never thought about political equality of the sexes whatever her views on parity in conjugal relations. Wives expected no rights or powers beyond those which they could exercise in the home. But the genial, welcoming, and omni-competent hostess, described in *The Winter's Tale* in a passage already quoted, is vividly and convincingly drawn in her labours and her levity. There could be many such.

In the dark months there was little recreation beyond the pleasures of gossip and party-going during the Twelve Days of Christmas. When travel by road was easy Stratford had its visiting troupes of players. That relief ended when the growing austerity and local dominance of the puritans put an end to these gaieties towards the close of the sixteenth century. Before that a number of touring companies had fitted a date at Stratford into the schedule of their Midland tours. If Mary Shakespeare did ever stand beside John while he performed his mayoral duties she had a chance to receive the Earl of Worcester's Men who were in the town when he was bailiff in 1564.

The players were reviled in the country as well as in London by those who accused them of collecting the riff-raff of the population and leading the young of both sexes into lewd thoughts and wanton practices. But if the queen took delight in seeing and hearing actors at court lesser women might reasonably follow the royal example and become part of the excited or hilarious audience. It is established that children came too. Robert Willis of Gloucester left an enthusiastic account of his boyhood play going in that city in 1570. He was allowed to stand between his father's knees and still remembered when he was seventy his joy in that experience.

There is record, fifty years later in date, of actors at Witney in Oxfordshire whose mixed audience of men and women held up the performance because they would go on dancing before the play began. A great day in Stratford was the arrival of Lord Leicester's Men in 1588. It is not certain whether their star comedian and later colleague of Shakespeare, Will Kemp, was with them. It is probable, since he toured widely with the team at home and abroad. If Mopsa and her kind could get leave from their farms and flocks for the day here was a colourful escape from the rustic routine. Her companion in the Bohemian episode of the play was entered in the text as Clown. Whoever came along when the players were there could watch in Warwickshire the acknowledged master of the tricks, quips, and antics of clownship in the London playhouses.

Mopsa is a peculiar name. It may have come from the Mop Fair to which those in search of work came to find an employer. If the girls wanted a domestic post they carried a mop or broom to advertise their line of work. The old name remained for Hiring Fairs attended by workers of all kinds. The farmers and householders gathered to look for likely lads as well as maids. When the engagements had been made there was the fun of the fair to follow the bargaining. The name of Mop Fair has not disappeared although its original purpose has passed with the coming of Labour Exchanges and plentiful employment.

For the country people there were many chances for a frisk. Some were Saints' Days, some agricultural celebrations such as the sheep-shearing at mid-summer and the harvest home rejoicings in August or September. If there was dancing, it is worth noting that Shakespeare expected the foot-work to be neat. The men were to be well dressed and the women 'fresh', a word which would then mean washed and brushed up and did not convey the sexual provocation implied in modern slang. In the masque in *The Tempest* the classical goddess Iris, summoning the revellers, says:

> *You sunburnt sickle men of August weary*
> *Come hither from the furrow and be merry,*
> *Make holiday, your rye-straw hats put on*

And these fresh nymphs encounter every one
In country footing.

This is followed by the stage-direction 'Enter certain reaper.
properly habited: they join with the nymphs in a graceful dance.
If there were hobble-de-hoys and slatterns at the Stratford revel
and fairs they were not to be shown so on the stage. Evidentl}
Shakespeare believed that the local girls could trip it 'featly'
Florizel finds Perdita's dancing a perfection of grace. Wh}
should Mopsa, so eager to join in singing a ballad, not be com
mendably nimble too when 'country footing' set her on her toes

The winters had their tedium for the women of Stratford anc
its farms. But from spring to autumn there were the holidays anc
fairs with the like of Autolycus and his pedlar companions parting
the spenders from their money to the advantage of their girls a
the receiving end of the revel. It is wrong to be sentimental abou
Stratford as a typical example of Merrie England and to forge
its plagues and perils. But there were times enough when th
women could relax or caper with the men on an equal level o
enjoyment and with some capacity to read about the wonders o
the world in a printed ballad.

CHAPTER III

The Married Man

THE DOCUMENTED facts about Shakespeare's marriage and his wife are few and the suppositions are many. Let the few facts come first.

The record begins in the Bishop of Worcester's Register for November 27, 1582. On that day a special licence was entered for a marriage with a single asking for banns instead of the usual three. The union proposed was specified as 'inter Willelmum Shaxpere et Annam Whately de Temple Grafton'. On the following day Fulk Sandells and John Richardson, described as farmers in the County of Warwick, stood surety for the legality of the marriage of Anne Hathwey of Stratford and William Shagspere. For the surety they put down forty pounds of 'legal English money'. The register is precise.

'The condicion of this obligacion ys suche that if herafter there shall not appere any Lawfull Lett or impediment by reason of any precontract consanguinitie affinitie or by any other lawfull meanes whatsoeuer but that William Shagspere on thone partie, and Anne Hathwey of Stratford in the Dioces of Worcester maiden may lawfully solennize matrimony together and in the same afterwards remaine and continew like man and wiffe according unto the lawes in that behalf prouided, and moreouer if there be not at this present time any action sute quarrell or demaund moved or depending before any iudge ecclesiasticall or temporall for and concerning any such lawfull lett or impediment, And moreouer if the said William Shagspere do not proceed to solennizacion of mariadg with the said Anne Hathwey without the consent of hir frindes, And also if the said William do upon his owne proper costes and expenses defend & save

47

harmles the right Reverend father in god Lord John bushop of
Worcester and his offycers for Licencing them the said William
and Anne to be maried togither with once asking of the bannes of
matrimony betwene them and for all other causes which may
ensue by reason or occasion therof, That then the said obligacion
to be voyd and of none effect or els to stand & abide in full force
and vertue.'

There is no record of where the marriage took place. If it had
been celebrated in the parish church of Stratford-upon-Avon it
would have been listed in the register. There is no doubt, however, that it did take place—somewhere. It was Anne Hathwey
and not Anne Whately of Temple Grafton who became the wife
of the young William who was then eighteen years and seven
months old.

To name Anne Hathaway (to use the now familiar spelling)
as 'maiden', if that implied virginity, was to pay her a courtesy
title. The next mention in the Stratford register is on May 26,
1583. The entry is 'C. (christened) Susanna daughter to William
Shakespeare.' Christening then followed birth after two or three
days. So Susanna was born round about May 23. If she was a
nine-months' child the date of her begetting was towards the end
of August, 1582.

In the same register there is entry of February 2, 1585.
'C. Hamnet and Judeth, sonne and daughter of William Shakspere.' The boy died at the age of eleven. The entry for August 11,
1596 was 'B. (buried) Hamnet filius William Shakspere.'
(The spelling of personal names at the time was completely vague.
The putative husband of Anne Whately was Willelmus Shaxpere.
For convenience I have kept throughout to the now usual
Shakespeare. Sir Edmund Chambers in his great and fully documented life in two volumes 'William Shakespeare' (1930) listed
eighty-three different spellings of the family name including
such oddities as Chacsper, Sashpierre, Shacosper, and Shadspere.
People then spelled as they happened to pronounce or mis-
pronounce a name.)

No more is heard of Anne Shakespeare until March 25, 1601
when her name occurs in the Worcester Probate Registry. She

was then mentioned in the will of Thomas Whittington, 'husband-
man' of Shottery, the village a mile from Stratford. There lay the
farm called Hewlands, a home of the Hathaway family and now
much visited as Anne Hathaway's cottage. The testator's words
were:

'Item I geve and bequeth unto the poore people of Stratford
40s. that is in the hand of Anne Shaxspere, wyf unto Mr Wyllyam
Shaxspere, and is due debt unto me, beyng payd to myne Executor
by the sayd Wyllyam Shaxpere or his assigns, accordying to the
true meanyng of this my wyll . . .'

Those who wish to put the worst possible construction on any
mention of Shakespeare and his wife assert that she was reduced
to borrowing from a shepherd and had not paid her debt of two
pounds. This is nonsensical. By that time her husband was
prosperous. She was the lady of New Place, the best house in
Stratford. If she was tight-fisted, of which there is no evidence,
she would hardly expose herself to public ridicule by bilking one
of the poorer members of her native village. Whittington's will
mentions a number of small sums owed by members of the
Hathaway family. Owed must be interpreted as held. There was
then no post office to serve as the poor man's bank and, if
Whittington was afraid of thieving neighbours, he would not
leave his money in his cottage when he went out to work. Anne
Shakespeare must have been one of those trusted with his shillings.

After this there is nothing documented except the brief
mention of 'my wyfe' in her husband's will made in 1616, of
which more will be said later. Anne survived William by more
than seven years. The parish record contains the fact of her
burial thus:

Aug. 8 1623 { B. Mrs. Shakespeare
Anne, uxor Richardi James.

This is no indication that she had married again and despite
her years had become Mistress James. Bracketing of names when
there were two interments on one day occurs elsewhere in the
register.

She was laid in the chancel of Stratford Church next to her husband's grave. A brass plate has the inscription 'Here lyeth interred the body of Anne, wife of William Shakespeare, who departed the life the 6th day of August 1623 being of the age of 67 yeares'. No month of her birth is stated. Accordingly we cannot certainly place her birthday since the church register begins its valuable chronicle in 1558. Anne must have been born in 1555 or early in 1556.

The inscription carries some Latin verses which may have been composed by her son-in-law, Dr John Hall, a scholarly medico and Latinist. In that language he wrote his case-book which was translated into English in 1657 with the title 'Select Observations of English Bodies'. There has been natural specula- tion as to the cause of Shakespeare's death; when he made his will on March 25, 1616 he declared himself 'in perfect health and memorie', but that may have been more a formula than a fact. If it is true, he sank rapidly. He died on April 23. Unfortunately, the case-book was not started until the next year. So it contains no post-mortem on Hall's great father-in-law. Anne, outliving William by seven years, could have come into it, but the 'Observa- tions' passed her by. Since the death evoked no comment we may presume a natural and peaceful death from old age.

The Latin tribute on her grave deplores the writer's inability to offer more than a stone in return for a mother's gift of milk and life to her children. The hope is expressed that a good angel may remove the stone that her image may come forth like the body of Christ. If the prayer is not granted may Christ come quickly so that the mother may rise again and seek the heavens. In the case of Anne's daughter Susanna sepulchral verses in English praised her qualities of wit and compassion. Of her mother's virtues there was no specific mention.

There is no more documentation, but Dowdall, an antiquary working at the end of the seventeenth century, recorded that in 1693 'at Stratford-super-avon I saw the Effigies of our English tragedian, Mr. Shakspeare'. He talked with the aged sexton at the church who was a boy of nine when Anne died. He was told that Shakespeare's wife and daughters earnestly desired to be laid in the same grave with him but nobody dared to disturb the poet's tomb owing to the cautionary verses set upon it.

> *Good friend, for Jesus sake forbeare*
> *To digg the dust inclosed here,*
> *Bles't be the man that spares these stones*
> *And Curs't be he that moves my bones.*

Dowdall related, presumably on the sexton's authority, that Shakespeare wrote this epitaph for himself 'a little before his death'. Only if he was failing badly could he have passed such doggerel. However, if the old man's gossip is true, the lines proved deterrent. So Anne lay alone, beside – not with – her husband.

With so few certain facts about the married life of Mistress Shakespeare there has naturally been a flow of fancy about her conduct, her temperament, her general way of life, and her view of a husband who was so long an absentee from home. The imaginative authors of what now is called a profile have equipped her with most of the known virtues and vices. To Frank Harris she was an intolerable shrew; to Edmund Fripp, whose two compendious volumes, rich in research into the personalities and practices of Stratford, appeared in 1938, she was almost a saint. But before this kind of surmise comes to be discussed the problem set by the Worcester register confronts us. Was there an actual Anne Whateley of Temple Grafton? Or must she be deemed a mythical figure, begotten by a careless clerk and mothered by his mis-spelling?

Could there have been a Battle of the Brides in which the Hathaways, powerfully backed by Sandells and Richardson, were victors at the last minute? The suggestion horrifies those who cannot admit to any reckless love-making on the part of their hero in his lusty youth. Shakespeare has been justly venerated by many not only as a genius but with less reason as a model of the English virtues. Bardolatry has its ethical side as well as its proper devotion to the supreme poet and playwright.

There he lies in the fine church at Stratford. To it on his birthday marches a procession of his townsfolk, young and old, carrying flowers for his tomb. There are Shakespeare sermons and addresses from the pulpit in Southwark Cathedral beside the Thames as well as on the banks of the Avon. I cannot agree that Shakespeare was throughout his life a convinced Christian proving his faith by his works. If he is to be almost canonised I can take no part in that.

He had of course to conform. As an important member of the Lord Chamberlain's Men, serving Queen Elizabeth, and later of the King's Men, serving King James, he was part of the Establishment which was firmly Protestant. Church-going was obligatory. It was a hard world in which to be accused of any kind of dissent, civil or religious, as Marlowe discovered amid menace at the end of his brief and fiery career. But Shakespeare had a private and wayward life as well as a public one of conformity. Throughout his writings there is revealed an intensely impressionable and sensuous nature. Beauty of all kinds and not least the beauty of women ravished him.

The voicing of passion in the plays has always the pulse of a passionate man. The story of the Sonnets does not suggest the work of a good and faithful husband. It has been maintained that the 'Dark Lady' was only an idea and the section about her fascination, cruelty, and treachery only an academic exercise. That is incredible to me. In his maturity Shakespeare knew all about 'the expense of spirit in a waste of shame'. That he had been at eighteen one of those whom Touchstone called 'the country copulatives' is undisputed. He was one month past his nineteenth birthday when he became a father.

His premarital, fruitful, and therefore unconcealable intercourse with Anne Hathaway can be reasonably defended by those determined to preserve the image of an exemplary Shakespeare. It is explained that such indulgence was regularly accepted if marriage followed. The church ceremony, we are assured, was a formal ratification of a plighted troth made in the presence of both families concerned. After the promise there was no censure of performance. Thomas Cranmer had announced that 'troth-plight is perfect matrimony before God'. The journey to the altar, if there was no evasion, removed all doubts and gave legal authority to the union. The Bishop of Worcester, by licensing the marriage in church with limited banns of William and Anne put them, as we now say, 'in the clear'. If it was generally believed in Stratford that 'troth-plight is matrimony before God' they may never have been out of it, assuming the pledge had been duly made with the elder Shakespeares and Hathaways consenting.

The rush to Worcester to get a special licence is explained by the oddities of ecclesiastical law concerning the season of Advent. From December 2 until January 2 no marriage could be celebrated without a costly special licence and on January 27, Septuagesima, there was a similar forbidden period which would delay until April 7 an ordinary wedding with threefold publication of the banns. These facts are familiar to readers of the many lives of Shakespeare.

Edgar Fripp, in his two comprehensive volumes 'Shakespeare Man and Artist' (1938) explained the situation. He was a profound student of Stratford's personalities and customs as well as of the poet's career. He was also a devoted encomiast of Anne's character as well as William's. But he candidly adds to his account of the excursion to Worcester 'Anne was with child and wanted her dowry'. Here we get the realistic side of the Shottery romance.

Her dowry was not large. Her recently deceased father had left her six pounds, thirteen shillings and fourpence 'to be paid unto her at the day of her marriage'. Sandells and Richardson had brought with them, despite the risk of robbery on the road, forty pounds in cash to make sure of the special licence. That was a very large sum at the time. Shakespeare's purchase fifteen years later of New Place, Stratford's principal house, cost him only sixty pounds. The purchasing power of Anne's little legacy was not inconsiderable and probably worth well over a hundred pounds in the steadily decreasing money-values of our time. When William first worked in the London theatres 'as a serviture', or 'hired man' as the minor players were called, he had to live on ten shillings a week. Six and a half pounds was more than a trousseau in the making.

The wooing at Shottery has been amply romanticised. Some of

the Shakespearian devotees would think it blasphemy to suggest that the elder party took the lead. To Fripp, who could be emotional as well as statistical, Anne was an admirable woman on her way to being a model wife. According to him she was and remained for William his 'Queen of curds and cream'. That lush complimentary phrase was paid by Camillo to Perdita in *The Winter's Tale* (IV.iii.161). It is a customary surmise that Shakespeare was proud of his two daughters and their looks and had them in mind when he was imagining the heroines of the later romantic comedies, but that he was thus saluting his now elderly wife is a less convincing supposition.

Fripp imagined that Shakespeare was always looking back fondly to the scene of his love-making and was describing with affection Hewlands Farm when he wrote some eighteen years later of 'a sheep-cote' with a ripple of water-music laid on and 'the rank of osiers by the murmuring stream' (*As You Like It*, IV.iii.79–81.) But he did not include Celia's following remark 'The house doth keep itself. There's none within.' The farm was very far from empty desolation. It must have been an exceptionally happy occasion if the lovers could find a solitary couch in a conveniently deserted home. The Hathaways were so many.

Anne's father Richard was twice married. After his death in 1581 his senior son and heir, Bartholomew, who married three months later, moved in with his wife. He was charged in his father's will 'to guide' the farm-management of his step-mother and to be 'a comfort unto his brethren and sisters'. He could hardly do that unless he were on the spot. In 1582 Anne was living not only with them but also with a nestful of younger brothers and sisters. According to the family tree compiled by Sir Edmund Chambers there were one sister and four brothers aged between four and thirteen. There would be abundance of work in looking after and feeding them. Also there was an unmarried sister of nineteen. If they all packed into the Hathaway cottage as it now is that must have been a crowded, noisy, and sometimes cantankerous household from which escape would be extremely welcome. Even if some were settled in a neighbouring cottage there would be little rest from labour.

If one follows Fripp's example and rakes round the plays for suitable quotations one might select as a fair description of Anne's daily round 'The maid that milks and does the meanest chares' (*Antony and Cleopatra*, IV.iii.78). For an elder daughter in a densely populated farm-house here was a long, hard day. She would have lost that curds-and-creamy look by the end of it. But looks can be repaired and Shakespeare could meet a sufficiently alluring companion when he paid one of his August evening calls and took her (or was taken by her) up the garden and into the fields. (The music of the murmuring stream was consoling, but an osier bed would have been rather damp for dalliance.) To be permanently released from Shottery's 'chares' was an attractive prospect to the elder daughter of a full house.

She may not have at once become mistress of a home of her own. Social historians tell us that it was a custom of the time for young married couples to go to live with parents. Accordingly it is generally assumed that after their wedding the young Shakespeares did not enjoy privacy but were accommodated at John Shakespeare's home in Henley Street now known as 'The Birthplace'. Within our own experience after wars when many marriages take place and few houses are built that kind of lodgment is common and frequently disturbing and even disastrous to conjugal as well as parental relations. But whatever Anne may have felt about sharing life with her in-laws in Stratford she may well have thought that preferable to her old existence at Shottery. However much Bartholomew tried to fulfil his father's request for comforting guidance of the farming and the children there cannot have been much comfort for those concerned.

The years were passing. She was twenty-six or close on that age when she took her amorous rambles with eighteen-year-old William. Girls then expected to be and usually were married young or even very young. It would not shock Elizabethan audiences to hear that the Capulets, though at first unwilling to marry Juliet to Count Paris before she had reached 'the change of fourteen years', later decided that she should be married at once and willy-nilly 'to that noble earl'. Quite apart from the pressure of living and working in the close-packed domesticity at Hewlands Farm, Anne, if she wanted a husband as well as a refuge, had good cause to look round and take action. It would be intolerable to be left, in the common phrase, 'on the shelf'.

When she proposed or agreed to be intimate with her William he could be considered, age apart, to be a good match. If, as some think, he was idle, feckless, a poacher of deer, and unable to earn a living Anne, however strong her desire to escape from spinsterdom, would not, unless she were madly infatuated, have mated with a youngster likely to make little money and much trouble. What he did after leaving school is uncertain. He may have become, as John Aubrey related in the gossiping way of his 'Brief Lives' 'a school-master in the country'. If that assignment was away from Stratford he could be home on an August holiday, a lively fellow with idle hours to fill.

I think it more probable that he was employed in a lawyer's office than in a class-room. Litigation was one of the major recreations of the Stratfordians and a promising and literate youngster could find employment without difficulty among 'the quiddits, quillets, cases, tenures, recognisances, fines, and double vouchers' mentioned by Hamlet as the burden of an attorney's desk and the matter of his law-books. Shakespeare's close acquaintance and frequent use of legal terms have been often remarked upon and strongly point to that kind of intended career. If he was a schoolmaster he thought poorly of his colleagues; the pedagogues in his plays are either ludicrous or pedantic creatures. He obviously did not care much for the procedures and jargon of the law, but he did know and long remembered the vocabulary of the suits and pleas.

Whatever his first profession he was a lad with a job of one kind or another and, if he stuck to it, he could be thought to have a respectable future. The present rewards might be small, but Anne was not accustomed to big money. The Hathaways could make the land yield a living, but it was not a rich one for them. To suggest that William was a desirable capture as well as a charming companion for a harassed and maturing daughter is not to be cynical. It is merely to face the facts which the carefully collected chronicles of the Hathaway family life reveal.

We owe much to the scholars who pursue such research with their indefatigable industry. But the academic mind is apt to forget the flesh and blood which lie behind the pedigrees and those workings of human nature which produced the marriages and births in the registers. It is no insult to the venerated Shakespeare to imagine that in the April of his years and in the flush of youth he could be off with one love and on with another. Few courtships are a continuous stream of honey. There is always the chance of speaking out and falling out. 'The Queen of curds and cream' may have turned sour in a fit of petulance despite her eagerness for marriage. Or William, suddenly more conscious than before of their difference in age, may have noticed and been noticed by another and a younger woman.

Temple Grafton was a short ride on a horse and a young man, if he did not own and could not borrow a mount, could walk the five miles with ease and be glad of it if there was a feminine magnet at the end of them. Suppose that he had met Anne Whateley when she was marketing in Stratford? There is ample evidence that the name was quite common in the district. If this second Anne was a considerable charmer meeting William on the rebound from a tiff she may have put a spark to a fire more powerful than that which had been kindled at Shottery. If so there could have been a conflict of loyalties which was carried as far as the bishop's register at Worcester. Later Shakespeare was to observe that 'Love is too young to know what conscience is'. That is not an opinion expressed by a character in a play. It is the poet's own voice in a Sonnet.

The mere notion of this shocks the ethical Bardolaters. In the note on Anne Whateley included in the vast and valuable 'Shakespeare Encyclopaedia' (1967) edited by the American scholar Oscar James Campbell, Professor Emeritus of English at Columbia University, with Edward Quinn as his associate, any belief in the existence of this person is to be one of the 'Detractors of Shakespeare'. Their offence is described as supposing that Anne Hathaway's mother and brother 'getting wind of the poet's plan to marry another woman forced him into a kind of shot-gun wedding'. Nobody has so far mentioned fire-arms. To introduce the punitive blunderbuss is to write in terms of melodrama, film-script, and show business. 'Annie Get Your Gun' has been the title of a widely popular musical piece. The idea of two Annies getting two guns may be entertaining but cannot be seriously entertained.

My writings about Shakespeare clear me of any charge of detraction. But I do believe for reasons now to be explained that an ardent and impetuous young man could—I do not say did— become foolishly entangled. The annals of village life are neither short nor simple. Hasty, necessary, and sometimes compelled marriages occur when a pregnancy can no longer be denied or concealed. Bitter feminine rivalries are not rare.

There would be no grounds for believing in the existence of Anne Whateley were it not for the precise statement of her name and home in the Worcester entry for November 27. This is followed by a different personal name about which there could be a muddle and by a totally dissimilar place-name in the entry for November 28. It has been repeatedly argued that the Whately of the first date must be a mistake and it is reasonable to say that the two family names have three letters in common, a, h, and w. A careless and hurried clerk could have confused them. But it is wholly impossible to say that Temple Grafton sufficiently re-sembles Stratford to excuse that blunder.

An explanation had to be invented. Anne Hathaway, according to Fripp, 'apparently went to live with her mother's people at Temple Grafton'. He gives no evidence for that. It is a surmise made to deny any possibility of a scandal. If we had any record that any Hathaways, about whose family we know a surprising amount, were living at Temple Grafton, the conjecture would be fair enough. But no such evidence is produced and Anne's home is named as Stratford, in whose parish was Shottery. Sir Edmund Chambers (Vol. 2, p. 51) says: 'Fripp conjectures that Anne's mother came from Temple Grafton and went to live there, but she is "of Stratford" in the bond. Mr S. O. Addy conjectures that John Shakespeare farmed at Temple Grafton for which there is no evidence whatever.

In two excellent books of recent appearance the affair gets different treatment. Dr Rowse in his 'William Shakespeare, a

Biography', 1963, followed Fripp and stated that Anne had gone to stay with her relatives at Temple Grafton. He makes no mention at all of Anne Whateley. Peter Quennell in 'Shakespeare, the Poet and his Background', 1963, admitted the possibility of her existence. 'Shakespeare's more speculative biographers,' he said, had put forward the claims of the two women 'on their too-impetuous lover' whom they were seeking to pin down. He did not decide the matter with Fripp's airy assumption of a Hathaway settlement in Temple Grafton but fairly concluded 'Whatever the truth may be, it was Anne Hathaway of Stratford whom Shakespeare made his wife.' That is agreed fact. But nobody knows where the wedding took place.

Here again is a mystery. Surely if Anne is 'of Stratford' in the register and her bridegroom was also a Stratford man it should have happened there. But there is no record of it in the Stratford Church register which fortunately gives us so much information about the Shakespeares. Fripp thought Temple Grafton likely and even named the officiating Vicar as 'old John Frith', who had been a Catholic priest in the reign of Queen Mary. Though he was bibulous and was deemed 'unsound in religion' he must have taken care to be sound enough to escape persecution. The Temple Grafton records did not begin until three years after the wedding. So that cannot be confirmed.

Other churches in the neighbourhood of Stratford have been suggested. Among the guesses the most plausible in my opinion is in Worcester where the couple may have stayed to make the speediest possible use of their special licence. There are church records for the parish of St Martin's in that city. It was discovered that two leaves of the register covering the likely date of the marriage had been cut out; an unscrupulous collector may have snatched this prize. The relic-hunter is sometimes a devotee whose devotion carries him into theft and vandalism. Shakespeare forgeries have been notorious; a pilfering of pages, even from a church, is quite possible. The site of the ceremony does not greatly matter. Somewhere it was celebrated and Shakespeare returned to Stratford a married man.

Anne Whateley, if she existed, disappears, but not into total obscurity. There is no limit to the imagination of those who maintain that Shakespeare cannot have been the author of the plays and poems. Claims have been put forward for more than fifty people or groups of people. Professor Campbell's 'Shakespeare Encyclopaedia' serviceably provides a list of those known as the Claimants although they put forward no claims for themselves since secrecy was their purpose. The nominees for the honour of the real Shakespearian authorship have been led by Francis Bacon and the Earl of Oxford as captain and second in command of the bi-sexual team which includes Queen Elizabeth, Mary Queen of Scots, assorted flowers of the literate nobility, the Jesuits, the Rosicrucians, and even Anne Whateley. With so much nonsense being talked it is astonishing that none of the fanciful stakers of these fantastic claims, while demanding justice for a neglected genius, should have thrown a laurel-wreath to Shottery. Anne Hathaway won her man but as a potential poetess is left out in the cold. So here is one victory, albeit of a preposterous kind, for Temple Grafton.

One assumption is that the back wing of the birthplace was the scene of Susanna's as well as her father's origin and that it had been turned into a separate dwelling with its own kitchen and staircase to the bedroom. Let us hope that such an arrangement was made. Sharing of kitchens in shared and crowded homes frequently sets trouble on the boil. However gracious John Shakespeare's wife Mary may have been and however cautiously the incoming Anne behaved the strains of proximity would have been eased by some such refuge for the young couple. Frith becomes ecstatic about the arrangement. 'Here among the apple-trees and early summer flowers, we will venture to think, Anne gave birth to her child in May 1583, and enjoyed the care of the Poet's mother with the loved name of Mary Arden.' Perhaps, but I have known Stratford when icy winds were doing more than shake the darling buds of May. But Mary Arden has previously been seen as a sensible and kindly creature. So we too may 'venture to think' that the pains which brought the infant Susanna into the world were eased as far as might be by the consoling friendship of two of Shakespeare's women.

CHAPTER IV

Husband and Wife

How DID it work out? The 'more speculative biographers'
mentioned by Peter Quennell have included one who was very
speculative indeed and confidently so. He was Frank Harris,
whose book on 'The Man Shakespeare and his Tragic Life Story'
was published in 1909 and welcomed by Arnold Bennett as an
enlivening contrast to the orthodox lives written by the high
academic authorities whom he described as mandarins and
whom Harris swept aside as 'Dryasdust and company'. If the
professors thus accused of stodginess and aridity made any state-
ments about the success or failure of Shakespeare's marriage they
had to be as conjectural as those of any speculator. There are no
letters which could indicate the temper of the 'troth-plighted' and
now wedded couple. The date of the first parting caused by
William's departure to London is a matter of guess-work. It
cannot have been immediate since he was in Stratford in May
1585 to beget the twins christened on February 2, 1586. The early
years may have provided 'the top of happy hours' imagined by
some or the regrets and despairs and even loathings imagined by
Frank Harris.

The ideas about the marriage have been totally contradictory.
To Harris it produced a hell, at least for the husband. To Fripp
the result was a heaven mutually shared and long continuing.
With his habit of extracting from the play-texts, some of which
were written a quarter of a century after the celebration at the
unknown church, he paraded a string of Shakespearian tributes to
holy wedlock, high wedlock, happy wedlock homes, and to the
presiding pagan deity of marriage-rites,

> *Honour, high honour, and renown*
> *To Hymen, god of every town.*

The wife was perfection, radiating tranquillity. Anne, according to Fripp, was 'godly, quiet, clinging, frail'. Her tongue did not clack. She was as quiet as Virgilia, the wife whom Coriolanus called 'my gracious silence'. This is, of course, nothing but surmise.

If Anne was sparing in her concession of conjugal rights to a highly sexed male there was still, for Fripp, a bed of roses. And bliss continued whenever they were together. William was thinking of that, we are told, when he came to write *Cymbeline*, a play usually assigned to 1609 or 1610. In it he made Posthumus say of Imogen (Act II.iv.9–12)

> *Me of my lawful pleasure she restrain'd,*
> *And pray'd me oft forbearance; did it with*
> *A pudency so rosy, the sweet view on't*
> *Might well have warm'd old Saturn;*

So any frigidity was forgiven, but Fripp, as was noted in the matter of the sheep-cote by the murmuring stream, did not follow up his quotations. The immediate sequel to these remarks about a rosy pudency is a violent and comprehensive tirade against the vices of women. It is absurd to say that he had Anne in mind when he thus raged against her sex; nor is there any reason for associating her with the rose-tinted pudency. She may have been as highly sexed as he was.

The fury of Posthumus was natural to the story of Iachimo's trickery and slandering of Imogen. So are the remarks about Imogen's prayers for 'oft forbearance'. They make her supposed treachery the more revolting to her husband. Shakespeare was a playwright and to sift the words of his invented characters for lines to back an argument can lead to ridiculous conclusions. Something may sometimes be gained by this method, but only if the selected speeches seem alien to the persons and the plot. Such cases deserve special attention.

Harris, always eager to contradict the orthodox, believed

strongly in the Battle of the Brides. Anne Whateley he confidently introduced as the loser. That defeat, he maintained, was an excellent thing, because if Shakespeare had married her, he might have been a happy and contented man, bedded down for life in Warwickshire. It was well, runs the argument, that he was tied to Anne in the galling chains of a marriage which proved to be a calamity. Her bad temper, her railing and scolding drove him to seek escape from the house. But how was he to make a living if he fled from Stratford? The temptation and the occasion to make a new career came when two teams of visiting play-actors were to be seen and heard in the town in 1587. So he put an end to his five years of wedded misery and was off with them to London. Thus the English stage and English poetry were enriched beyond measure. That the world has been vastly indebted to the tantrums of the irascible Anne Hathaway was Harris's view of the marriage in disruption.

One part of this guess-work may well be correct. The date and cause of the departure are plausible. Acting companies carrying the name and protection of royalty or great nobles were frequently in Stratford during the fifteen-eighties. Some of the mandarins and Dryasdusts agree with Harris that two 'fellowships of players', those under the nominal patronage of the queen and the Earl of Leicester, were in Warwickshire in 1587; they fascinated Shakespeare, noticed him as 'a likely lad' when he approached them, and took him away as a promising recruit. So far, so reasonable. But evidence of the young husband's domestic torment has to be found or invented.

Harris had inevitably to play the customary game of Shakespearian biographers and pick his quotations. Since he constantly stressed the impetuously passionate elements in Shakespeare's character he seized on the salty comments of the shepherd who has discovered the exposed child Perdita. 'I would there were no years between ten and twenty-three or that youth could sleep out the rest; for there is nothing in between but getting wenches with child, wronging the ancientry, stealing, fighting.' (*The Winter's Tale*, III.iii.16–20.) Why, it is asked, the allusion to three-and-twenty? Why select that age instead of the more natural twenty-one? Because, the argument continues, that was a date of particular significance and long remembered as his year of liberation. In 1587 Shakespeare was twenty-three and that number slipped out subconsciously while he wrote this speech.

He had certainly got a wench with child. If there is any substance in the now usually discredited legend about his escapade as a poacher in the deer-park at Charlecote he had wronged the ancientry in the person of Sir Thomas Lucy. There had been four and a half years of the matrimony alleged by Harris to be utterly miserable. The year is a probable one for his removal from an irksome profession and a more than troublesome wife. If he was accepted as a promising tyro by Lord Leicester's Men or by any other troupe on tour about that time he would have four years as a 'servitor' player and apprentice playwright before he began to emerge as the busy and soon successful 'Johannes Factotum' in the early fifteen-nineties. The supposition is fairly plausible, but it is not an indication of the bitter domestic contention which Harris alleged.

Accordingly he had to hunt round for passages in which a married woman is portrayed as a virago. Yet he did not concentrate or even mention 'Kate the curst' in *The Taming of the Shrew*. The fact that she yielded in the end did not assist his case. Harris could not quote from Katharine's final speech her admission that a husband is his wife's lord, life, and helper, since William in his opinion had been down-trodden. But he could have extracted the lines about a dreadful spouse

> *froward, peevish, sullen, sour*
> *And not obedient to his honest will,*
> *What is she but a foul contending rebel*
> *And graceless traitor to her loving lord?*

There is punning in the Sonnets and also probably in *Love's Labour's Lost* on the word will used both as noun and personal name. So 'honest will' as the victim of domestic revolt could have been brought in. But Petruchio's shrew was tamed and Anne was not. William was not her lord and keeper. Therefore another picture of the turbulent wife had to be produced.

It was found by Harris in *The Comedy of Errors*. That is an early play and the date of its composition is uncertain. It was certainly in the repertory of Shakespeare's company when it was performed just after Christmas at Gray's Inn in 1594. It was kept in hand or produced in revival by 'His Majesty's Players' for King James to see it at court in 1604. But one does not hear any more of it until it appeared in the First Folio in 1623. It was a juvenile crudity and may well have been written at the outset of Shakespeare's authorship. However that may be, Harris saw in the arrival of Antipholus of Syracuse at Ephesus a self-portrait based on memories of the raw young actor arriving in London, 'stiff and weary' after 'long travel' but anxious, like any country-man with an inquiring mind, 'to view the manners of the town', watch the traders and see the buildings while remaining wary of the 'cozenage' practised by 'disguised cheaters, prating mounte-banks'.

The lines have a personal quality and do suggest the recollection of a revealing and exciting day which had never lost its glamour and excitement for the retentive mind. Here, after petty Stratford, was the city of opportunity, a raree-show of strange types, the thieving 'nips', the prosperous merchants, and the foppish, swaggering grandees with their costly elegance. Shakespeare was at large, probably seeking the cheapest of lodgings, but with the freedom of a bachelor. He was now a Londoner and on leave from the status of a husband. If conscience gnawed at the new-comer for desertion of a wife and family he had the compensations of liberty in the capital hitherto known only by report. In another early play, *Two Gentlemen of Verona*, there is another young man who rejects caution and is determined to see 'the wonders of the world abroad' instead of being 'dully sluggardised at home'.

One character in *The Comedy of Errors* is well suited to Harris's purpose in the denigration of Anne. She is Adriana, the wife of the second Antipholus for whom the first is mistaken on the assumption that a Twin Set farce justifies any confusion of this kind. Antipholus falls in love with Luciana who thinks he is Adriana's real husband. There follows, without much reason, a lurid picture of a jealous, scolding woman with a violent temper.

It is odd and may be significant that she resents her 'homely age' and 'decayed' beauty. Why should that grievance of the years be introduced unless there was here a memory of Anne who was about thirty when her husband of twenty-three was going to town? Harris quoted, with obvious pleasure, the cry of Antipholus

> *She that doth call me husband, even my soul*
> *Doth for a wife abhor.*

Abhor is a word often occurring in Shakespeare's texts and he did not use it lightly.

At the end of the play Antipholus takes refuge from his troubles in an abbey. Because of the confusion of personalities Adriana thinks that he has gone mad. The lady abbess becomes a judge. In her adjudication she shows a most surprising knowledge of what the poor man had endured at Adriana's hands:

> *And thereof came it that the man was mad:*
> *The venom-clamours of a jealous woman*
> *Poisons more deadly than a mad-dog's tooth.*
> *It seems his sleeps were hinder'd by thy railing:*
> *And thereof comes it that his head is light.*
> *Thou say'st his meat was sauced with thy upbraidings:*
> *Unquiet meals make ill digestions, —*
> *Thereof the raging fire of fever bred;*
> *And what's a fever but a fit of madness?*
> *Thou say'st his sports were hinder'd by thy brawls:*
> *Sweet recreation barr'd, what doth ensue*
> *But moody and dull melancholy,*
> *Kinsman to grim and comfortless despair;*
> *And at her heels a huge infectious troop*
> *Of pale distemperatures and foes to life?*
> *In food, in sport, and life-preserving rest*
> *To be disturb'd, would mad or man or beast:*
> *The consequence is, then, thy jealous fits*
> *Have scared thy husband from the use of wits.*
>
> (*The Comedy of Errors*, Act. v.i.68–85.)

Where did the lady abbess get these harrowing details of extreme distress? Nobody has advised her of the case to which she comes in ignorance. 'Wherefore throng you hither?' she asks of the noisy contestants. Yet she quickly provides a full list of the husband's many sufferings.

Harris had a point here. Out of Shakespeare's angry memories of domestic humiliation, he argued, there poured subconsciously the astonishing catalogue of his physical and mental pains. dyspepsia and fever, sleepless nights, and 'sweet recreations' interrupted and barred by a brawling woman. She has scared him out of his wits—and scared him out of Stratford too if this interpretation be correct. Harris repeatedly maintained that we can learn much about Shakespeare's own feelings and opinions if quotation from speeches in the plays is based on the irrelevance of the chosen passage to the plot of the play and purpose of the scene. Fripp's unjustifiable method was to extract phrases here and there without discussing their context. Harris may have been guessing quite wrongly, but he could reasonably assert that this explicit description of wrongs and endurances is impossible to explain unless the dramatist had forgotten the possibilities of the abbess's knowledge and was breaking away from the drama of Ephesus to get his own domestic drama off his chest.

Abhor is a strong word and it is hard to believe that incompatibility had passed into such a fury of indignation. The view of the complete rift put forward by Harris is more ingenious than persuasive. Common sense suggests that, if the move to London followed a series of quarrels, both parties contributed to the parting. Matrimonial squabbles could come in the natural course of events without violent loathing as their cause or sequel. Should there have been abhorrence on Shakespeare's side it was not sustained over the years. If his life had been made intolerable why did he ever return to this hornet's nest?

John Aubrey drew some of his material from Christopher Beeston, an actor who died in 1681 and was the son of William Beeston, a player in Shakespeare's company. If there was gossip at least it came in a direct line from the actors. Aubrey was a tattler but the source which he used for his jottings on Shakespeare was quite a good one. His statement that Shakespeare 'was wont to goe to his native country once a yeare' can fairly be believed. How soon he began these to-and-fro journeys from London is not stated but it is evident that the idea of a regular return to Stratford was not repulsive to him. It is documented fact that he bought New Place in 1597. There was no reason to do that unless he wished to settle Anne and the children in the station of life which he thought due to them and which he could now afford and readily provided.

The idea of a strife heavily charged with hatred contradicts what we know of Shakespeare's career and character. Jealousies, grievances, resentments are common dissolvents of partnerships, professional as well as matrimonial. They are frequent in the theatrical world. But the facts of his stage-career prove that he avoided any schism or separation. The Revels Accounts of the royal household show that by 1594 he was an important member of the Lord Chamberlain's Men. With them, later known as the King's Men, he stayed for the rest of his working life. Other dramatists moved from one management to another while he stayed with 'the fellowship'.

Some of the playwrights were fiery fellows, sudden in quarrel, ready with their swords as well as their tongues. Marlowe was in trouble as a brawler. In 1592 two constables of Shoreditch petitioned for security, swearing that they were in terror while he lived thereabouts. Ben Jonson, who revered the classics and behaved like a romantic, fought a duel in 1596, killed a man, and was lucky to get away with his life after a term in the Marshalsea prison. Gaol sentences for writing deemed indiscreet or seditious were frequent. Jonson suffered that way in 1605 because of his share in a play called *Eastward Ho!*

As actor-playwright Shakespeare kept peaceable company and never lost his freedom by losing his temper. We hear nothing of him as a swordsman. None of his fiery characters, such as Tybalt, were self-portraits. There was some contention with an ill-tempered and corrupt magistrate in South London, Mr Justice Gardiner, who maintained that Shakespeare, along with Francis Langley, the owner of the Swan Theatre, was endangering his life. But Gardiner was an unprincipled liar and scoundrel and there is no evidence that he needed 'the sureties of the peace' for which he asked or that he got them.

The general impression to be derived from contemporary allusions is of an affable, companionable Shakespeare who did not 'blow his top' on provocation. He was praised for his 'civil demeanour'. He never revealed personal animosity in his work and there is no example in the records of his life of his hating and pursuing hatreds. He was deeply pained, as the Sonnets show, by what he thought the treachery of a dear friend and soon forgave him. In so far as he could be called a preacher in his plays his call was to mercy and forgiveness. Aubrey, after his talks about Shakespeare with Beeston, reported that he was 'very good companie and of a very readie and pleasant smooth Witt'. In other words he had suavity of manner and was what is called 'a good mixer'. If so calm and self-contained throughout his career why should he have been so rancorous in his youth as to profess abhorrence of his wife?

That Anne and the children were left unprovided for by a conscienceless deserter is one reading of the events in Stratford when he left it in 1587 or thereabouts. It is taken for granted that he had no money to leave behind him. But that is not certain. Aubrey said that he had been 'a school-master in the country'. It has been suggested that this kind of work could have included a tutorial position in a great house. The nobility did not as a rule send their sons away to school (Philip Sidney at Shrewsbury was an exception) but engaged private instructors for their sons until they reached the age of university entrance at fourteen or so.

On the western fringe of the Cotswolds, country familiar to Shakespeare as several mentions of it in the plays attest, was Berkeley Castle, which is named in *Richard II* with the curious additional detail of its 'tuft of trees'. It is hard to explain this piece of landscape painting unless Shakespeare had seen and remembered the timber. Furthermore the Earl of Berkeley kept a troupe of players who went on tour and were five times in Stratford. It is a likely scene for a tutorial engagement which also stimulated theatrical interests. If William left Anne for a while to work in this household she must have felt that he was doing well for himself and for her. There was the chance, if he gave satisfaction, to receive a gift of money in addition to his salary. A tutor in a rich home who knew his way about was not working on stony ground.

The plausible idea that he was employed in his home-town in a lawyer's office does not exclude the chance of additional occupation in a tutorial job. He had eight or ten years to fill between leaving school and going to London. Even if we accept the now dismissed deer-poaching escapade that is no proof of a generally idle life. Throughout his years in London Shakespeare was astonishingly industrious, quick and constant with his pen, busy with the cares of administration as 'a sharer' in the house-management as well as the theatrical policy and performance of his company. He was continuing to memorise and rehearse parts and to appear as an actor in 1603 in a play not his own when there was no need for him to do so. If he was so energetic then he is unlikely to have been a complete idler in his earlier years, especially if there was money to be made. He may have been bored by the legal chores, but there were good rewards to be made in a community with such a zest for taking debts and disagreements to court. In addition to the wage or share of fees there would be 'pickings' for a hard-working and astute young man who proved his possession of both qualities later on.

To say that Shakespeare was astute is not to demean him as avaricious. Some people are horrified at the thought of a genius who mingles calculation with inspiration. But the history of literature has many examples of the good writer who was also a good business man. Throughout his later life he was careful and thrifty as were others of the Chamberlain's Men who bought houses in the suburbs or the country. What he earned he looked after, investing steadily in land, and proud to be a man, or rather a gentleman, of property. His placing of his steadily rising capital will be discussed when we come to the purchase of New Place.

Frank Harris was strangely ignorant of this side of Shakespeare's character. He was far off the mark when he said that Shakespeare was 'extravagant to lavishness' and 'free-handed and careless'. There is no evidence that he was mean. There is abundant proof that he advanced steadily in moderate wealth and used it with the shrewd tenacity of a countryman who likes to own his own land and buildings and add to them. He saw to it that his family were finely housed and had their sizeable inheritance. There had to be lean years at the start, but not so lean, I think, as has been supposed. Since he had a keen sense of values, in money as well as in his majestic use of words, it is reasonable to suppose that his life did not involve a complete change from juvenile indolence and squandering to acquisition and retention of money hardly earned. Would Anne have been so eager to marry a mere boy if she had known him to be a wastrel?

The surroundings of Shakespeare's boyhood were those of a small-town commerce which was frequently contentious. There were quarrels and hard bargains. The shop-keepers ran the affairs of his town where his father, a glover by craft and seemingly a zealous public servant, held various offices and finally became in 1568 bailiff or mayor. The Hathaways were not farmers on a large scale and small farmers have no chance to be careless about money. The plays do not reveal contempt for retail trade. Usurers he did not like, but the fair dealer in the market gets no derision from him. His was a middle-class and bourgeois world and he accepted it. One of the traditional stories provides a picture of a capitalist in the making.

Dowdall was told by the aged sexton that Shakespeare was received into the playhouse as 'a servitor'. It was elsewhere said that he was first employed in 'a very mean rank'. The acting companies were divided into boy-apprentices, hired men, and sharers. The hired men were poorly paid and all the players were hard worked since there were no long runs and new pieces had to be continually found and rehearsed. But there would be chances for a keen-witted man to make money on the side.

What was Anne's position when he decided to join the players? There had been a stream of touring troupes in Stratford while she was growing up. They kept on returning; obviously they were popular with their lively additions to small-town pleasures.

Only in the eyes of the law were they 'rogues and vagabonds' and from the law they were protected by the name of the nobleman who gave them his support but did not necessarily finance them. There is no record of the visiting troupes practising roguery, being riotous or otherwise misbehaving during their regular appearances in the town. Shakespeare's father had welcomed the Queen's Men and the Earl of Worcester's Men during his year as bailiff in 1568-9. The local puritanism which was later on to spread and ban players from Stratford was not yet powerful in civic affairs. So there was no cause for Anne to be ashamed if her husband enlisted in a company protected by one of the lordships. The patronage was august.

The risk was more of finance than of reputation. If my view of Shakespeare's thrifty nature and ability to save during his first occupations is sound he could leave something in Anne's purse when he went. That he should wantonly desert her and the children with nothing in hand and no provision is completely contrary to the man's character as later established. Only if we accept the Harris portrait of domestic abhorrence and of recklessness with money could he have walked out with a callous lack of consideration for his family. To use a word once employed by Shakespeare, Anne was doubtless 'frampold' at times. (This was an adjective applied to ill-tempered horses; Mistress Ford in *The Merry Wives of Windsor* is said by Mistress Quickly to lead 'a very frampold life' with her 'jealousy' husband.) In the normal way of married life there would be frictions which stimulated his resolve.

Angry protest when he did insist on making the break was likely enough. Anne could fairly protest that he was taking a chance; he could reply that it was the calculated risk of one who knew that he had it in him to write fine words and to speak them too, that he knew what he was doing, and was confident of his power to get rapidly ahead. He could not guarantee to send money back during the beginning of his career, but he could use his wits to see that no opportunities of earning were lost. I do not see him madly jumping for joy when he crossed the Clopton Bridge with an outgoing company, especially if his boy and girls were there to see him go. Except in his passion-fretted sexual life he was in all else and throughout his life a man with both feet on the ground.

Sir William Davenant told the actor Betterton (1635–1710) a story about the theatrical recruit's earliest years in London. The tale was omitted by Shakespeare's first critical editor and biographer, Nicholas Rowe, who acknowledged his debt to Betterton's conversation when compiling his 'Some Account of the Life, etc., of William Shakespeare' published in 1709. Dr Johnson accepted it. The report was of an enterprise in horse-holding undertaken by Shakespeare on the fringe of his theatrical career. The mounted play-goers required someone to hold their horses during the performance. The significant part of this tradition, which had come down through the actors, is that Shakespeare was not only doing an odd job but organising a business. The venture went so well that he had to take on a staff. If he was engaged as a small-part actor he could not be thus occupied himself when the play was on, but setting up as an employer got round that difficulty. The story of this equestrian parking-site included further detail that the lads offered their services by saying 'I am Shakespeare's boy, sir.' If so, the organiser was sensibly careful to publicise his name.

That part of the Shakespeare Mythos, as Sir Edmund Chambers called reports of this kind, has not been widely accepted. But it has considerable plausibility. The invention of anecdotes was common in Stratford during the eighteenth century when the salesmanship of relics was being developed by the unscrupulous exploiters of the newly arrived 'Bardolatry'. The stories naturally went best if they had some 'news value'. So the local hero had poached and been whipped for it. He had joined in drinking matches and slept out as the result of it. He planted a mulberry tree whose wood became the raw material of countless mementoes. Anne played her part. She put Shottery on the tourist's map.

But the idea of a smart commercial undertaking is neither romantic nor picturesque. It fits the character of an enterprising youngster on the look-out for extra money. He certainly needed an addition to the meagre rewards of a minor actor or a commencing playwright. The dramatists received only a pound an act in a piece put together by collaborators or five pounds for a full-length piece which was all their own work. The script was bought outright and these fees covered all rights in the work, which became the property of the acting company. Shakespeare may have had better terms when he had scored some successes and made a name. But at first he needed every penny he could pick up. The player who was one of 'King James's Men' and was to become a groom of the Royal Chamber may have been glad at another time to be a groom of a humbler sort. Can one see Shakespeare as a crudely insensitive and callous father who would leave three small children as well as his wife without provision after a fit of temper and because of a hazardous ambition?

He could rely on their having a roof over their heads, preferably with his parents in Henley Street or back in Shottery with her family. It is arguable that during the fifteen-eighties John Shakespeare was unlikely to welcome a continuing domestic burden. He seems to have lost status and some of his money during the latter part of his life but his actions at that time are mysterious and have evoked much disagreement. The various scraps of fact gleaned from local records are confused and cause contradictory opinions. What matters is that John Shakespeare never had to sell his home or his business and that he had been honourably restored to the borough council from whose membership he had been dropped owing to long absence from its meetings. Almost certainly his troubles were more the product of religious views and disputes than of financial failure. When he died in 1601 he was not in disgrace or distress.

There was bitter contention among the Churches. The recently established Church of England was facing and endeavouring to suppress two kinds of opposition. The Roman Catholics, some openly and some secretly loyal to the Old Religion, were dissidents on one side. The puritans, on the other, were steadily rising in numbers and fanaticism. The Anglican Ecclesiastical Commission appointed in 1576 had powers to imprison or punish by seizure of property persons 'wilfully and obstinately absenting themselves from church'. There was an immediate persecution of those who would not be church-goers and that was intensified in

1577 in the see of Worcester when John Whitgift, a rigorous Anglican, became its bishop.

The recusants, as the absentees from church services on Sundays and feast days were called, were now in danger of going to gaol and losing their property. John Shakespeare was named as a recusant. Whether he was in revolt as a Catholic or a puritan has never been settled. He was bailiff of the borough in 1568, but he did not resign in protest when the Gild Chapel of Stratford was stripped of its Romish equipment and decorations and the parish church was deprived of its vestments. That suggests a zealous protestantism. On the other hand he had married into a Catholic family which had suffered for its faith and the traditional account of him, coming from Sir John Mennis and found among the manuscripts of Thomas Plume, Archdeacon of Rochester, provided the picture of 'a merry-cheek'd old man' who was always ready to 'crack a jest' with his son Will, 'a good honest fellow'. This is not reliable since Mennis was a child of three when John Shakespeare died, but it is interesting to note that Will was not remembered as a good-for-nothing but given a good character and a certificate of integrity. It is hard to see his father as a square-toed and austere puritan. The commonly held opinion attributes the recusancy to Catholic sympathies.

Whatever the recusant's reasons for refusing church attendance and for missing the meetings of the council of whose membership and actions the Stratford records give us quite a lot of information, he had to be careful and evasive. It was the common practice of those in danger of Whitgift's investigations and attacks to alienate or 'devise' their property in the hope of quietly retaining it. In the year of Whitgift's arrival John Shakespeare ceased to attend the council for which he had worked in various posts for twenty years. In the following year he mortgaged his wife's Wilmcote property and sold her share in the Snitterfield estate. One deduction from this is that he was covering up his tracks as a landed gentleman. A clear and compact analysis of the events is to be found on pages 14–25 of 'Shakespeare' published by M. M. Reese in 1953. It is not a book often quoted, but I find it excellent in scholarship and judgment. Reese decided that Whitgift's

Visitors, as they were called, when they went on their rounds found themselves provided only with 'the helpless riff-raff of the town-gaols' and that, when they wanted to pounce on solid citizens, they were put off with deceits and excuses. Reese called these devices 'transparent' but they must have been ingenious. The Visitors had eyes. There had to be some cunning to frustrate this inquisition.

There was natural and commendable sympathy for those menaced. Stratford was mainly a Protestant town and some of its people were drifting towards puritanism, but they were tolerant and did not carry their faith into abuse and unjust treatment of their Catholic neighbours. Men of radically different beliefs sat on the council. George Badger, a known Catholic, was actually bailiff when the hunt was on. It was explained that John Shakespeare like others stayed away from church because he feared arrest if he went out on Sunday. This was a kindly but absurd pretext. Was legal process out of action six days in the week? His fellow-Stratfordians were playing on his side. He had not lost popularity even if he could be called a Papist or at least sympathetic to Rome.

He still had money in hand. He faced a fine of as much as forty pounds which he could have avoided. That does not suggest ruin. When he was bound over to give sureties to keep the peace he managed to hamper collection of these by spreading them over three dioceses. It was an intensely worrying time, but he came through it unbroken. Moreover, he had obtained his coveted coat-of-arms in October, 1596, and was then certified a man of property. The plea for the grant of a coat was accepted by the Garter King-at-Arms with stated reasons. John Shakespeare, it was explained, had lands and property to the value of five hundred pounds.

His wife did not have to beg her bread and the home in Henley Street was not molested. If they shared that roof Anne and her children were in no danger of destitution during the first years of separation. John and Mary Shakespeare had their pride as well as their home in Henley Street, and sufficient money. William could leave them for his great adventure without appearing to be a defaulting scoundrel. The difficult years were round about 1590. After that the actor-dramatist of promise was 'making friends and gaining influence'. Fighting his way up in the theatres and winning favour with the generous Earl of Southampton he could send money home or bring it with him on his annual journey. It was difficult to make return journeys at first, but it is wildly improbable that he was not most anxious to see the children as often as he could. The case for domestic misery can be argued. Frank Harris made the most of Adriana. But the facts are stronger than the fancies. The subsequent events in Shakespeare's life show him to have done his utmost to provide security and status for his family. That his marriage had been disastrous and bitterly regretted, and that he had been a callous father content to leave his wife and children to be kept by others, is an idea effectively contradicted by his behaviour when he became, at the age of thirty-three, a man of property, contented to end his life in the comfortable home which Harris took to be a shrew's nest.

CHAPTER V

A Death and a Move

ON AUGUST 11, 1596, the Stratford parish church register recorded the burial of Hamnet, son of William Shakespeare. The boy died at the age of eleven years and five months. The Lives of his father have mainly been written by men absorbed in the masculine career; in times of trouble and grief it is William's suffering of which we read. His wife could not put her sorrow into words of unforgettable power and haunting music. He spoke for her whose grief cannot have been less and may have been more terrible and durable. She had lost her only son and, at thirty-nine or forty, she was unlikely to bear another.

It is true that losing children was a common experience of Stratford life. In the year after Hamnet's death the plague, which had decimated the population of the town in the year of Shakespeare's birth, struck again. In February and March funerals were constant and some were of boys of ten and eleven. Even without an epidemic infantile and juvenile mortality was high. The Shakespeares, as has been explained, were accustomed to early bereavements and burials.

While William was in London Anne was left with the two girls, Susanna now thirteen and Judith, Hamnet's twin. There had been time for the begetting of others. It was an age in which families were large. Gaps were quickly filled. The denigrators of Anne have mentioned as the cause of her failure to be a prolific mother refusal of cohabitation by one party or the other owing to mutual dislike or even the abhorrence suggested by Harris. That is only a guess and a mean one: also, considering the events of the following year, it is a foolish one. Shakespeare was not thinking only of London. He bought Stratford's major home, New

Place, nine months after the loss of Hamnet. Anne gained at least a material compensation for her bereavement. At last she had more rooms than she needed under a roof of her own. And so had he when he was back at home. There are no signs of mutual loathing in that transaction.

The play of *King John*, dated by most authorities as the work of 1596, contains the mourning speeches of Queen Constance, tremendous first in a turgid kind of verbal elaboration and then in a most moving simplicity. She believes that her boy Arthur is dead. He is in fact in prison. It is generally agreed that her farewell to the lost child was written by Shakespeare after Hamnet's end and poured out from a dark abyss of sorrow. This I confidently believe and it surprised me greatly to find that M. M. Reese, a biographer so excellent in many ways, would not accept that. He dismissed the queen's outcry as a routine poetic lament 'the accepted mediæval mode for the expression of tragic feeling' and said that 'it does no honour to Shakespeare's grief to identify it with the parade of a rhetorical convention'. Admittedly when Constance is desperately praying for an end to her own life she delivers the over-loaded oratorical eloquence which the poet could at any time majestically discharge.

> *Death, death:—O amiable lovely death!*
> *Thou odoriferous stench! sound rottenness!*
> *Arise forth from the couch of lasting night,*
> *Thou hate and terror to prosperity,*
> *And I will kiss thy detestable bones;*
> *And put my eyeballs in thy vaulty brows;*
> *And ring these fingers with thy household worms;*
> *And stop this gap of breath with fulsome dust;*
> *And be a carrion monster like thyself:*
> *Come, grin on me; and I will think thou smilest,*
> *And buss thee as thy wife! Misery's love,*
> *O, come to me!*
>
> (*King John*, III.iv.24–36.)

Shakespeare had a ready command of such gruesome imagery. He could turn the tap at will and set flowing the sonorous lamentation. But Hamlet is not being insincere when he cries out in this vein to his father's ghost

> *Let me not burst in ignorance; but tell*
> *Why thy canonized bones, hearsed in death,*
> *Have burst their cerements; why the sepulchre,*
> *Wherein we saw thee quietly inurn'd,*
> *Hath oped his ponderous and marble jaws*
> *To cast thee up again! ...*

(Hamlet, I.iv.20–24.)

But he suddenly passes to a superb economy of phrase when he thinks of men as fools horridly shaken

> *With thoughts beyond the reaches of our souls.*

The same thing happens in *King John*. The poignancy of authentic grief is intensified by the sudden change from the panoply of the play-house rhetoric to the austerity, almost the nudity, of unbedizened speech and the plainest of plain words. When Queen Constance is harshly rebuked by King Philip and Cardinal Pandulph for overdoing her agony and uttering 'madness not sorrow' her answer has the devastating power of the language which any parent might use in moments of extreme distress. Her speech needs full quotation.

> *For since the birth of Cain, the first male child,*
> *To him that did but yesterday suspire,*
> *There was not such a gracious creature born.*
> *But now will canker-sorrow eat my bud,*
> *And chase the native beauty from his cheek,*
> *And he will look as hollow as a ghost,*
> *As dim and meagre as an ague's fit;*
> *And so he'll die; and, rising so again,*
> *When I shall meet him in the court of heaven*
> *I shall not know him: therefore never, never*
> *Must I behold my pretty Arthur more.*

CARDINAL PANDULPH. *You hold too heinous a respect of grief.*
CONSTANCE. *He talks to me that never had a son.*

KING PHILIP. *You are as fond of grief as of your child.*
CONSTANCE. *Grief fills the room up of my absent child,*
  Lies in his bed, walks up and down with me,
  Puts on his pretty looks, repeats his words,
  Remembers me of all his gracious parts,
  Stuffs out his vacant garments with his form;
  Then have I reason to be fond of grief.
  Fare you well: had you such a loss as I,
  I could give better comfort than you do.
  I will not keep this form upon my head,
  When there is such disorder in my wit.
  O Lord! my boy, my Arthur, my fair son!
  My life, my joy, my food, my all the world!
  My widow-comfort, and my sorrows' cure!

                              (*King John,* III.iv.89–106.)

When Shakespeare was moved and was most moving he knew (and never better than when he wrote the final speeches of *King Lear*) the overwhelming impact of monosyllables with only the occasional admission of a longer word. I cannot see this as the conscious planning of a contriving writer. Instinctively he understood when rhetoric, pounding on the ears, would fail to drive at the heart and when the words of everyday use could be raised to a higher power and evoke the 'thoughts beyond the reaches of our souls'.

And so there comes quietly the language that Anne too might have employed on that August day. 'Dim and meagre', 'Hollow as a ghost'. The pinched limbs and pallor of the boy are there before our eyes.

          Grief fills the room up of my absent child,
          Lies in his bed, walks up and down with me,
          Stuffs out his vacant garments with his form.

Stuff is as ordinary a word as could be found. But it creates with its very crudity the vision of the coat and shirt of the schoolboy hung on a peg. The ague's fit brings up the stuffy smell of the sick-room on a hot day before the parents went out into the garden with grief as their walking company. How such writing can be called 'the parade of a rhetorical convention' defeats my comprehension. Rhetoric had resounded in this scene. Reality followed. Shakespeare was speaking simply for Anne as well as himself while in his play he was also speaking rhetorically to the groundlings and the gentry in the galleries of a theatre. The talk of Stratford and the tastes of London are fused in the high-flown and the homely style of this unforgettable passage.

Much has been written rightly and inevitably about the Shakespeare of the Sonnets, the enticed, enraptured, and tormented lover. Much less about Shakespeare the husband and the father. It seems on the surface that there is far too little material for a confident picture of the domestic life. None the less there is far more than a shadow of his affection for children to be discovered in the plays. With his love and knowledge of gardens he could always make some exquisitely touching comparison of childhood's brevity with the beauty 'whose action is no stronger than a flower'. He had often his roses in mind.

Their lips were two red roses on a stalk,

says a murderer of the Princes in the Tower.

Of nature's gifts thou might'st with lilies boast
And with the half-blown rose

says Queen Constance to her son. Such lines which linger like bars of music in the mind might have been written anywhere in any company. But many of the boys in the plays have the stamp of close, personal observation. They are not all models of behaviour, innocently gambolling 'as twinn'd lambs that did frisk i' the sun' and, like Peter Pan, thinking of no future except to be 'boy eternal'.

There was, by contrast, that nasty young Marcius, son of Coriolanus, who liked to chase and persecute 'a gilded butterfly'. He would catch and release it over and over again. Then, when he once more caught it after an escape, he was enraged, put his teeth to it and 'mammock'd' it. Mammock is explained as a dialect word, meaning a shred if used as a noun or tear to shreds

when made into a verb. It has a countryside look. Did they
mammock their neighbours' reputations in the shops, streets and
taverns of Stratford? Many good judges, including Granville-
Barker, have thought that *Coriolanus* was written at Stratford and
sent up to London. I suspect direct reporting of this garden
mammocking, repulsive to our humanitarian feelings but
applauded by Virgilia, the boy's mother and not, I hope, by
Anne, if she had ever seen a butterfly nibbled by her boy long
ago or by some young visitor to New Place while Shakespeare
was working on the play during a summer day in his garden at
New Place.

Virgilia spoke of her boy as 'a crack' which my Shakespeare
glossary defines as an urchin. The 'cracks', whether alluded to or
appearing in the plays, are given distinctive character by one who
was a fascinated observer of childhood. I agree with Fripp that
Hamnet in his early years was being remembered by Shakespeare
when he wrote *Titus Andronicus*. It is not often realised that
amid the horrors of that juvenile fabrication, much relished
in the author's lifetime but now little read or revived, there
lurk some exquisite and tender lines typical of a master's finest
touch.

> *Those lily hands*
> *Tremble, like aspen leaves, upon a lute*

and

> *Come and take choice of all my library*
> *And so beguile thy sorrow*

might occur in any of the nobler reaches of the Folio. Not so
exquisite in phrase but likeable in a simple, affectionate way is the
reminder given to young Lucius, grandson of Titus.

> *Come hither, boy: come, come, and learn of us*
> *To melt in showers: thy grandsire loved thee well:*
> *Many a time he danced thee on his knee,*
> *Sung thee asleep, his loving breast thy pillow;*
> *Many a story hath he told to thee,*
> *Meet and agreeing with thine infancy;*
>
> (*Titus Andronicus*, v.iii.160–6.)

If that play was written in 1590, as is generally supposed, Hamnet was then five. The 'merry-cheekt' John Shakespeare fits into the picture of a children's hour in Henley Street with Anne glad to have the boy and the two girls off her hands while she gets on with her work.

One view is that before Hamnet's death Shakespeare had brought his family to London and that the boy became ill there and was taken back to Stratford to recover, if he could. There is no evidence at all for this. It is certain that Shakespeare was for a while living in Bishopsgate in the parish of St Helen's. It was what the estate agents call 'a much-favoured district'. Among its residents were the Lord Mayor of London at Crosby Place. Sir Thomas Gresham (1519–79), the merchant who laid down an economic law of enduring fame and founded the Royal Exchange, had had a fine house there. One neighbour was also a colleague. That was Thomas Morley, organist at St Paul's and a gifted composer of airs for madrigals and for the lute-players. He made a setting for 'It was a lover and his lass' which he published in his 'First Book of Ayres' in 1600. This was used, and still should be, in *As You Like It*. Also from Morley came the setting for 'O Mistress Mine' in *Twelfth Night*. It is not known whether Shakespeare wrote the words for the music or whether Morley wrote the music for the words. In any case there was a superb co-operation between the two neighbours.

That Shakespeare had a family house and not just a room or two in Bishopsgate has been assumed because he had paid (or rather failed for some time to pay) a higher tax assessment than those prominent members of his company Richard and Cuthbert Burbage. He was rated as owner of property worth five pounds and was due to meet a demand of only thirteen shillings and fourpence a year. This hardly suggests a large well-furnished home. The rate-collecting system was chaotic and probably corrupt. The fact that Shakespeare defaulted for a while may have been his protest against the muddles of petty officialdom. That he found the neighbourhood a good place to live in for a while is all we know. He left it a few years later for Southwark. That was obviously convenient. A lodging on the South Bank was far handier when the Lord Chamberlain's Men were playing at the Swan Theatre and later at the Globe, both on the South-wark shore.

He could afford at this time to be a family man in London but between 1592 and 1594 he had lived through or escaped from a savage epidemic of the plague. In 1593 there were eleven thousand deaths. It would have been a criminal folly to bring Anne and the children to the city even when there was sufficient freedom from infection to allow the reopening of the long-closed theatres. Stratford people knew what the plague meant and had always to fear recurrent attacks. But they could not visualise the greater horror of life in London when the city became a mortuary for month after month and the funeral bells were tolling day after day. In those years it was no place for women or children if there was no necessity for them to be there.

Moreover Shakespeare had no time for cares outside his work in which he was now busy as never before. In 1594 he had become an actor sharer in the Lord Chamberlain's company. His position was important, responsible, and exacting. New plays by other men had to be frequently chosen to keep the stage occupied since no piece, even if well liked, could expect more than a few performances after its first showing. Shakespeare was himself memorising and acting parts and fully engaged as a dramatist. To 1595 and 1596 are attributed *Romeo and Juliet, Richard II, A Midsummer Night's Dream,* and *King John.* He could not have been more arduously occupied and he is not to be blamed, indeed posterity must gratefully applaud his decision, if he rejected any suggestion of Anne that she should bring the children to Bishops-gate. A man may genuinely miss his family and yet not want it on top of him or clustered round his writing-table when the work in hand is devouring all his energy and attention. It is far more likely that he was called back to Hamnet's sick-bed than that the boy had to be taken away from London, only to die in Stratford.

Back to London William had to go. But in Stratford there was to be a new future in a new home for Anne. On the way to the church taken by the mourners at Hamnet's funeral stood New Place, 'a praty house of bricke and tymber', as the traveller

Leland had described it more than fifty years earlier. It had been built by Sir Hugh Clopton who had been Lord Mayor of London in 1491 and had given notable service to the people of Stratford by restoring the Gild Chapel for the benefit of their souls and the great bridge over the Avon for the convenience of their movements and advantage of their commerce. Sir Hugh died in 1496; so the house was over a hundred years old.

It was more than 'praty'. It was spacious with a frontage of sixty feet and a depth of seventy. Sir Hugh called it 'my grete house'. To be owner of it would satisfy two urgent desires. It would give Anne a home of which to be proud and in which to forget. Not grief only would fill the room up of her absent child. The new possession would also be a crushing reply to all who had jeered and sneered at a young husband whose excessive ambition had led him on a fruitless journey across the Clopton Bridge with poverty and obscurity as the likely result. It was good to be able to make this decisive retort in the form of bricks and timber and the land around them.

In the middle of the century New Place had been in 'great ruyne and decay'. The Clopton 'manour' was bought in 1567, and presumably restored to a habitable condition, by William Underhill, a lawyer of the Inner Temple in London and a considerable landowner in the neighbourhood. He died in 1570. His son, also named William, sold it to Shakespeare in May 1597 for sixty pounds. The purchase included two barns and two gardens. From an incident soon to be discussed it seems that possession may have been taken before that.

The fanciful might say that the Shakespeares were also acquiring for dubious company the ghost expected by the superstitious to haunt an ancient building associated with a violent or vicious crime. Two months after the sale the second William Underhill was poisoned by his son of eighteen, called Fulke, who was later hanged at Warwick for the murder of his father. Neither of the victims had died at New Place; only if spectres are naturally inseparable from their old home and return to it would the house be infested by one or even two of the Underhill family. Some local gossip of that kind is imaginable.

The size of the house was considerable. It had ten fire-places which meant an unusual number of rooms. It was largely rebuilt in 1702 but a description of the house as Shakespeare knew it was left by an old Stratford shoemaker. He spoke of a porch at the end near the Gild Chapel and of 'a kind of Green Court' which had to be crossed before entering the house. We also know of a 'Greater Garden' and a smaller one.

Shakespeare was now 'generosus', Gentleman, in the eyes of the law, and Anne, if she chose to be so, could figure as the leading lady of the town. Hers had been a hard way up from Shottery, but suddenly a new life lay ahead. There was no more dependence on the older members of the family. The situation was reversed and, if the seniors found the burdens of age too heavy in their own homes, it was Anne who could say that rooms were waiting for them at New Place. But her mother-in-law made another choice. Surviving her husband John by seven years she died in 1608 at the home of her daughter Joan, who had married William Hart, a hatter.

So began a term of residence for Anne which lasted over twenty-three years. The documentation of changes in the use of the house is scanty, but the signposts all point the same way. There was a steady growth of affluence and there was no break in the marriage. With William back in London Anne's first task was to supervise some repairs. For these more stone had been bought than was necessary. The borough accounts record the purchase from Mr 'Shaxpere' of 'a load of stone'. (The garden of New Place was not a quarry; there must have been over-ordering.) The sum paid was tenpence. The prices of the time are puzzling. Naturally with building material cheap the buildings were cheap too. Other charges seem comparatively high. While a large house with barns and gardens could be had for sixty pounds one 'grey trotting mare' cost forty-five shillings, considerably more than one thirtieth of the outlay on 'the messuage' and its surrounding amenities.

There was no need to worry about money and there was masculine advice available. Anne had three brothers-in-law. Gilbert, the eldest of them (1566–1612), may have worked for a

while in London as a haberdasher but he was back at home in
1602 and acting as William's agent when the latter made a substantial purchase of land in a district known as Old Stratford.
Nothing is known of Richard except that he was christened in
March 1574 and buried in February 1613. He may have occupied
one of the empty rooms at New Place and been a useful lodger.
The youngest brother, Edmund, born in May 1580, followed
William's example and went to London as an intending actor. As
to what parts he obtained, and with whom, there is no information; there is no mention of him as one of William's colleagues of
whom the editors of the First Folio gave an ample list.

Perhaps he was a failure and a nuisance; if so, he did not trouble
the family long. He died in December 1607 and was buried in the
actors' quarter in the church of St Mary Overies, now Southwark
Cathedral. He may have been the father of a bastard child,
entered in the register of burials in St Giles's Church, Cripplegate,
as 'base-borne' son of 'Edward (not Edmund) Shackspeere,
Player'. There is no more news of him. The Shakespeares, with
one exception, were ordinary folk. Anne had one genius on her
hands and would be content if Gilbert had a level head in the
handling of business; this he could have shown in the stocking of
malt.

There was some commotion in Stratford at the beginning of
her arrival in New Place. There had been an investment in malt.
There were the two barns. Why not use one of them? Anne was a
farmer's daughter and could see the signs of hard times for the
growers of crops and of good times for those who had grain to
sell. There had been a series of bad summers from 1594 to 1596
in which the fields were flooded and

> *The ploughman lost his sweat and the green corn*
> *Hath rotted ere his youth attained a beard.*

A shortage of cereals followed, prices rose, there was an outcry
of 'malcontents' and an official inquiry was ordered into the
holdings and 'engrossment' of malt in the neighbourhood. The
'Noate of Corne and Malte' made at Stratford early in February
1597 stated that ten quarters of malt were held by 'Wm. Shacke-

spere in Chapel Street ward', i.e. at New Place. This suggests
occupation before the purchase was completed in May.

It was taken for granted that buying was a sensible move. If
this was wrong it was not thought so in high circles. The local
grandee, Sir Thomas Lucy, High Sheriff of the County, had
twelve and a half quarters and Alexander Aspinall, the headmaster
of the Grammar School, eleven. In all there were six hundred and
fifty-nine quarters recorded by the investigators. Stratford,
bidden to fix a price for malt, replied that malting was its 'especiall
trade with many servantes amonge us hyered onlye to that
purpose'. Nothing much happened. The harvests improved and
by 1600 'no lack of corn' was reported. Presumably Anne made a
profit. William need not worry. He had plenty in hand in London,
The Merchant of Venice, the two parts of *Henry IV,* with *The
Merry Wives of Windsor* royally commanded as a Falstaff sequel.
He was also acting in plays not his own; Ben Jonson's *Every
Man in His Humour* was one of them. He was making a satisfactory
amount of money and preparing to invest it at home.

The acquisitions accumulated. In 1602 the large sum of three
hundred and twenty pounds was sent home for the purchase of a
hundred and twenty acres of land from William and John
Coombe in Old Stratford, an agricultural area to the north of the
borough. The deed was 'sealed and delivered to Gilbert Shakespere to the use of the within named William Shakespere'. Later
in that year Anne, who can hardly have lacked housing space, was
provided with more. The new premises were a cottage with a
garden in Chapel Lane, adjacent to New Place. The tenant to
whom it was let is unknown. A gardener is a fair guess since two
orchards had been added to the two gardens of the big house.

The Shakespeare properties were increased again in the
following year by an investment of four hundred and forty
pounds in a lease of tithes 'in Stratforde, Old Stratford, Welcombe
and Bishopton'. In 1608 or 1609 Shakespeare became a sharer in
the fully-roofed and prosperous Blackfriars Theatre. This could
be used in the coldest weather which would put the Globe out of
action. With the dividends on his holdings in two London playhouses together with the rents and tithes at home the family

income was large by Stratford standards, but so was the house. A room became vacant in June 1607 when Susanna was married to Dr John Hall and went to live near by in the large and pleasant house now known and much visited as Hall's Croft. Part of New Place was lent or sub-let to Thomas Greene who had a wife and two children. He was a lawyer who became town clerk of Stratford in 1603. It is not clear when this arrangement began but in 1609 he wrote that 'he might staye another yere at newe place'. If he left in 1610 the obvious conclusion is that Shakespeare, who was making recurrent journeys to and from London almost to the end of his life, was now spending much more of his time with Anne. His second daughter Judith was still with them since she did not marry until 1616.

To be a hostess, but financially assisted in the supply of liquid refreshment, was now a duty shared by Anne with her husband. Distinguished visitors to Stratford were entertained by the borough council not only in inns but also in the homes of eminent citizens. The town's Christmas account for 1614 includes 'Item for one quart of sack and one quart of clarrett winne geven to a precher at the newe place, twenty pence'. Sir Sidney Lee said that the guest was 'of Puritan proclivities'. To that unlikely suggestion Sir Edmund Chambers replied that there was no evidence and headed his note on this incident 'A Preacher's Thirst'. Unless there was company assembled, the needs of the visiting divine were well slaked at no great expense to the rate-payers.

Those who insist on a disastrous marriage have to face the fact that it lasted. In answer to this they habitually quote two passages from the plays which seem to reflect a personal view and not one essential to the story and the situation. The observations of Prospero in *The Tempest* are taken by some as Shakespeare's thoughts in 1611. On the anticipation of the marriage ceremony Prospero speaks with striking severity. Ferdinand, seeking to marry his much-loved daughter, is told that as a wife she will 'outstrip all praise and make it halt behind her'. Yet for no obvious reasons Prospero, suspecting him of an impatient passion and seduction before wedlock, delivers this extremely brusque warning of the fate which befalls too hasty lovers,

If thou dost break her virgin-knot before
All sanctimonious ceremonies may
With full and holy rite be minister'd,
No sweet aspersion shall the heavens let fall
To make this contract grow; but barren hate,
Sour-eyed disdain, and discord, shall bestrew
The union of your bed with weeds so loathly
That you shall hate it both: therefore take heed,
As Hymen's lamps shall light you.

(The Tempest, iv.i.17–25.)

There is no talk here of justification by a troth-plight which is said by the defenders of Susanna's begetting to have made that affair respectable. But was Shakespeare really condemning himself and saying that he was rightly punished by a 'loathly' marriage for the doings of twenty-nine years ago? It seems to me more probable that some local girl, possibly his own daughter Judith, who did not marry until she was thirty-one, had been taking chances with a reckless breaker of virgin knots who was unlikely to be a tolerable husband.

The other lines which are supposed to express resentment of Shakespeare's marriage occur in *Twelfth Night*. They are spoken by Orsino, Duke of Illyria, when Viola, masquerading as a young man, tells him that the lady for whom she is pleading is of the same age as himself,

Too old, by heaven: let still the woman take
An elder than herself: so wears she to him;
So sways she level in her husband's heart.

(Twelfth Night, ii.iv.28–31.)

This is a mild observation compared with Prospero's sudden, savage outburst and it is hard to see in it good evidence for an unhappy married life. Orsino adds that men's fancies in love are 'giddy and unfirm' which is true of Shakespeare's life in London at the turn of the century when *Twelfth Night* was written. It is worth noting that just before the opinion voiced about difference of age the fidelity of a true, abiding affection has been acknowledged and admired. The lovers are described as

Unstaid and skittish in all motions else
Save in the constant image of the creature
That is beloved.

The exception should not be overlooked. If the quotation game is to be played there are certain to be contradictory conclusions. The tribute to the constancy of one beloved can be taken as a compliment to the kind of wife whom some now call 'a steady' quite as reasonably as the counsel to take a young wife can be regarded as the grievance of one who failed to do so.

Shakespeare had still his urgent work, his keen theatrical interests and the enduring company of his inseparable and still prospering fellow-players in London. The team were not only the King's Men; they were indeed often acting at royal command, but they were as much the favourites of the public as of the court. He could have stayed comfortably with them in the town. Why should he return if this country home was a battle-ground?

There is abundant proof of his addiction to Stratford. Though never taking part in local government as a councillor he was helpful in 1611 as a Stratford contributor 'towardes the charge of prosecutying the Bill in parliament for the better Repayre of the highe waies'. He looked after his expanding property, leasing a barn to a Mr Johnson of Henley Street, quarrelling with the Coombes, and yet, with peace made, getting a legacy of five pounds from one of them. He was involved in the controversy over enclosure of land at Welcombe. It was a long and tangled dispute his attitude to which remains uncertain.

It is curious but significant that he never considered himself to be a Londoner even when he was dealing with affairs in London. In 1612 he had to testify as a deponent in the dispute between Christopher Mountjoy, his one-time landlord of a lodging in Silver Street, Cripplegate, and Mountjoy's apprentice and aggrieved son-in-law, Stephen Belott. The witness's name appeared in his statement as 'William Shakespeare of Stratford-upon-Avon'. In 1613 he invested a hundred and forty pounds in the purchase of property in Blackfriars known as the Gatehouse. Again he was named 'William Shakespeare of Stratford-upon-

Avon'. In both cases the spelling of his name was that now
familiar to us and used by his colleagues Heminge and Condell
when editing the First Folio. At Stratford he could be Shaksper
or almost anything else. Presumably he did not fuss about that.
He was and remained a Stratford man. This he would never have
done if the town with its gardens and water-meadows had been
made intolerable by an 'abhorrence' of the woman with whom he
chose to spend his last years.

The Stratford air was not always free of worry and danger.
Fire as much as plague was an intermittent but severe peril. In
the two decades between 1594 and 1614 there were three devasta-
tions. Anne, whether she was living with John and Mary Shakespeare in Henley Street or in some house or cottage close to
them, had reason to remember the first of these disasters. It
came on a Sunday, September 22, 1594 when the conflagration
raged round her and the children. Many houses in four streets,
including Henley Street, were damaged or destroyed as a strong
south wind spread the flames. The 'Birthplace' escaped narrowly.
Fortunately there was then an intervening stream between the
old Shakespeare home and the worst of the blaze.

In August of the following year there was another outbreak,
especially in the Sheep Street area. In these two great fires two
hundred buildings, including one hundred and twenty homes,
were wholly or partly destroyed and the damage was assessed at
twelve thousand pounds. There were collections of relief funds
in the adjacent district and even in counties as far away as Kent,
Derbyshire, Berkshire, and Leicestershire. These operations produced some curious conduct. Fripp, usually eager to look on the
sunny side of Stratford life, wrote that the collectors, who were
leading citizens, thought themselves entitled to the first fruits of
this benevolence and filled their pockets. When starting out as the
envoys of charity they 'raised immediate loans on the expectation
of what they would get'. They could reasonably claim that they
were leaving the occupations which provided a livelihood for
their families and that the advances on expected receipts were
needed to fill the larders while the hats were being passed round
far and wide. But further acquisition was bad enough to merit a

judicial inquiry. The puritan preachers blamed the sins of the people, especially Sabbath-breakers, for these afflictions, two of which came on a Sunday. In their view God was a righteous as well as wrathful fire-bug, with Stratford's homes his justified fuel. Such theology did not ease the pain or mitigate the sufferings of the towns house-wives

New Place was spared then and spared again in July 1614 when fifty-four dwelling houses and many outlying barns and sheds were destroyed by the flames with 'the wind sitting full upon the town'. The occasion was a Saturday. The godly had to attribute the divine vengeance to other transgressions. The scene on that frightening day must have resembled an English town in 1940 after the German raiders had passed dropping their incendiaries. It was a bad time for the women, especially if their men were absent. Dr Hall was frequently away on long journeys to see the patients of wealth and title who spread his practice over several counties. Shakespeare was sometimes in London. There was no chance of help from Gilbert and Richard Shakespeare since both had recently died. Thomas Greene had left for a house of his own. The spread of the fire must have been watched with great anxiety. Fortunately New Place was not thatched and the chief danger came from Stratford's large quantity of inflammable straw after a spell of hot and dry weather and when the wind was as oddly described, 'sitting' on the roofs. The three great flare-ups all occurred in summer.

Our idea of what New Place looked like in the Shakespeares time comes from an artist and antiquary called Vertue. He visited the town in 1737. That was more than a century after Anne's death and twenty-five years after the house had been completely rebuilt by Sir John Clopton. Vertue made a pen-and-ink sketch based on information obtained in talks with Shakespeare Hart, a descendant of William's sister Joan. His memories of New Place as Anne knew it were fairly good evidence for its structure and appearance. The house as depicted by Vertue was a solid building with three stories and five gables. It was not closely surrounded and the roof, more likely to be tiled than slated, was free of the dry straw which was so risky in a town if people were careless with their fires and their simple forms of illumination by candles or rush-lit oil lamps. The methods of coping with a blaze were quite ineffective when a fire had begun to burn fiercely. One simple device was to use a long fire-hook to pull away parts of a burning house. This could do something to stop a spread of destruction, but it extinguished nothing. Long and efficient hoses attached to piped water were unknown. Things called 'spouts' were attached to the domestic wells, but they were of little use against any large fire.

The local justices reported on the calamity of 1614 and commanded the borough council to have more buckets, spouts, fire-hooks, and ladders ready in future. They also sent a petition to the Lord Chief Justice in London asking that thatched houses should no longer be built since 'the wynde taketh the Thatch and carries it very far of and there fireth other thatched howses'. They added that owing to the air-borne straw 'very many fair tyled howses have byn burned to the ground'. (New Place was in luck.) The request was obviously ineffective. One has only to look at many old English villages with cottages built long after that. Now house-agents advertise a thatched roof as an 'olde worlde' attraction for a country cottage. There was once more a campaign to rake in gifts of money for relief and once more a shabby scandal. When the collectors' accounts were examined by local magnates who were above all suspicion they discovered 'every one prefferring his owne private benefittes before the generall good'.

There is no record of Shakespeare taking part in these necessary but ill-used excursions; nor did he share in the inquiry made by eminent men into the financial chicanery which had been cloaked with the name of charity. He looked after his own affairs and gave assistance occasionally to those public causes which concerned him. Still a traveller to and from London he showed by his already-mentioned contribution of money that he resented the wretched condition of the roads. It was a quiet, walled-in life at New Place where he had his family, his gardens, his mulberry-trees and the company of such Stratfordians as he found agreeable. All his neighbours were not congenial in the town which was increasingly dominated by the play-hating puritans. No touring companies were now allowed to perform in Stratford. That was an insult to its leading citizen but there are no signs of his resentment. He did not dramatically shake the Stratford mud off his feet and go back to enjoy the society of the tavern-wits and the liberties of London. He stayed on, but not for long. He died in April 1616 and was buried in the parish church on April 25, just fifty-two years after his christening.

Anne was beginning to feel the load of her years. It was a burden which came earlier than it does now. Longevity was rare in Stratford. Now the obituary lists contain many who have passed the eighty and some the ninety mark. Dr Hall, according to repute, gave confidence to his patients, but there was then no science of gerontology, the study of old age, and no specialisation in geriatrics, the alleviation of its aches and pains.

Did Anne require such care? The doctor treated patients for depression; he had his pills and potions to purge melancholy, then a fashionable ailment and sometimes an affectation. Anne had lost her male heir in childhood and her husband in what we should call middle age and the Elizabethans regarded as the gateway to senility. Close to her was Susanna, cheerfully married to a prosperous man who had a pharmacy on his premises. There was her grandchild Elizabeth to watch at play. She had, until two months before William's death, Judith to help her in the house. It is supposed, without any certain evidence, that when she was widowed the Halls left their home and came to New Place. That is likely since the house was far too big for her and she may have needed attention as well as companionship. She survived William by five years and died early in August 1621 after twenty-four years in New Place. She was then sixty-seven.

The only mention of his wife in her husband's will, the interlineated bequest of 'my second-best bed with the furniture' has given intense delight to the denigrators. That Anne was being cruelly deprived of a legacy is nonsense. She had the widow's right of dower. This entitled her by common law to a third interest in her husband's heritable estate and to residence in his principal house. She was well provided for.

Nonsensical too is the idea that the adjective applied to the bed was written with an ugly sneer. The best bed may have been in the guest-room. (Was the preacher couched there to sleep off the fatigue of his sermon and the excellence of a convivial supper?) Sir Edmund Chambers suggests that when the draft was read over Anne 'asked for the bed; it had come from her old home at Hewland'. The insertion of this item as an after-thought may have been due to a special request made by Anne. Whatever the explanation such a mention was not unique. Mark Eccles in his carefully compiled book on 'Shakespeare in Warwickshire', reveals that William Palmer of Leamington, who made an affectionately worded will and was obviously not in a mocking mood, bequeathed 'unto Elizabeth my wief all hir wearing apparell and my second-best featherbed for hir selfe furnished and one other meaner feather bed for hir mayde'. The meaner bed would provide a luxury. The mattresses in most homes were then filled with rushes. Second-best could be as good as any.

Is it conceivable that a man known for his civil demeanour and gentleness would use his last testament as though it were a sardonic script for a bitter and satirical comedy? He had begun the will by commending his soul 'into the handes of God my Creator' and affirming his belief that he might partake of life everlasting 'only through the merittes of Jesus Christ my Saviour'. That he would use this solemn document as the vehicle of a cruel and vulgar joke is beyond belief.

The matter has so often been discussed at length that there is no need to say more about it. Anne was neither deprived nor derided and, as long as health allowed, could sleep comfortably in New Place, whatever the classification of her bed.

CHAPTER VI

Susanna

SUSANNA, child of the hasty wedding, emerges from the mingled sunshine, cloud, and mist of Shakespearian Stratford more clearly than does Judith, Hamnet's twin and her junior by two years. Dr Johnson's remark that 'a writer of lapidary inscriptions is not on oath' is a just warning against too much credulity in the often fulsome compliments paid to the dead, sometimes in a servile adulation of the great and more often in likeable but excessive affection for lesser folk. None the less we need not suspect a major perjury in the tribute on Susanna's tombstone in the church. Posterity was told of her inheritance of her father's wit, of her piety, and of her awareness of salvation to be earned. Praised also were her compassionate nature and her practical common sense which extended charity from words to deeds and provided for suffering people 'comforts cordiall'. We may, if we choose, diminish this encomium by regarding it with Johnsonian caution as an unsworn statement. Even so, Susanna is to be accepted as a good companion with a ready tongue and as a likeable and congenial addition to the life of the town.

At the age of twenty-four, on June 5, 1607, she married Dr John Hall, who was then thirty-two. He was much esteemed and his services were in wide demand. She lived to be sixty-six, six years longer than her husband; thus she was a widow for nearly fourteen years. The Latin epitaph on the doctor's tombstone in the chancel of the church called her his most faithful wife. That could be a routine compliment, but it may contain a reminder that her fidelity had once been rudely challenged.

In July 1613 she brought an action for slander in the Ecclesiastical Court of Worcester against John Lane, the twenty-three-year-old son of a landed gentleman, John Lane of Alveston Manor, two miles up the Avon from Stratford. The malicious gossiper had said five weeks previously that Susanna 'had the running of the raynes and had bin naught with Rafe Smith at John Palmer'. Smith was a haberdasher and hatter, then aged thirty-six. Robert Whatcott, who was later to be a witness of Shakespeare's will, was the principal witness for Mistress Hall. Lane put up no defence. He failed to appear in court and was excommunicated. Susanna came out with a stainless character. This did not curb his reckless impudence. In 1619 he was sued for libelling and also attacking Wilson the puritan vicar of Stratford. In court the churchwardens testified that he was a drunkard.

As the doctor's wife and also as Shakespeare's daughter and the expected heiress of New Place Susanna was an important figure in Stratford society. Since the demands on her husband's services were many and came from a long distance she was frequently alone with her daughter Elizabeth who had been born in 1608. If calls came for medical aid she could turn to Matthewe Morris, once the trusted 'man' of her father-in-law, William Hall, who had been a doctor in Acton near London and owned a collection of books on 'physique' as well as on alchemy, astronomy, and astrology. This library was left to Morris with the request that the legatee should instruct his son John Hall in such matters if the latter intended to continue in these studies.

After William Hall's death in 1607 Morris came to work for John at Stratford and married there in 1613. He named his first two children Susanna and John, which declares his respect and affection for his new employer and his wife. It is likely that Morris, with this experience, acted as secretary, could make up his master's prescriptions, and was there to offer some medical advice if it was hurriedly sought in an emergency during the doctor's absence. Later there was an apothecary called Court working at Hall's Croft.

Also there was a Mr Joseph Boles, M.A. of Cambridge, living opposite New Place. Dr C. Martin Mitchell, who included a detailed biography of Dr Hall in his book on 'The Shakespeare Circle', suggests that since Boles was left Hall's manuscripts he

99

was also a medical assistant. Here too was escape for Susanna if there were a noisy knocking on the door and urgent seeking of help for people suddenly smitten. The wife of a general practitioner can badly need a support of this kind.

In order to attend patients it was not necessary to have the M.D. degree. A reasonably qualified man could be licensed to practise without it. Dr Mitchell pointed out that John Hall had no university medical degree though he had been at Queen's College, Cambridge. He is generally written about as Dr Hall; that is a courtesy title. But to call him Doctor is realistic as well as polite. There is no question of his ability and standing in his profession. He was called in as a consultant by the Earl of Warwick's doctor when the earl was seriously ill. He had many titled patients among the Midland aristocracy. Bernard Shaw, in his preface to 'The Dark Lady of the Sonnets', partly accepted and partly countered Frank Harris's opinion that Shakespeare was a snob. He was not, said G.B.S., a parvenu. As a member of two families who thought well of themselves, he was resuming what he conceived to be his natural position. This he did when he had enough money to claim his status of Gentleman and maintain it.

If that is so Susanna had played her part to her parents' satisfaction when she chose her husband. I take a chance in making her the active and decisive party to the match, but in that I am complying with the Shavian view that the woman marries the man. If John Lane was wrong in his allegations of Susanna's infidelity he may have been near the truth in his remark that she 'ran the reins' and was of a managing disposition. However that may be, her father's will showed complete confidence in her good sense and business ability. She had her wits, as well as her wit, about her.

With Morris on the premises at first and later the trusted Mr Boles, Susanna was free to look after her daughter and her home without constant interruption. Some of the doctor's calls demanded exhausting travel and riding across country. Dr Mitchell mentions journeys of twenty-six miles to Worcester, thirty-nine to Gloucester, forty-two to Northampton and sixty to Ludlow. Hall's 'Case Book' included among the English bodies observed those of the Earl of Northampton, relieved of a pleurisy, and his dropsical countess. That sadly swollen lady was 'perfectly cured and brought to a good colour in twenty days'. The remedy had been drastic, a purging so violent that she had forty-one 'stooles' in three days 'without any loss of strength'. (We may suspect the doctor of occasional optimism about the ease, speed, and durability of his cures.) Visiting the Northamptons meant journeys to Ludlow Castle in Shropshire where he stayed nine times. Her ladyship was heiress of a Lord Mayor of London and the fees should have been substantial.

Susanna saw him trot away with his medicine-chest. 'Surgeon's box' is the term for this piece of luggage used in *Troilus and Cressida* by Thersites whose vocabulary contains a whole catalogue of diseases. Calls were made on the Bishop of Worcester and Sir Thomas Temple at Wolverton in Buckinghamshire. Not so distant were Warwick Castle, where Hall's services were much valued, and Clifford Chambers, the still delightful village across the Avon from Stratford. In the long topographical poem 'Poly-Olbion' by Michael Drayton it was described as 'many a time the Muses' quiet port'. There Drayton comfortably anchored several times, being a favoured guest of Sir Henry and Lady Rainsford; the latter, a scholar and linguist, had been the admired 'Idea' of his sonnets. In their home Drayton was smitten with a tertian fever, which was 'a fever or ague characterised by the occurrence of paroxysm every third (i.e. every alternate) day'. Hall's treatment was an emetic infusion in which some strange elements were mixed with syrup of violets. Working 'upwards and downwards' it prevailed. Dr R. R. Simpson in his book on 'Shakespeare and Medicine' was so much astonished by the other ingredients that he would not name them.

The doctor also coped with the sufferings of a scorbutic Lady Underhill who endured 'as it were the biting of ants in many parts of her body'. Her tortures were ended by an apozeme or concoction of herbs which she thankfully praised as magical. Treatment of the itch was constantly needed.

The major afflictions of Stratford were visitations by plague and fire. A third pest, less lethal but ineradicable, was scurvy.

Susanna herself was one of the sufferers. When she was forty-seven she was troubled with 'scurvy, pains in the loins, and melancholy' for which her husband found relief. The cause of that would now be called vitamin deficiency. Such terms were not in the doctor's lexicon but he knew that the remedy lay in the juices of fruit, herbs, and flowers. His patients with money to spend ate heartily and sometimes suffered for it. After the autumn they had to feed monotonously. There were no artificial food-cakes to carry live-stock through the winter and turnips were scarcely known. When winter came there was a general slaughter of beasts except those kept for milking and breeding. Without refrigeration the meat had to be salted to keep it through the winter and spring. There was little variety of vegetables and no canned or imported fruit for use when the summer and autumn crops had been eaten. The intake of the anti-scorbutic Vitamin C was thus far too small and scurvy was common as much in the wealthy homes as in the poorest.

Dr Hall's understanding of this was emphasised by Dr James Cooke of Warwick who translated from the doctor's Latin and published in 1657 a number of the 'choycest' of the 'Case Book' notes with an introduction 'to the Friendly Reader'. In it he wrote

'It seems the Author had the happiness (if I may so stile it) to lead the way to that practice almost generally used by the most knowing, of mixing Scorbuticks in most remedies: It was then, and I know for some time after thought so strange, that it was cast as a reproach upon him by those most famous in the profession. He had been a Traveller acquainted with the French tongue, as appeared by some part of some "Observations," which I got help to make English. His practice was very much, and that amongst most eminent Persons in the County where he lived, and those adjacent, as may appear by his "Observations". '

It was absurd that Hall should be criticised by his less percipient colleagues for specialising in the treatment of a malady then so prevalent. But his concentration on the causes and relief of scurvy did not prevent him from dealing with all the ailments to be met in a general practice. Gastric troubles were frequent when drinking water was taken from wells in undrained towns. Susanna knew the advantage of having a doctor in the house. In addition to her treatment for scurvy she had to be rescued from a tormenting colic. Her daughter was saved from distressing attacks of twisted neck and convulsions of the mouth, probably the result of severe chills. An 'Observation' of Dr Hall recorded the incident.

'Elizabeth Hall, my only daughter, was vexed with *tortura oris* or the convulsion of the mouth, and was happily cured as followeth . . . 5 January 1624/5. In the beginning of April she went to London and returning homewards the 22nd of the said month she took cold and fell into the said distemper on the contrary side of the face, and although grievously afflicted with it, yet, by the blessing of God, she was cured in sixteen days as followeth: . . . her neck was fomented with *aqua vitae*, in which was infused nutmegs, cinnamon, cloves, pepper; she ate nutmegs often. In the same year, May the 24th, she was afflicted with an erratic fever: sometimes she was hot, by and bye sweating, again cold, all in the space of half an hour, and thus she was vexed oft in a day . . . Thus was she delivered from death and deadly disease, and was well for many years, to God be praise!'

Elizabeth had been rash. For the recent victim of a serious facial disorder to drive to London, two hundred miles there and back, in the ferocity of English spring weather and in the travelling conditions of the time was indeed a folly. But her parents were to blame for letting her go. She was not then a married woman. Her mother may have yielded to importunate requests and taken her to town to see the sights and do some shopping. It would be a great adventure but it had painful results.

Elizabeth was an only child. Susanna had been married on June 5, 1607, and her daughter was christened on February 21, 1608. Since the custom then was to baptise almost immediately after birth Elizabeth anticipated by a few days the full nine months of pregnancy, but there is no need to suppose that her parents had anticipated the 'sanctimonious ceremony' on which Prospero was later to insist in Miranda's case. They were both looked to as virtuous. Dr Hall has been described as a puritan but he was not so strong in his protestantism as to be a recusant refusing to attend Church of England services. He carried his piety into his medical practice; though his 'Case Book' showed him to be proud of his cures he continually gave thanks to God as the powerful source of his successes.

There was to be no further issue of a marriage in which there is no sign of any early unhappiness. A son for Hall's Croft and a grandson for New Place must have been keenly desired by all the family. Anne had not been able to replace Hamnet and Susanna was also barren after her first-born. The Shakespeares had no luck at all on the male side of their stock. John and Mary had four sons and never a grandson except through their daughter Joan's marriage to Hart. William lived to see Judith married to Thomas Quiney, but he never saw any of her three sons; his death spared him further grievous disappointment, since the first died in infancy. There was the added irony that he had been christened with the family name. For his brief life of six months he was 'Shaxper Quiny.' Judith's other boys died at twenty-one and nineteen. Shakespeare's will testifies to his expectation of and longing for a surviving male heir. But again and again 'the great bell tolled' in the church-yard.

It is possible that the delivery of Anne's twins had left her with a frustrating internal injury or a determination to endure no further agony. It is possible also that Susanna had had great difficulty in labour and that it was decided with her husband's advice that the risk should not be taken again. We cannot tell. A warning against quotation-picking from the plays has been made, but I cannot help noting that in Shakespeare's magnificent building up of the play *Pericles*, so feeble at the start which is obviously not his, the Prince's wife Thaisa is taken for dead after the birth of Marina during a tempestuous storm at sea. Pericles cries

A fearfull labour hast thou had, my dear!

after he has called in his distress upon Lucina, the pagan goddess of women in labour,

> *Divinest patroness and mid-wife gentle*
> *To those that cry by night convey thy deity*
> *Aboard our dancing boat; make swift the pangs*
> *Of my queen's travails!*

Shakespeare's work on *Pericles* is generally attributed to 1608, the year of Elizabeth's birth. It may of course be an idle fancy that he had his own daughter in mind. But it could be so.

On April 22, 1626 Elizabeth married Thomas Nash, a member of a prosperous Stratford family. She was just eighteen and he was thirty-three. There was no child. Nash died in 1647 and two years later she married John Barnard, a land-owning widower with property in Northamptonshire. She was then over forty and probably no issue was expected. There was none. Except through Joan Hart and her descendants the Shakespeares of Stratford had disappeared while there was normal fertility in the families of their fellow-townsfolk.

Susanna became an heiress at her father's death. Her entailed share of the estate included New Place, the Old Stratford acres, the Henley Street houses, the Chapel Lane cottage, and the Blackfriars Gatehouse. If she had married a man of position he had married a lady of means. But he continued busily in his practice. If they moved into New Place, there was one request or demand which Susanna, as mistress of the house, could make and claim to be entirely reasonable. Her husband must not bring his dispensary with him. Why should she tolerate on her premises the astonishing and sometimes revolting ingredients of his prescriptions? Nobody could object to the frequently used syrup of violets and the plentiful assortment of herbs and flowers necessary for the treatment of the scorbutic patients and for many other mixtures to be taken by mouth. There was a pocket-money occupation for the boys and girls of Stratford in combing the fields and hedges for their yield of 'simples'.

For his poultices and applications the doctor drew on a witches' cauldron. Dr Mitchell reminds us that in 'The London Pharmacopeia', first issued in 1618, there were still listed in the edition of 1721 such items as worms, blind puppies, crabs' eyes, and the excrement of dogs, cats, geese, and mice. The renowned Culpeper thought to relieve cataract by blowing on the eyes the ashes of a black cat burned in a new pot. Hall showed great sense and was far ahead of his time in his preparations of doses to get rid of scurvy. But in ointments for external use he was a mediaevalist and accustomed to an alchemy which was no better than black magic. A famous Dr Mayerne recommended an 'apozeme' made up of powdered human skull, the blood of weasels, and balsam of bats. That was by no means all since Dr Mitchell wrote of other more loathsome and offensive prescriptions which he would not name since he wished to spare the readers' feelings.

It is not suggested that Dr Hall was a close and trusting student of the 'Pharmacopeia'. But he did specify some of his materials boiled up and sieved for poulticing. They included spiders' webs, swallows' nests taken with their dirt and dung unremoved, white dog's turd, hen's dung, frogs' spawn, and a powder of earth-worms. Sulphur and the flesh of vipers were also required. The youngsters who went 'simpling' would earn an extra tip if they could bring in a few of our English snakes. The apothecaries of the day had much need to stuff their nostrils and wash their hands continually. Doubtful as we may be concerning the ablutionary standards of the time it is a fair guess that Masters Morris and Court were carefully watched by their mistress when they had finished their work among the pots, pans, and crucibles. Their workshop was a chamber of horrors that could not possibly be accepted in New Place. Fortunately there were the outlying barns and the fresh air of its gardens around.

The number of herbs used was enormous. The apothecaries were kept busy selecting, grading, and boiling them down when they were not to be taken raw. There were 'blunderbuss' medicines for discharge in a massive volley into the patient's stomach. One known as theriacum, from which we get our word treacle, had more than sixty ingredients. Dispensing even with the inoffensive blossoms and plants was hard labour.

An agreeable contrast to the fouler elements of the concoctions were the powdered metals taken internally. A Romish priest, in danger of death from a strange fever, was given a powder of precious stones, including 'prepared pearls' and 'fragments of iacynth and rubies, each of three grains'. This 'cured' the Catholic beyond all expectation'. Much as he disliked Roman doctrines and rituals Dr Hall was determined to save his man with no sparing of his salves, animal and mineral as well as vegetable. The dispensary was both a dung-heap and a treasure-chest. Susanna could be as much fascinated by the precious metals as disgusted by the chopped-up snakes and earth-worms.

In 1626 she might have been Lady Hall. Her father perhaps and certainly some of her neighbours must have thought the doctor stubborn and discourteous when he refused to enter the market established by King James who, to cope with the effects of his grotesque extravagance, was putting titles up for sale. Hall was obviously not averse to aristocratic company; his ordinary patients had reason to resent his long absences when attending the nobility. But the king's commendation of sports and games on Sunday afternoons was resented by the strictly inclined churchmen of whom the doctor was one. Odious also to the rigid Protestants was the royal advice that those who did not like this liberty of play, be they Papists or puritans, should leave the country.

The canny Scottish king had it both ways. If the gentlemen approached would not buy a handle to their names they were fined for their contumacy. The refusal of a knighthood cost Hall ten pounds and some of his wealthier neighbours rather more. What Susanna thought of that we cannot tell. Few wives regard titles with disdain. The epitaphic words 'Wise to Salvation' could imply that she thought more of earning her place in heaven than of acquiring honours on earth. She may have exercised her wit at the expense of a commercially-minded king, commended her man for remaining plain John, and been happy to remain Mistress Hall of Hall's Croft and New Place.

After tranquil years there was grave anxiety to come. In 1632 or thereabouts the doctor's wife had to send hurriedly for two friends and colleagues in his profession. One of the 'Observations'

107

records that he 'fell into a most cruel torture of the teeth and was driven to bed with a burning fever which was raging and killing all that it did infect'. He became emaciated and lost control of his limbs. Among the remedies employed was the application to his feet of 'a live pigeon cut open'. This was then commonly thought to be a therapeutic in cases of plague. That the recurrent pest had once more struck the district is a natural conclusion from the symptoms and sufferings recounted.

Hall wrote that he was 'rescued from the very jaws of death' and added his customary thanks to God. He stated that he recovered his former health after five weeks. Nothing is known of the infection passing to Susanna and Elizabeth. If there was an outbreak of bubonic plague they had learned in a doctor's home the elementary defensive methods then known, isolation, sprinkling of herbs and so on. But these were largely ineffective, as we know in the case of epidemics in London when thousands died. Mother and daughter, however active in precaution, were lucky.

Further domestic worries were to follow, provoked by bitter local disputes in politics and religion. Hall had refused in 1617 and 1622 invitations to be a member of the borough council. He replied with good reason that he was too busy looking after his patients. It would have been wrong of the doctor to divert his energies into the petty feuds of the local rulers. But after his escape from his very severe illness he was at last enrolled as a council member. Then, as Susanna must have known to her distress, he had become fractious, choleric, and even unruly. When he thought his fellow councillors to be fools he did not suffer them gladly. He spoke out fiercely. It was minuted after one meeting that he had been acrimonious and quarrelsome and had violently abused the mayor. This led to his expulsion from the council by nineteen votes to three for 'breach of orders, sundry misdemeanours and continual disturbances'.

Stratford could have been found a quiet spot when Shakespeare returned to it, but it became a hot-bed of religious as well as civic contention ten years later. Into these stormy waters Hall had plunged and continued to splash. The doctrines of the vicar and the conduct of the services were in dispute. The puritans of the town were advancing in numbers and strength but they met with pugnacious opposition. It was a triumph for them when Thomas Wilson was inducted as vicar in 1619. He was a powerful preacher on the puritan side and so bitter in his hatred of Rome that he was later accused of desecrating the old Gild Chapel by letting in pigs and hens. He did not deny this and pleaded guilty.

His arrival had caused a riot and on his first appearance in the church he was chased into the chancel while a menacing anti-puritan crowd added window-breaking to their clamorous protest against his appointment. He stayed on, at first backed by the council, and long championed by Dr Hall. The town was divided by a degrading series of verbal squabbles and even physical brawling. Susanna had to watch her husband wasting his energy and losing his temper while the sectarian strife was simmering and sometimes boiling over.

Completely unworthy of the eminent doctor of medicine was his participation in a 'battle of the pews'. The private seats in the church were eagerly sought and jealously held by the leading families. Hall insisted on moving from the Shakespeare pew to a position occupied by the leading aldermen and their wives who angrily refused to budge. There was pushing and jostling as well as a warfare of words. The sordid wrangling had to be settled by an inquiry conducted by the vicar-general to the Archbishop of Canterbury. The doctor's claim was upheld and Wilson was still the incumbent. But while the puritan wing of the churchmen won the day, the doctor completely lost his dignity. It is hard to believe that his sensible wife enjoyed so ridiculous a victory and took her new seat with pride and pleasure.

It seems plain from her husband's conduct after his 'rescue from the jaws of death' that his claim to have completely recovered was a piece of self-deception. There had been no previous signs of the ungovernable petulance which he displayed after 1632 in the council room and in the affairs of the Church. Dr Mitchell, considering this behaviour as a medical man, suggested that the raging fever and temporary paralysis had caused serious patho-logical damage to the doctor's brain. In 1635, three years after his illness and his first disastrous entry to the council, he died suddenly. They were years of affliction for his wife who had to watch him losing his balance and dissipating the well-earned respect of so many of his fellow-citizens. Cerebral injury is the most likely explanation of this collapse.

He had hurriedly dictated to his son-in-law Nash and the curate Simon Trappe a will of the oral kind legally known as nuncupative. He divided his goods and money equally between his wife and his daughter. There were also separate bequests. He left to Susanna the house in Acton, inherited from his father, and to Elizabeth some meadow-land in Stratford. Nash inherited his 'study of books' with the right to dispose of them as he chose. The doctor intended his 'papers' to go to 'Master Boles' but as Boles was away at the time Nash was to do as he pleased with them and could burn them if he chose. Fortunately the 'Observations' survived this foolish and impetuous dismissal of his own work by a man who was mentally disturbed and at the point of death.

Susanna, when two years later she had to meet a legal claim against her husband's estate, said that his property had been worth a thousand pounds. This may have been a cautious under statement. Certainly with her two inheritances from her father and her husband she was a wealthy lady by Stratford standards and her views would be respected. Though a queen had recently reigned over England and done it with such a mixture of prudence and audacity that she earned the title of Gloriana, women of ability had no share in the national or local forms of government. Milton wrote in 'L'Allegro' of

> *ladies whose bright eyes*
> *Rain influence.*

They could exert their pressure privately and Susanna, with or without persuasive glances, creates the impression that the lady of New Place was capable as well as amiable and commanded attention for her views.

John Hall died at New Place on November 25, 1635 and was buried in the chancel of the church which he had loved and had assisted financially. He had fought zealously over the conduct of its services as well as stupidly over its seating. His grave was next

but one to that of William Shakespeare. This does not suggest
that his religious opinions had ever made a breach between them.
The idea has been put forward that the indignant puritan destroyed
his father-in-law's manuscripts and plays printed in Quarto,
despising them as the works of the devil. This is nonsense. Hall
was not a barbarian and Susanna would not have allowed such an
insult to her father.

The Latin epitaph on 'Hallius' described him as most celebrated
in the art of medicine. It said that he died expecting the joys of
God's kingdom and that he deserved to outlive Nestor but was
snatched by the levelling hand of death. More about his life
would have been useful to students of Stratford history.

Susanna continued to live on in New Place. Elizabeth and
Thomas Nash owned a house close by in Chapel Street. Nash did
not share Dr Hall's political opinions. When the Civil War came
he was a devoted Royalist and made the largest of the Stratford
contributions to the king's war-chest: he gave a hundred pounds
in plate and cash. During the campaigns Stratford loyalties were
divided; varying too were its occupying armies. Not far from the
sharp escarpment of Edgehill where the first battle was fought in
1643 the town received wounded soldiers of the Parliamentary
army and voted money for their relief. Five months later it was
entered by the Cavaliers. Queen Henrietta was brought there by
Prince Rupert with an army of three thousand and quartered at
New Place. The corporation obediently supplied her and her
servants with poultry, meat, cakes, cheese, beer, and fodder for
horses to the value of fifteen pounds. The queen left after three
days. She was said to have preferred New Place for her brief stay.
The king was one of Shakespeare's admirers and she had enjoyed
command performances at court of some of his plays. Presumably
Susanna moved out to the conveniently adjacent home of her
married daughter.

Nash died suddenly in 1647 and was honoured with a grave in
the chancel. He was by no means poor and Elizabeth had her
right of dower as well as the house. He proved his friendship for
the whole family by leaving money to three of the Hathaways,
none of whom had appeared in Shakespeare's will. He also gave

fifty pounds to Susanna. This was unnecessary unless she had been wasting her money, which is improbable. The bequest was evidently a sign of his affection; he had not suffered from an oppressive mother-in-law.

In June 1649 Elizabeth married again. Her new match brought a social promotion. Her husband John Barnard (sometimes spelled Bernard) was a country gentleman with no need to earn a living. He had a house at Abington in Northamptonshire where he was Lord of the Manor, but Susanna only just lived to see them married. The Stratford parish register's entry for July 16, 1649 notes the burial of 'Mrs Susanna Hall, widow'. She was laid beside her husband and her father. The lines on her grave-stone related the good qualities of her mind and heart.

Except during the period after the doctor's devastating attack of fever her life had been as serene as might be. She may have been to London with Elizabeth on that ill-fated journey. For the rest she had her Stratford grass-roots. The lack of a son was tragic: despite this galling deprivation one gets no impression of an empty or frustrated life. Her husband, with his renown spreading across the Midlands, had been for nearly thirty years a source of pride and a good help-mate until he became 'a handful' and an invalid. The Barnards stayed on at New Place until 1653. The honour which Susanna lost when John Hall had refused to pay for it came to Elizabeth when Barnard was knighted after the Restoration, presumably for his services to the royal cause and not as a cash transaction. Lady Barnard died in 1670. So ended the direct descendants of William Shakespeare.

CHAPTER VII

Judith

MUCH LESS is known of Judith, Susanna's younger and less fortunate sister. She hovers, an elusive character, on the fringe of the copious Shakespeare biographies. Her girlhood is a secret matter. So is Susanna's, but the curtain was lifted on her married life. Not until she was thirty do we get documented information about Judith and then the news is sad. We learn of a partnership that was probably more harassing than happy and of bereavements certainly cruel. She did not wear out easily despite the worries at the time of her wedding and the bitter loss of two sons in her middle age. She lived to be seventy-seven, twenty-five years older than her father and nine years older than her mother. She had much to take and she took it, but it is difficult to think that she enjoyed the length of her years.

For Judith there was only a precarious rung on Stratford's social ladder. She did not share the Shakespeare celebrity and the status which her well-married sister had sustained. After her death she was not interred with her parents and her sister in the chancel of the church. The entry of her burial was made for February 9, 1662—'Judith, uxor Thomas Quiney, gent.' The site of her grave is unknown. If there was a benignant epitaph, left in the usual way to inform posterity of her good sense and good nature, it has vanished. The phrase 'odd man out' may here be applicable to the other sex. In the Shakespeare family chronicles Judith seems to be more an item in the index than an inhabitant of the home. She was outside and perhaps looking away rather than in. Her luck was out too. One naturally wonders about her relations with the successful Susanna and her daughter. Did Elizabeth, away in Northamptonshire and a lady of title when the news of Judith's death reached her, think of her as 'Poor Aunt Judy'? There was some reason for that.

Shakespeare had left Stratford when both the girls were small. If that, as is generally thought, happened in 1587, Susanna was four and Judith two. The idea that their mother was encouraged to take, or insisted upon taking, the children to London to join their father in Bishopsgate has been discounted. Except during his annual vacation visits, which must have been brief, they were their mother's children. On Shakespeare's returns there would be great affection, a parcel of presents, and a happy time in the garden when New Place was theirs; but that was an incident. The regimen for eleven months in the year was Anne's with the grandparents in the background. The amount of schooling then available for girls has been discussed and the conclusion drawn that it was not negligible. The signatures of Susanna and Elizabeth Hall have survived. Both wrote a good literate hand. In 1611 Judith twice witnessed a deed made between two friends of the family, Elizabeth Quiney and her son Adrian. She did so by making her mark. That, as has been explained, is not a sure proof of illiteracy. But it is surprising that she did not sign her name in the ordinary way.

She did not marry until she was nearly thirty-one. Her mother is regarded as a late starter because she was unmated at twenty-five. In another way Judith followed Anne who had paired with a youngster of eighteen. When she went to her wedding her man was twenty-seven. Again there was no observance of her father's cautionary canon about the woman taking an elder than herself. There was a curious parallel to her parents' enforced journey to Worcester to correct an omission. There was a complication about Judith's wedding-date and need for a special licence. The parish church's register recorded '1616, Feb. 10, M. Tho Queeny two Judith Shakspere'. There was trouble to come about the requisite permission from Worcester and domestic tragedy was imminent. In less than three months her father had died.

It is strange that she had been single so long. Marriages were not only love-matches. The nobility set an example of deliberate calculation of dowries and the middle class were not neglectful of marriage-portions. The delay in the mating of Anne Hathaway is understandable. She came of a comparatively poor family and had enough domestic and farm-house work on her hands in the full homestead at Shottery to limit party outings and well-dressed appearances in Stratford company. There was no financial attraction; young men with an eye to a silver, if not golden, nest-egg in the future home could have small expectation here.

Judith's case was very different. The Shakespeares had taken over New Place when she was twelve. She matured as a daughter of 'the grete house'. In the following years Shakespeare was adding steadily to his Stratford properties. When he came back to be more or less a resident he was wealthy by local standards. There could be substantial masculine hopes when Judith, rising thirty, was being considered as a match.

Perhaps she was slow, shy, and awkward in her girlhood, overshadowed by her elder sister. It does not need a profound psychology to suspect that when Hamnet died she could feel that her father and mother unconsciously resented the survival of the second daughter when they lost her twin-brother who was their only son. She was then eleven and old enough to be sensitive to any slight imagined by her and of course not intended by her mourning parents. After as well as during the first grief she could fancy herself to be unwanted and inferior. The unhappiness would be worse if Susanna was mentally more alert, more spirited, better-looking, and more attractive. Shakespeare used the odd little word 'sprag' to describe a lively and quick-witted youngster. Was Judith incapable of being sprag? There may also have been clumsiness in her mother's handling of a backward and difficult girl. We can only guess. Such an atmosphere in the home is more than possible.

After growing up Judith seemed (to use words of her father's) to be the lingering blossom

> *Which, withering on the virgin's thorn,*
> *Grows, lives, and dies in single blessedness.*

Contrasted with that had been the poet's opinion

> *But earthly-happier is the rose distilled.*

The distillation of Judith was a long time in coming and, when she took a husband, it was a bad choice. Earthly-happiness there may have been at times, but it was not an immediate acquisition.

The Quineys were a middle-class Stratford family, neighbours and old friends of the Shakespeares. Richard, father of Judith's Thomas, had been Mayor of Stratford in 1592 and 1601. He was thought capable of representing the town on business in London. He was there in 1598 and wrote to Shakespeare from the Bell Inn in Carter Lane asking for a loan of thirty pounds 'in helpeing me out of all the debettes which I owe in London'. He got his assistance. Probably the money was repaid. Shakespeare was no usurer, but it is known that he collected even small sums owing to him in Stratford. Richard's father Adrian advised him to bring this or other money home and invest in the hosiery business at Evesham where there was a brisk trade in 'knit stockings'. When Richard died in 1602 he had again been elected mayor, but he was not wealthy and his widow had to conduct a vintner's business. Carting wine to the Midlands must have been a slow, laborious business, but there was a market for it and it paid. Later her son Thomas worked with her and leased a tavern. The Quineys were representative of the Stratford trading community. Woollens or wines, hosiery or sack, they would deal where there were customers. On the whole they were solid folk. So far there was no disgrace and no distinction in marrying one of them if there was nothing against him. But there was soon a very black mark to be set against the name of Judith's Thomas.

There were signs of a hasty ceremony. Why otherwise was the wedding on February 10? This came within the period for which a special licence had to be obtained. It was not a rule strictly observed in Stratford at the time. The assistant minister, Richard Watts, did not bother much about the date and three similar marriages were recorded. But in the case of the Quineys there was trouble. The ecclesiastical administration in Warwickshire was oddly confused. For two years out of three the local vicar had the right of episcopal jurisdiction and could grant marriage licences. But for one year in three the Bishop of Worcester took over the ight. The marriage of Judith to Thomas Quiney seems to have come at a disputed date. They had the vicar's permission and took that as valid. The bishop did not agree.

Perhaps Thomas should have done some tipping and oiled the palm of the summoner or apparitor of the diocese who was subsequently found guilty of corruption. To us the squabble between the bishop and the vicar over the issue of licences seems trivial, but bishops can be prickly and resent any slur on their authority. So Thomas had to go before the consistory court at Worcester. Either careless or contumacious, he failed to appear, was fined, and excommunicated. That was not a punishment as terrible as it sounds. This is shown by the christening of the couple's first child in the church at Stratford on November 23. Thomas's conduct must have been grievous to Judith and her parents. Certainly it would not please the Halls. Judith, however, did not have to hurry to the altar because of pregnancy. The dates of the wedding and christening do not indicate an anticipation of the wedding. But if Judith had not yielded too early to Thomas's seductive charms, another woman had.

On May 21, 1964, Mr Hugh A. Hanley, Assistant Archivist in the County of Kent, published in 'The Times Literary Supplement' his account of a discovery made among the Sackville papers which had come from that family's mansion at Knole to be deposited at Maidstone. (The Sackvilles had acquired the documents through a marriage with a family who had bought them from the Grevilles who were territorial magnates in the Shakespeare county.) Included was an ecclesiastical 'act book', written in Latin, which put it on record that on March 26, 1616, Thomas Quiney of Stratford was 'presented for incontinence with a certain Margaret Wheelar'. Cited in person by the lawyer Greene he confessed to 'carnal intercourse with the said Wheelar'. He could not evade the charge since the consequences of the affair had been both fruitful and fatal. The woman and her child had died, either in childbirth or through one of Stratford's frequent infections.

Quiney submitted to the correction of the judge who ordered him to make public penance, clothed in a white sheet, for three

Sundays in the parish church. (If such appearances were at all
frequent they must have diminished the unwillingness of local
recusants to make the attendance at services demanded by law.
Sin does more than sermons can to attract the scandal-loving
man and gossiping woman.) The Church, militant against
licentiousness, could be pacified by repentance of a financial
kind and its price was not high. For the sum of five shillings
Quiney escaped the white sheet of humiliation, but he had to
admit his guilt in his own ordinary clothes before the minister
of Bishopton, a 'chapelry' within the parish of Stratford and
presumably the home of the Wheelars or Wheelers. The time-
table of Judith's unhappy marriage is thus scheduled by Mr Hanley. In January 1616 Shakespeare made the first draft of his will.
On February 10 the marriage of Thomas and Judith took place.
On March 15 Margaret Wheelar and her child were buried. On
March 25 Shakespeare altered his will to the disadvantage of
Judith and suggesting distrust of Thomas. On March 26 the
latter faced the charge of incontinence with Wheelar with the
results described.

Thomas had managed to get his wedding celebrated. He was
marrying into a prosperous family; if his father-in-law was
already a sick man he had hopes of a good share in his property.
But there is no evidence to suggest that Shakespeare was a dying
man in February; if his end came suddenly we cannot accuse
Quiney of that calculation. He must have known that Margaret
Wheelar was very soon to be a mother. He could hope that she
would go away and be delivered of her child secretly before the
storm broke. If it did break, it was necessary to have his marriage
into the Shakespeare family settled before trouble came. He could
hardly risk calling in the efficient Dr Hall to cope with the result
of his 'incontinence'. Did some local mid-wife attend the wretched
Margaret Wheelar with disastrous consequences and bring the
whole squalid affair into the open?

This wretched business is not one of the Stratford legends
or concoctions. The Sackville papers are genuine and explicit.
They explain the changes in Shakespeare's will caused by lack of
trust in his second son-in-law. He was still hoping for a grandson

from Susanna, to whom now went all his personal property, New Place and holdings of land. These were entailed upon her eldest son or heir male. (That would be Dr Hall if he survived her and she had no son.) In the event of Susanna's lacking a son the property was entailed upon the heirs male of Judith who herself came poorly off.

The immediate bequest to her was only one hundred pounds as her dowry, with fifty pounds more if she abandoned her claim to the cottage in Chapel Lane. This increased her deprivation if she and Thomas were expecting to be the cottagers. If she or any child of hers was living three years after the date of the will, another hundred and fifty pounds was to go to her or her children; but she was only to get the interest accruing from this money. Her husband was not to touch this sum unless he settled land of the same value on her and their children. Of the chattels she was only to have her father's 'broad silver-gilt bole'.

For a while certainly the Quineys stayed together. Thomas was given a place on the borough council and became chamberlain in 1621. That meant some trust in him since that office put him in charge of the accounts. It was usual for the chamberlain to proceed, as John Shakespeare had done, to the high post of bailiff or mayor. But Thomas was not promoted and Judith never was mayoress. Something went wrong, as they so often did with her. Quiney was for some time landlord of a tavern called 'The Cage' at the corner of Bridge Street and High Street; in recent years there has been a café on the site bearing Judith's name. In 1630 he was fined for using bad language and misuse of his premises by toleration of drunkenness. One can imagine the distaste of the Halls for a relative of this kind. He stayed on trading in wine. Dr Mitchell said of this member of the Shakespeare Circle that he was 'an undesirable' and deserted Judith, but other accounts deny that he flitted. The date of his death is unknown. Whatever happened he was not a commendable husband and his dying father-in-law had a correct intuition of his character.

When Judith died in 1662 she had lived in four reigns as well as under the protectorate of Oliver Cromwell. Country-town women when there were no newspapers or broadcast news could not be keenly political. National affairs only excited them when they produced local events. Queen Henrietta Maria had been very briefly the talk of Stratford. The gossips would know that a title had come to Lady Barnard. Beside the Avon families rose and declined in their trades and crafts. Stratford life went changeably on its Warwickshire way. Memories were short. Even her famous father had soon become a shadowy figure of the past. He was a name in the chancel and had his monument, but an incoming vicar knew little or nothing of the man who was to put Stratford on the map of the world, and make it a magnet for tourists of all nations and a cultural shrine.

When John Ward was inducted to the parish in 1662 he confessed that he was unaware of Shakespeare's fame. He admitted this by entering in his diary that he must remember to peruse the plays 'that he might not be thought ignorant in this matter'. He discovered that Shakespeare 'had but two daughters' and then mentioned Mistress Hall and her Elizabeth. Judith did not count. He had indeed been told that, if he wanted to learn more, he should see 'Mrs. Queeny'. But, unless he arrived before her death at the end of January, he missed her. Had they met she could have corrected the report that Shakespeare 'spent at the rate of a thousand pounds a year'. That, he wrote, was 'what I have heard'. It was absurd. The sum was impossibly large.

Judith must have known the extent and value of her father's possessions and compared them with her share of the inheritance. One of the obvious facts of life in her time was the favour shown to the eldest child. It was a hard world for younger sons and a younger daughter might suffer for the same reason. The rule of primogeniture prevailed and Shakespeare exposed this injustice at its worst when he wrote of his own Arden country and its practices in *As You Like It*. Orlando complains bitterly of the deprivation suffered by junior members of families with property to settle. He has been left by his wealthy father 'but poor a thousand crowns', has been kept by Oliver, his eldest brother, 'rustically at home, stalled like an ox', and deprived of travel. His gentility has been 'mined' by lack of education.

That is cruelty, but Orlando admits that such treatment is traditional. 'The courtesy of nations', he says to his grasping, tyrannical senior, 'allows you are my better in that you are the first-born', and he admits that precedence of birth brings Oliver nearer to his father's 'reverence'. When Falstaff is describing the sad medley of forced and untrained men whom he must lead to the wars he includes impoverished gentry, 'younger sons of younger brothers', with 'discarded unjust serving men, revolted tapsters, and ostlers trade-fallen'. (Orlando who could throw a professional wrestler would have made a lusty addition to this ragged regiment.) In the bequeathing of a family estate there was no equality and Judith could not reasonably expect any parity in her father's disposition of his goods. None the less the inequity in this case was great and the will rankled.

She was at last a newly married wife setting up house and that was not in the family's cottage in Chapel Lane from which she had been excluded. Furnishing was needed and her husband was not a man of substance. She had her 'silver-gilt bole' but that did not go far towards the equipment of a new home. Susanna's inheritance was not limited to houses and land. To the Halls went the whole residue of the estate, 'goods, chattels, leases, plate, jewels, and house-hold stuff'.

It is true that Judith could manage since the cost of living was extremely low. Schoolmasters and parsons might be locally regarded as considerable persons but they did not get considerable salaries. Twenty pounds a year was thought to be a large reward. That was for a long time the emolument of the headmaster of Stratford's grammar school which had a series of university men in charge of it. If Judith got a good rate of interest on her financial legacy the few pounds coming in bought quite a lot and were a help. There was the tavern where Thomas Quiney later permitted the excessive consumption of liquor which he presumably did not sell at a loss. But there were galling circumstances.

After Susanna's death she had to watch the Barnards enjoying New Place and the gardens to which she had come as a child in 1597. That had been an entry to a happy splendour unknown during the hard times before it when she was five or six and her father was still a junior actor and stripling dramatist and not yet the favoured beneficiary of the Earl of Southampton. While he was working his way up in the theatre and making any other money which his industry and ingenuity could provide the amount of it returning to Stratford was very small. The rise in wealth and the promotion to New Place must have been glorious to the children. Now the married Judith was to have no share in that. She was at the tavern along the street. The name, 'The Cage', seems unkindly apposite.

It is not to be thought that Shakespeare wished to humiliate Judith by the allotment of his property. There is no sign of cruelty in his character. But he was a dying man and understandably vexed by her match. His views of Quiney's character were already being justified. The date of the wedding which he did not welcome was being muddled. Whether or not we share Frank Harris's view of him as a snob he shared his father's keen feeling for the dignity of the family. He had his Arden as well as his Shakespeare blood and the pride which went with it. He was not mean but he had strong opinions about the use of the money for which he had worked so hard and which he had thriftily saved and carefully invested. He had no intention of allowing a wastrel to squander it.

Twenty years ago he had unforgettably praised the quality of mercy. In *The Tempest*, not his last play but obviously written in a valedictory frame of mind, he had made the wronged and angry Prospero say:

> *Though with their high wrongs I am struck to the quick*
> *Yet, with my nobler reason, 'gainst my fury*
> *Do I take part; the rarer action is*
> *In virtue than in vengeance.*

Had he lived longer he could have displayed Prospero's magnanimity. He could have forgotten the offence and remembered the tie of blood as well as the duty of benignity. It was too late. While the lawyer was drafting his will there was no time for a change of mood. To his sick-bed came the news of Thomas

Quiney's misconduct and disgrace to intensify his scepticism about the stability of his son-in-law. Judith, he thought, was being a fool while her husband was being exposed as a knave. The timing of the affair was disastrous; once more Judith had no luck. The contrast with Susanna was inescapable. She had proved her judgment by her marriage and shown herself to be a true daughter of William Shakespeare, gentleman. Judith was neither enhancing the family name nor securing for herself a prosperous and agreeable future. As at New Place, so in the will she was the 'Odd Woman Out'. And then she had to face thirty-six years of life in the chilly air of the Shakespeare fringe.

Susanna as the elder daughter of course had her right to the chief consideration, but the disproportion in the distribution is striking and obviously indicates strong apprehension that Quiney did not deserve any confidence as a husband. The income which would come from Judith's capital was something at that time and would be more if Quiney was to put up the investment required. There may have been doubts before the affair with the unfortunate Wheelar had confirmed the fears about his character. It is not known whether Quiney ever made the required purchase of land. The hasty wedding is explained if Quiney wanted to be married before his affair with Margaret Wheelar leaked out.

Judith's humiliation when her husband was arraigned and exposed must have been intense. After the terms of the will had become known she had further cause for regretting her marriage. And then there came to the unhappy woman the loss of her infant son in the following November. There was hope again when she bore two more sons, but both were lost in what was probably an epidemic since they died in rapid succession in January and February, 1639. Judith was fifty-four. Shakespeare's hopes of a male heir had now completely gone.

CHAPTER VIII

Women About Town

A VIVID picture of London in Shakespeare's time has been left us by Thomas Platter of Basel. This Swiss traveller's report reveals his excited interest in all matters of English conduct, the eagreness of his curiosity, and the thoroughness with which he took notes. Fortunately his diary has been preserved. It can be read in translation in a book by Clare Williams called 'Thomas Platter's Travels in England in 1599'.

One thing which immediately surprised the Swiss visitor must also have impressed Shakespeare when he came from the country to the capital. That was the freedom enjoyed by women. They could go about the town, watch its spectacles, and sample its various forms of gaiety and conviviality in a way little known at that time on the mainland of Europe. This liberty was not restricted to the rich and titled ladies on the exalted fringe of society or to those on the lowest level, the types whom Shakespeare said should be set down as

> *the sluttish spoils of opportunity*
> *And daughters of the game.*

The middle-class wives also had what Dickens called 'the key of the street' and were not restricted to watching the swirling tide of life by taking a peep from their windows. If London was, in the idiom of today, 'swinging', they could join the dance.

Legally and politically they had no rights. The property given or left to them by their parents passed to their husbands when they married. A wedding in the right quarter was an investment in valuable land if the girl's father was a territorial magnate or in money at the bank if he was a prosperous merchant. Platter was immensely struck by the number of ships in London's harbour, the extent of the seaborne commerce, the richness of the cargoes, the high rate of interest, ten per cent, and the prosperity of the money-changers and goldsmiths who acted as bankers. He said that they occupied nearly all the buildings in one long street (Cheapside) and were in control of 'inexpressibly vast treasures'. There was plenty of money about in this corner of England and daughters were coveted for their inherited share of it. In the matrimonial game a dowry could be a trump card.

Foreigners who came to London either as political and diplomatic emissaries or for business reasons commented with surprise on the extent to which women shared in the general pursuit of refreshments and recreations. Father Busino, who was sent to the Venetian embassy at the Court of King James, recorded that the theatres were frequented by a number of respectable and handsome ladies who came in and took their seats beside the men with no shyness or hesitation. Evidently there was no veto on priests attending performances since he was a play-goer himself. When he was at the Fortune Theatre he had for neighbour 'a very elegant dame' whose respectability could be questioned. Whatever her morals he approved of her appearance. To this he gave close attention. He remembered all the details of her sumptuous attire, the yellow satin bodice, the petticoat of gold tissue with stripes, the robe of red velvet lined with yellow muslin with broad stripes of pure gold. Her head-tire was highly perfumed and the collar of white satin beneath her ruff struck him as very pretty.

The lady was quite ready to exhibit her wealth as well as her wardrobe. She took off no less than three pairs of gloves (the London colleagues of John Shakespeare had a good customer here) and then displayed the diamonds on her fingers. The Father added that he turned a deaf ear to what she said and did not specify the suggestions made. He had to remember his office and he had come to see a play. The lady may have thought him churlish. That she became so rapidly familiar suggests that the holy man was not in the uniform of his calling and to avoid attention had changed into layman's clothes. However that may have been we have a good picture of the elegance of the audience in the galleries as well as of the customary feminine participation in the pleasures of play-going.

Platter also remarked on the presence of women in theatres. He decided that a thirst for information was as much a motive for a trip to see the players as was the normal desire for two hours of excitement and laughter. 'Indeed', he wrote, 'men and women folk visit such places without scruple since the English for the most part do not travel much and prefer to learn of foreign affairs and take their pleasures at home.' This is a compliment, perhaps not fully merited, to the intellectual curiosity of the native play-goers who, if they were seeking such further education, must have received from Shakespeare some strange ideas about the customs and behaviour to be found in Busino's own Italy. The Father, as a Venetian, could hardly accept as a realistic guide to local practices the matrimonial arrangements made for Portia of Belmont. Doubtless he missed that play and her casket scene.

The Swiss observer had preceded the Venetian in his admiration of London's *couture* as met in the receptions which he attended in the streets, or at the theatres across the Thames. To him it was a well-upholstered city. The wherries in which he was ferried to and from the South Bank had embroidered and very comfortable cushions and were covered over to protect the customers from rain or a blazing sun. Platter made his journey in September when he was unlikely to be roasted, but he gratefully acknowledged the defences against all types of English weather about which he made no complaint.

The Elizabethan grandees were exhibitionists. Men and women were ready to spend with a wild extravagance on their wardrobes. If their male escorts wore rosettes and even jewels, as did Sir Walter Raleigh, on the shoes beneath their corseted waists, the beauties of the town were not going to betray the standards of elegance established by the men. In that flashing world which met the eyes of the man from Stratford to be foppish was not to be effeminate; the sparkish milord sumptuously dressed mixed brawn and brains. He was as ready to pen a sonnet of quality as to draw his sword for his queen or in personal quarrel. He would have music wherever he went, even on his wherry-trip to the Southwark suburb and its raree-show of the theatres and the bull-ring. And there on the stage the ladies and gentlemen coming from the great river-side mansions on the North Bank might see their own grandeur, perhaps a little tarnished, but deemed essential to the proper mounting of a play.

The actors, said Platter, are most expensively and elaborately dressed. Some of the manager Henslowe's accounts of payment have survived. He was a careful, acquisitive man who paid his dramatists five pounds for all rights in a five-act play with no royalties to follow. Yet he would lay out twenty pounds for one copper-lace robe for his money-spinning star, Alleyn, who was deemed worth the investment since he was the most magnetic of the players until Burbage arrived as Shakespeare's colleague among the Lord Chamberlain's Men. Such a splashing of money on a single garment was exceptional and Platter discovered one of the methods employed in financing a lavish production with thrift.

There was a side-line commerce in costumes. The fops, he said, were in the habit of handing their clothes, by gift or bequest, to their servants who then went to the back-doors of the theatres and sold them to the actors. If the ladies followed their example and also passed on their discarded finery to their maids and the maids preferred cash to costume a feminine spectator of moderate height might see the boy appointed to play a queen or princess robed in splendour by the disposal of her own modish dresses. Shakespeare's Cleopatra must have been wearing on the stage the tightly fitting costume of Jacobean fashion since she had to cry to her maid of honour, 'Cut my lace, Charmian' when she was distressed almost to swooning by the news that Antony was leaving her and off to the wars. So in the case of many a play there could be a female complaint heard in the galleries that the crafty lad had got hold of her last year's 'creation'.

It has been maintained, against a mass of evidence, that the women were a small minority in an Elizabethan audience or were limited to prostitutes on the prowl. The presence of the latter provided opportunities for the puritan opposition to rail at the 'picking-up' which went on. In 1583, well before Shakespeare had come to London, Stubbes in his 'Anatomie of Abuses' had denounced the men's itching and shouldering to sit by women and 'such tickling, such toying, such smiling, such winking'. When the play was over 'every mate sorts to his mate, every one brings another homeward of their way, verye freendly'. This friendliness he also believed to be homosexual. 'They play the Sodomits or worse.' The latter practice would naturally meet with a furious rivalry among the prostitutes, who were playgoers for professional reasons. We hear of no homosexual scandals in the theatres. The Court of King James was not so innocent.

But the thunders of the square-toed critics of Londoners' conduct must be kept in proportion. The play-house public was more bourgeois than raffish. Professor Harbage in his book on 'Shakespeare's Audience' disputes the view of Sir Edmund Chambers that the galleries were frequented by 'light women who found them a profitable haunt' and a few 'ladies of position probably in the private rooms and possibly masked'. Platter's scrutiny of an audience found it to be mixed in class as well as in sex. When Philip Julius, Duke of Stettin-Pomerania, wrote his diary of an English journey in 1602, he visited three theatres and found them to be attended by many respectable women. Ben Jonson in *Every Man Out of his Humour* showed his expectation of a serious audience and asked 'the modest matron' as well as 'the grave wise citizen' not to be offended by two of the characters in the piece. One of the play-hating scolds, Robert Anton, wrote in the year after Shakespeare's death that the theatres were attended by 'swarms of wives'. Father Busino paid a tribute to silent and courteous listening. The great majority who had paid to come in wanted value for their money and angrily resented the interruptions of the unmannerly gallants who had seats on the stage, gagged, made jokes, and 'mewed'.

It was customary to go well dressed to the play-house. In the numerous references to the audiences there are descriptions of a well dressed cross-section of the community who put on their best clothes. That was stressed in 1617 in the outburst of an 'arch-priest', William Harrison, who must have been to this supposed parade-ground of male and female vanity before he denounced theatrical attendance as unseemly for one of his calling.

> For few of either sex come thither, but in theyr
> holy-dayes appareil, and so set forth, so trimmed,
> so adorned, so decked, so perfumed, as if they made
> the place the market of wantonnesse, and by
> consequence too unfit for a Priest to frequent.

Shakespeare himself makes it very difficult to believe that the women who came to his plays were limited to ladies of high rank or common sluts. Whether he or another wrote the epilogue to *Henry VIII*, the appeal is to respectable women and it is implied that they have a powerful influence in determining the failure or success of a play.

> Tis ten to one this play can never please
> All that are here: some come to take their ease,
> And sleep an act or two; but those, we fear,
> W' have frighted with our trumpets; so, 'tis clear,
> They'll say 'tis naught: others, to hear the city
> Abus'd extremely, and to cry, 'That's witty!'
> Which we have not done neither: that, I fear,
> All the expected good w' are like to hear
> For this play at this time, is only in
> The merciful construction of good women;
> For such a one we showed 'em: if they smile,
> And say 'twill do, I know, within a while
> All the best men are ours; for 'tis ill hap,
> If they hold when their ladies bid 'em clap.

When Shakespeare wrote the Epilogue to *As You Like It* he had in mind a mingling of the sexes and classes. He sees them in holiday mood and disposed to be affectionate within proper limits. The lines delivered by the boy-player cast as Rosalind are aimed at the average man and woman.

Rosalind. It is not the fashion to see the lady the epilogue; but it is no more unhandsome than to see the lord the prologue. If it be true that good wine needs no bush, 'tis true that a good play needs no epilogue: yet to good wine they do use good bushes; and good plays prove the better by the help of good epilogues. What a case am I in, then, that am neither a good epilogue, nor cannot insinuate with you in the behalf of a good play! I am not furnish'd like a beggar, therefore to beg will not become me: my way is, to conjure you; and I'll begin with the women. I charge you, O women, for the love you bear to men, to like as much of this play as please you: and I charge you, O men, for the love you bear to women (as I perceive by your simpering, none of you hates them), that between you and the women the play may please. If I were a woman, I would kiss as many of you as had beards that pleased me, complexions that liked me, and breaths that I defied not: and, I am sure, as many as have good beards, or good faces, or sweet breaths, will, for my kind offer, when I make curtsy, bid me farewell.

This was surely not intended only for women of high rank and low morals, the dames and drabs envisaged by Sir Edmund Chambers. The dramatist and the actors knew that the shop-keeper took money from the till to spend at theatre-doors and that his wife came too.

Familiar examples of the tradesman and his household in search of pleasure are the grocer, his wife, and his stage-struck apprentice Ralph in *The Knight of the Burning Pestle*. The authors, Francis Beaumont and John Fletcher, were not men of the people. The former's father was a gentleman of title, and the latter's had been thrice a bishop, of Worcester, Bristol, and London. Both dramatists had been to the university. So the members of the grocer's party are seen from an upper distance and laughed at for their simplicity. They misunderstand the plot of the play which they are seeing. The wife is a cheerful creature in her chattering way. Her dramatic criticism is of a naïvely practical kind. A statement about sharp practice in shops sets her wondering about the honesty of her own dressmaker. Did that woman really use all the material that was handed over to be made up?

The grocer's wife is having her first outing of this kind although Ralph the apprentice is a fanatical play-fancier. Her husband is not a puritan sternly keeping her from Satan's workshop. He has merely made promises of an excursion and failed to keep them for reasons not explained. He could hardly grudge the money since they appeared to go in among the groundlings who stood round the stage for a penny. Being so close to the centre of things the wife wants to be nearer still. She demands to be up and on the stage and gets her way. None of the 'gatherers' demands extra payment for their climb to join the men of means who have paid sixpence for their privileged seat beside the players.

She is enraptured when the shop-bound Ralph, a frustrated actor with Shakespeare's lines frothing on his lips, is allowed to butt in and take a leading part which he delivers with a flourish in the grand histrionic manner. Both she and her husband are so unsophisticated and so entranced that they take the characters in the romantic drama to be real persons. If there are scoundrels they give warnings to Ralph of their villainy while they warmly encourage the young hero in his gallantries. A complaint in the text about feet afflicted by travel evokes the wife's description of her favourite treatment for chilblains. She detests the filthy tobacco-smoke of the sixpenny bucks but in the end is so delighted by the occasion that she asks them to her home with the offer of wine and even of more tobacco.

The grocer first complains about the dramatist's usual habit of girding at citizens', i.e. ridiculing his own class of merchants and tradesmen. He cries for a break with that old vice of the snob-writers and asks for a play 'notably in honour of the commons of the city'. In a way his wish is met. The point is interesting to those concerned with the theatrical trends of the time. The fashion in comedy was changing from aristocratic to middle-class themes and characters. It was a mode to which Shakespeare had once contributed in *The Merry Wives of Windsor*, but he did not continue to offer familiar surroundings and bourgeois persons. Others did and the new kind of play which was not 'girding at citizens' appealed to the citizens' wives as well as the men when they saw their own way of life shown. It was not done with what we would

call total realism but at least with recognisable standards of rank
money, and behaviour. The result was gay and exciting withou
derision of the men and women who were making the new
commerce of the town.

The women of this class did not come to the play as illiterates
Parents could pay the small fees asked for attendance at th
growing number of girls' schools. Some of these were conducte
by immigrant school-teachers. Owing to the persecution o
Protestants in neighbouring European countries there wer
many refugees who brought their skills with them. The textil
workers from the Low Countries found occupation with th
London clothiers. There were others, especially women, wh
were qualified to teach if they already possessed or had acquire
good enough English. Dorothy Gardiner, in her book alread
mentioned, describes several schools of this kind. In 1571,
Dutch woman who married an English husband was earning
living by taking pupils in the parish of St Ethelburga. Joh
Sterling and his wife kept a girls' school in the parish of S
Bride. Little academies of that kind throve and multiplied. At th
great and long-continuing charity of Christ's Hospital co
education was practised.

Thomas Platter was taken to see it and approved of it. Thi
foundation, 'ordained' in 1553, had begun life as the Grey Friars
House for 'poor and fatherless children'. He put the total numbe
of boys and girls 'given food, clothes, lodging and learning' a
seven hundred. The girls at that time fed with the boys and share
some of their class-rooms. They had accommodation in a bi
house of their own looked after by a matron.

The tradesmen's children would not of course be beneficiarie
of Christ's Hospital unless they were destitute orphans. But her
was set a standard of instruction for both sexes which ha
reasonable quality, and there is evidence that the fee-payin
schools were soon turning out girls who could write with a fai
hand, do the housekeeping accounts, and were good reader
creating a market for the many books which were now bein
printed. Along with the romantic story-books there was a flo
of instructional publications about cooking and housekeepin

nd other domestic duties written in the 'Do It Yourself' style.
Most of the women who came to the theatre were by no means as
simple as the grocer's wife whose innocence at the play was a
device for getting laughs. At home she doubtless displayed a
shrewdness in business and capacity for getting things done.

In his book on 'Shakespeare's Public' Martin Holmes maintained that Beaumont and Fletcher's character is an abiding
London type whose 'genial, ready tongue is not stilled even yet,
but may be heard today in queues, at jumble sales, and in train or
omnibus regaling total strangers with intimate, good-tempered
discussion of her private affairs'. To the dramatists such women
could be a profit when they were no longer made a source of easy
laughter. They persuaded their husbands to pay for places in the
theatre. If they liked what they saw, which they probably did,
being so eager to be entertained and ready with a laugh, their
gossip contributed to 'the word of mouth' commendation. This,
as our theatre-managers know, is the best kind of publicity for a
play. Even the best notices in the Press are soon forgotten. The
talk of the town goes on.

The playwrights in Shakespeare's time did not have to face
dramatic criticism except in the tattle of the taverns and the
street. The young men of blood and money for whom the Inns of
Court provided a continuing university when they left Oxford and
Cambridge in the teens were also unappointed arbiters of the
plays to which they thronged. The authors and actors were
spared the occasional praise and often more frequent humiliation
of widely-read reviews which can kill a new piece and wound
with a sarcastic quip the tender sensibilities of touchy artists.

Men who wrote both plays and pamphlets (pamphleteering
was the journalism of the day) spat their fury at the fools in the
audience after they met a failure on the stage. Dekker cursed the
groundlings as 'stinkards' who understood nothing. After the
poor reception of *The Faithful Shepherdess* Fletcher's fellow-poets
wrote with sympathy for him and contempt for 'the rout of
riffles' who decided the fate of a play. Women were not singled
out in these attacks for special condemnation. They did not give
trouble. They came as devoted play-goers and not as rowdy

exhibitionists. Shakespeare through the mouth of Hamle
scorned bad actors in lines which are irrelevant to the play an
may have been cut if his own players were annoyed or though
that Will was going too far should this be a side-slap at thei
rivals. But there is no record of his damning the audience witl
the comprehensive abuse delivered by some other playwrights

To speak of one ill-received piece, not specified as his own, a
'caviare to the general' was not to be scathing about the publi
and may have included some justified criticism.

The dramatists could write over the heads which were not a
thick as they thought. The laboured classicism of Ben Jonso
when his 'learned sock' was on would be intolerably stodg
fare for the average woman. What Shakespeare said over th
cups in a tavern after an occasional experience of a bad 'firs
afternoon' we do not know. If he was caustic in private abou
feminine taste in the theatre he took care to be courteous in th
publicly spoken words of his Epilogues. He understood al
tastes and wrote for them, including the tradesman's wife. H
knew those women. His mother was one of them.

The Epilogue to *Henry VIII* mentions 'good women' whos
'merciful construction' is expected to determine the fate of a
new piece since the husbands would not dare to hold back whe
'their ladies bid them clap'. This was tactful talking, but there i
no evidence that the women were the larger or even a significantl
large part of the audience. We cannot imagine Shakespear
deliberately angling for the women's vote when he devised a
plot or drew a female character. Bernard Shaw suggested that h
did write down to the public and confessed it in the titles of *As Yo.
Like It*, *Much Ado About Nothing* and *What You Will,* his alternativ
name for *Twelfth Night*. If that is so, the dramatist apparently faile
to make condescension pay, whether it was crafty or reluctant.

We can make a rough estimate of the popularity of his play
from the time of their writing until the closing of the theatre
during the Civil War. Such a calculation is not wholly reliable
The record of performances may have omissions in the list o
Court commands. Sundry allusions made in native writing or b
foreign travellers to the public productions or to revivals b

Shakespeare's own company are useful but not conclusive.

More definite information, however, comes from the list of publications of play-books in Quarto form. Judging by the taste of play-goers today, which gives enormous runs to musicals and farcical scampers round the bedroom, one would expect Shakespeare's make-believe comedies to have been more profitable than his excursions into the tragic depths. The known facts about the reading of stories denounced as light and lascivious by the moralists show a large demand for 'romance fiction' typified by re-written legends of traditional heroes with breaking hearts at last mended and for invented tales of true love on the rocks and reaching calm waters. Accordingly Rosalind and Viola should have packed the theatres and especially enraptured the women to whom Rosalind appealed in her Epilogue.

But that did not happen. Let us take the Quartos first. Neither *Twelfth Night* nor *As You Like It* had any separate publication before they were fortunately preserved for us in the First Folio of 1623. That was not because it had then ceased to be profitable to publish play-books. The great tragedies which followed the comedies most popular in revival today were much printed, with or without the author's or his company's permission. If that was refused, they were worth stealing. But nobody made piratical raids on Arden and Illyria. Yet *Hamlet* was immediately pirated and was still wanted in print in 1637 when the Fifth Quarto appeared. *Othello* had three Quarto editions before 1635 and *King Lear* was twice printed before it was available in the Folio.

The report of performances also reveals no 'box-office success' for one of the gaily fanciful pieces so frequently staged today. *Twelfth Night* was played at the Hall of the Middle Temple for the benefit of the men of law and perhaps their ladies in 1603. It was commanded at court, in 1618 and 1623. By that time it was called *Malvolio* and in 1640 Leonard Digges mentioned Malvolio as a character who could fill the house. He did not name the piece *Twelfth Night*. Viola's steward had stolen her play. The music and 'the food of love' were not the favourite baits for public consumption. The drolls had supplied the tit-bits.

Far more surprising is the fate of *As You Like It*. After a performance, not completely authenticated, said to have been given by the King's Men on tour at the Pembroke mansion at Wilton, there is no mention of any performance either at court or in a public theatre. On the list of royal command performances *The Winter's Tale* appeared six times. Illyria had some attraction at the court at Whitehall, Bohemia far more, and Arden none. Nor was Rosalind restored to the stage at the Restoration. She and Orlando vanished from the public theatres until 1723 when a hashed version by Colley Cibber was staged at Drury Lane. The whirligig of time has brought its revenges to the exiled lovers. If 'feminine interest' was intended it was long absent but has been at last and abundantly won.

Shakespeare, when writing his tragedies, wished to get a load off his chest as well as to provide tremendous parts for Burbage and other members of his fellowship of players. It cannot be imagined that *King Lear* was written to please. And that it failed to do in the nineteenth century. An embittered poet discharged a fit of misanthropy in his searing portrait of a misanthrope when he wrote or took a major part in writing *Timon of Athens*. He could not possibly have been thinking then of gratifying either sex and expecting a good play-house response to follow. He certainly got none. In F. E. Halliday's 'Shakespeare Companion' the known productions and revivals of plays are carefully listed. For *Timon* the entry is short. 'No record of any pre-Restoration performance.' But in the comedies Shakespeare did have his eye on the audience and in his Epilogues he says so.

When Prospero speaks the farewell lines of *The Tempest* he as frankly asks for approval and 'a big hand' as does Rosalind in her parting words.

> *With the help of your good hands*
> *Gentle breath of yours my sails*
> *Must fill; or else my project fails*
> *Which was to please.*

It is commonly believed that Shakespeare's own voice is directly heard in Prospero's speeches. If that is so, there is the candid confession of a playwright working for his company and himself who must give pleasure if they are to survive. He had done his best to meet all tastes. The public had been offered a Boy-Meets-Girl story, a storm, a shipwreck, plots and clowning in a more or less desert isle, a savage monster, a masque, songs, and conjuring tricks. Dramatist and management could hardly do more. Prospero in his last words made no special appeal for feminine approval by show of clapping hands, as had been done in other Epilogues, but we may be sure that he could have the ladies-in-waiting applauding with the royalties and courtiers when *The Tempest* was produced at Whitehall in November 1613.

That the project had not failed and that pleasure had been given was shown by its selection in the following winter as one of twenty plays, eight by Shakespeare, acted during the wedding celebrations of Princess Elizabeth and the Elector Palatine. About these the bride would naturally be consulted as to what she willed. The West Indies, not Arden or Illyria, were as she liked it. A further feminine vote in favour of *The Tempest* would surely have been given if the grocer's wife saw it on a summer's afternoon at the Globe or on a winter day at the roofed-in and comparatively luxurious Blackfriars Theatre which the King's Men had taken over three years before.

That was a play-house with a special appeal to the ladies. It was warm in the months when the Globe was an uninhabitable ice-box; the seats were more expensive, and the company as a rule more refined. There was no need to cross the river. The coach-owning or coach-hiring class were driven to it in such numbers that there were traffic-jams which greatly annoyed the neighbours of the play-house and the merchants with businesses adjacent. Several appeals were made in the years following 1608 to the Privy Council to close it altogether. The protest failed because 'it worked to the prejudice of the players, his Majesty's servants'. They were the King's Men and their public was influential. Queen Henrietta Maria was as much interested as her husband in the Blackfriars Theatre and was a regular attender. She also gave the company costumes for their wardrobe.

The ladies who were carried in their numerous carriages to Blackfriars could enjoy some amateur acting if they appeared in a masque at court or as part of some celebration at a great house. Women got no footing on the public stage in Shakespeare's time unless one or two were smuggled in pretending to be boys. That possibility has been several times put forward in stories and plays, most notably by Emlyn Williams in his piece called 'Spring, 1600'. That was a case of fancy free. It could possibly have happened, but there is no documented mention of the professional actress making her entrance to the long-forbidden stage until thirteen years after Shakespeare's death. That was at Black-friars and it was a disaster.

It was recorded in 1629 by Thomas Brande that 'certain vagrant French players', including women speaking their own tongue, presented 'a certain lascivious and unchaste comedy' which he did not name. He added that it gave 'just offence to all vertuous and well-disposed persons in the town. . . . Glad am I to say that they were hissed, hooted, and pippin-pelted from the stage'. This leaves one wondering. Did the 'vertuous persons' have no French as well as no manners? Had there been some masculine trade union spirit among the boy-players who saw their careers threatened and organised a riot? Did the pippin-pelters bring their missiles with them by previous intention or were they so suddenly infuriated by the appearance of the women that they seized the chances provided at the apple-counter in the theatre's catering service? Whatever the source of the fusillade of apples it won its unchivalrous victory. The women had to wait for the Restoration to seek stage-careers and then, by a coincidence, a girl in the fruit-trade was one of the first to put her personal charm and possible talent on view. A blow had been struck for the equality of the sexes and there is no news of Miss Gwyn's being hissed, booed, and orange-pelted from the stage.

Equality of opportunity for women was to be denied in most careers for over three hundred years after Shakespeare's time. The professional actress of 1660 was centuries ahead of others. But in addition to their permitted play-going, there was another emancipation enjoyed by the women about town. As much as their male escorts they could take a drink in public without hindrance, embarrassment, or disgrace. One of Platter's surprises

was to find himself surrounded by reputable feminine company
when he relaxed and refreshed himself. Discussing the taverns
and beer-gardens he was astonished by both their number and
their mixed clientèle.

'The women', he wrote, 'count it a great honour to be taken
there and given wine with sugar to drink. If one woman only is
invited she often brings three or four other women and they
gaily toast each other.' The mixing of wine, which was already
sweeter than ours, with a helping of sugar, does not seem attractive to the more astringent palates of today, but the uninhibited
gate-crashing is still practised at certain kinds of drinking party
where 'anything goes' and to which anybody, of either sex,
comes. There is no reason to doubt the accuracy of the keenly
interested tourist from Basel with his note-book or 'table' in hand.

This table-carrying is several times mentioned by Shakespeare;
it could be a princely habit and was practised by Hamlet even
when meeting his father's ghost. Like a reporter seeking an
interview he cries

> *My tables, meet it is I set it down*
> *That one may smile and smile and be a villain.*

In the Bishopsgate hostelry where he lodged, Platter 'tabled' the
amount of the amenities; there was constant music and the house
was 'visited by players almost daily'. He commented on the
abundance of ale-houses and pleasure-gardens, adding that the
women to be found in them were often more numerous than the
men. There is no suggestion that the women were 'loose'. He
knew that open prostitution was extremely dangerous; the
women arrested and convicted on this charge were taken to the
Bridewell prison and flogged in public. King Lear had that
atrocity in mind when he cursed the hypocrisy of the beadle
with his bloody hand who lusted while he scourged.

There were naturally some refuges for men who preferred
masculine conversation about affairs of state and the conflicts
of the poets and play-wrights to the lighter gossip of mixed
society. Such was the Mermaid Tavern in Bread Street. Here the
English 'table-keeper' Thomas Coryate recorded the drinkings

and diversions of 'a worshipful company of Sireniack gentlemen' (Sirena meant mermaid). The main consumers of Canary and leaders of discussion were Ben Jonson, Beaumont, Drayton, and Donne. Shakespeare has not been mentioned in the tributes to this tavern where, according to Beaumont, the talk was so brilliant that it fired and illumined the subsequent 'pot-valiant' customers however crass.

> *We left an Aire behind us which alone*
> *Was able to make the next two Companies*
> *Right witty; though but downright fooles, more wise.*

The landlord of the Mermaid was William Johnson who was discovered by Dr Hotson to be a friend of Shakespeare's; it is difficult to imagine that the latter, although he seems to have been averse to heavy drinking, was never there. If he did attend the gatherings he would not have brought feminine company. There was room enough for the women to sweeten their wine and dulcify conversation elsewhere.

There were no licensing justices to declare that inn-keeping was an improper occupation for the gentle sex. So in the serving of liquor as in the consumption of it there was some fair sharing among male and female. Christopher Sly spoke of the obese ale-wife at Wincot who had some tough 'bezzlers' with whom to cope. There was no legal difficulty for Shakespeare's Mistress Quickly at the Boar's Head; her best customers were more addicted to potations of sack than to the swilling of ale, but they were as turbulent in their cups as torrential in their talk. It is true that the Quickly management is dated back to the reign of Henry IV, but Falstaff was based on a character of the Elizabethan century and the Boar's Head seems to be a replica of an Elizabethan tavern. No ladies would be expected, but women were part of the entertainment, and not for gross purposes only. The Quickly tongue could keep up with Falstaff's and no poet of them all could have bettered Doll Tearsheet's rebuke to the Knight 'When wilt thou leave fighting o' days and foining o' nights and patch up thine old body for heaven?' At the Boar's Head there was as much equality of the sexes in the flow of the English language as in the swallowing of Spanish wine.

CHAPTER IX

Great Ladies

THE HEROINES of Shakespeare's comedies live in (or are ejected from) exalted homes before they join their amorous encounters or comical-pastoral adventures. They do not emerge from a crude, uncultivated luxury. They have their store of learning as well as their liveliness of spirit. They carry their wit into kingdoms and landscapes of romance, but their background is that of an Elizabethan reality, a life in which for the young of both sexes in wealthy families amenity and intelligence have been richly mingled. Their author had been given a side-view and some interior knowledge of the great houses quite early in his career and he knew that its ladies were as ready and even as anxious as its lords to welcome a dedication from a rising poet. Spenser prefaced 'The Faerie Queene' with eighteen dedicatory sonnets. Of these fourteen were offered to 'Various Noblemen', three to individual Ladies, and one 'to all the gratious and beautifull Ladies in the Court'.

The feminine patrons might expect to be given the routine praise of their good looks, but their other qualities frequently were as commendable as their features. To have some erudition was not rare; good tuition stimulated good taste. The distribution of their patronage was welcome, but it was not that of Lady Bountiful throwing alms to the needy. To be on the visiting list of the Countess of Pembroke at Wilton was admission to an Academe whose presiding hostess was a woman of great gifts and keen perception, too sensible to favour any writer only because he displayed an aptitude for flattery.

The ladies of rank who took pleasure in the arts and supported the writers on terms that did not humiliate or make them kept creatures had been brought up in homes with books in plenty. They received instruction of the best. Lady Pembroke had shared tuition with her brother Sir Philip Sidney at Penshurst. Girls of this class did not attend the public lessons of a 'petty' teacher as did the daughters of their tenants in the country. The models from whom Beatrice, Rosalind, and Viola were drawn were never 'three little maids from school' and 'fresh from a ladies' seminary'. Had books of reference existed they would have replied to queries that their education was 'private'. The leading ladies in Shakespeare's comedies, whether set in Italy, France, Illyria or the curiously Anglo-French and semi-tropical Arden (here are lions) have, without becoming bookish, made their acquaintance with the books to be found in what our auctioneers still call 'A Gentleman's Library'.

A natural conclusion to be drawn from these roles is that, when they were written, there had been recruited to Shakespeare's company one or more boy-players who could do more than memorise long parts, point their lines, and speak the English of well-educated people. They could impersonate women of position with a convincing carriage of their bodies and a natural management of a farthingale. Clumsiness would be disastrous. In the 'breeches parts' to be boyish came easily but Beatrice and Olivia demand a performance well graced and well dressed and not only well spoken. It is significant that three of these star parts were written in two or three years, between 1598 and 1600.

Their author would not have been so lavish with the taunting wit and tenderness of affection which he bestowed on them if he had feared that his bounty of words would be squandered. The ability to be at once lively and lady-like were there, probably trained by himself. He had had time by now to mark the play of mind and quality of conversation as well as the taste in dress and decoration prevailing among the highly placed Elizabethan families.

To the fringe of that wealth and cultivation Shakespeare had been promoted by the friendship and generosity of the Earl of Southampton and by his leading position among the Lord Chamberlain's Men with their close attachment to the Queen, the courtiers, and the ladies-in-waiting at Whitehall. They on their part were realising his capacity to give pleasure with a narrative poem or a personal sonnet in their circle while he entertained his larger public in the theatres. He was near enough to their splendour to depict the privileged class in its glitter. His plays are a series of painted cloths of Elizabethan life which has been transported for dramatic purposes to other countries. The feminine characters who sparkle in the comedies are as true to their own ambience in their thoughts and speech as they are out of any world in their fictitious adventures, misunderstandings, and masquerades.

The assiduously tutored queen had set a fashion in classical education for women. Lady Jane Fitzalan, daughter of the Earl of Arundel, afterwards Lady Lumley, translated into Latin the Greek orations of Isocrates and into English the Greek tragedy of Iphigenia by Euripides. Her script of the latter has survived. She wrote a fine, clear hand, without alterations or erasures. Such proficiency was doubtless exceptional, but it proved the respect for academic attainments: there was no idea that the feminine accomplishments should be limited to music and needlework. If Lady Jane was what would have been called in later English homes 'a swot' she was not to be laughed at for her delight in mastery of ancient literature read in the ancient languages.

Art has been well defined as 'exaggeration à propos'. Shakespeare gave the young milady a spontaneous liveliness of wit and speed of delivery which gallops beyond belief; but there was actuality behind their animation. The ducal daughters of his invention spoke for a number of highly educated women who have been called the Tudor Paragons. They were not prigs and they could carry their learning lightly. When girls of this type were put by Shakespeare into doublet and breeches for the purpose of a fantastic play-house story their hose was not the Blue Stocking. Their creator did not care for pedantry and for the drudgery in the library. That

> *Small have continual plodders ever won*
> *Save base authority from others' books*

may be taken as his own opinion. He realised that he himself had been seized by the theatrical possibilities of the old myths and legends, but he took the classics with a smile. So did Rosalind and Beatrix whose learning was a compost of old names and new laughter.

First of the series, if we give the first version of *Love's Labour's Lost* an early date, is Rosaline, a sparkling and audaciously free-spoken owner of the nimble mind and darting tongue. If the heroines are to some extent replicas of the girls of good family, whom the queen chose to be her maids of honour and ladies of the court and sometimes had to dismiss for conduct unfitting to their birth and her dignity, they were free with a form of conversation which admitted the bawdy with the brilliant. There was a vogue for the quips and word-play known as conceits and the exchange of these ripostes between Rosaline and Berowne is as breath-taking as the volleyings, smashes, and recoveries of our lawn-tennis champions. Some of the verbal attack and defence is difficult for us to appreciate; words, as T. S. Eliot wrote, 'slip and slide and will not stay still'. Meanings and innuendoes which diverted an Elizabethan courtly audience evade us now. But it is obvious that the wit of the ladies had been as keenly sharpened in their years of pupilage as the blade of a razor.

Rosaline does not display a classical education, but Rosalind in *As You Like It* knows something of Julius Caesar and can draw for amorous examples on the myths and legends of Venus and Cupid, Troilus and Cressida, Hero and Leander. Whoever arranged for her further studies after literacy was acquired, whether it was her banished father or usurping uncle, had not neglected her education. Beatrice in *Much Ado About Nothing* makes less reference to the ancient world but is well up in the history and geography of her own. For Shakespeare there was no distinction of the sexes in capacity to fashion a phrase. The mint which provided the glitter and the tinkle of the gold pieces owed something to the imported metal of Renaissance scholarship, something to that astonishing acceleration of the mind and enlargement of vocabulary which came in with the New Learning, and more to the peculiar genius of one man for whom, as Beatrice would have said, a singular star was shining, if not dancing, when he was born.

The first three British kings called George have been absurdly flattered by the turning of their name into an adjective applied to their period. During this Georgian age the national standards in the arts, learning, and oratory were set by such men as Pope, Gibbon, Dr Johnson, Burke, Sheridan, Garrick, Reynolds, Hogarth, the Adam brothers, and the incomparable craftsmen who furnished and decorated the great houses surrounded by their superbly planned gardens. What had the monarchs done to earn the enduring label of Georgian for such splendour? The first Queen Elizabeth, on the other hand, was a true Elizabethan. The name and the epithet have been justly united.

She was as scholarly as shrewd and drew on a vocabulary as rich as her wardrobe. She could rival the musicians of her household and she encouraged her actors as well as her poets because she understood as well as relished the entertainments which they provided. If she had regarded the drama as trifling nonsense for 'the niffles' Shakespeare's life and those of his fellows would have been completely different and perhaps wholly frustrated. To be a member, as was Shakespeare, of the Lord Chamberlain's Men was to write and perform for a team which, when commanded to appear, had to be on its toes and at its best. They were not at court merely to add drollery to a banquet. At the summit of society was the best educated woman in the land, a premier paragon.

Today juvenile vandalism and criminal conduct are mercifully attributed to and even excused by 'a disturbed childhood' and emergence from bad homes. The homes of Henry VIII had hardly been exemplary and if ever there was disturbance of girlhood and youth Elizabeth had it to the full. Her mother and the step-mother who had been Catherine Howard were be-headed. She grew up in a world where the axe was busy and no powerful neck was safe. She was moved from place to place amid incessant uncertainties and intrigues. After reaching fourteen she had a long spell of bad health; she was afflicted with migraine and pains in the eyes. Her privacy was subjected to the boisterous and lecherous inroads of the Lord Admiral Seymour.

As Elizabeth Jenkins put it in her biography of 'Elizabeth the

Great' 'the cowering under bed-clothes, the struggling and running away culminated in a scene of classical nightmare, that of helplessness in the power of a smiling ogre'. The nervous and physical strain were intense and caused later reports that her monthly periods were very few or none. Probably the whole of her sexual life was affected. Here indeed was 'disturbance'. By the calculations of the modern psychologist she should have been turned into an unteachable and ungovernable law-breaker. The queen's moods were volatile throughout her life. But if she could not rule her temper she ruled her country with an ability which made her age her monument.

During these harassing years of her girlhood she was put through a course of instruction which was astonishing in its range, variety, and thoroughness. With the wise and kindly backing of her governess, Katherine Ashley, she was introduced to a severe measure of 'the grand, old fortifying curriculum'. William Grindal of Cambridge was summoned to teach her Latin and Greek. Under the general supervision of the eminent scholar and educationalist Roger Ascham she worked at history, geography, and mathematics. She practised music at the virginals. She was instructed in the elements of architecture and astronomy. Especial attention was given to modern languages, of which she mastered four, French, Italian, Spanish, and Flemish. It seems that she acquired some Welsh, as befitted a Tudor, from a Mrs Parry who was a member of her household and became Keeper of the Royal Books. The least unlucky of her succession of stepmothers, Catherine Parr, encouraged her in her studies and included in their scope the teaching of the doctrines of the Reformed Church. That was politically important. Most valuable of all was the care of the last of Henry's queens, the sensible and kindly woman who so combined authority with tact that she could manage even her turbulent husband in his last years of infirmity and galling pain.

There may have been some flattering and calculated exaggeration of Queen Elizabeth's multitudinous attainments. But undoubtedly she had a comprehensive knowledge of ancient and modern languages; probably she had no less Latin and Greek than was owned by some of those university wits who sneered at Shakespeare for his scarcity in that department of education. That she could discuss the intricacies of her foreign policy with a number of foreign ambassadors and emissaries in their own language is certain. That she had the good fortune to be endowed with a photographic memory is likely. How otherwise could she have absorbed and retained so much knowledge during a girlhood of such confusion amid the doubts and bewilderments of politics above her head and the terrors inflicted by Seymour in her bedroom? The fact is clear that she acquired an admirable intellectual equipment for one who was to be the land's First Lady and set a cultural standard which others of her sex were anxious to reach.

Yet there was nothing of the prim girl-graduate about the gusty and free-spoken life to follow. She could laugh; she loved a play and gave protection to the players. What words she exchanged with Shakespeare himself is unknown, but as he was a leading member of her favourite company at the age of thirty and honoured with commanded performance of his plays he must at one time have been given some of her vigorous commentary and conversation, humble though his status was in social ranking. The Lord Chamberlain's Men acted before the queen six times between December 26, 1596 and February 1597. It was then, no doubt, that she was fascinated by the figure of Falstaff.

That she ordered a further play about him for performance at Windsor is not attested by any contemporary record. Two mentions of this episode were made in the first decade of the eighteenth century. In 1702 John Dennis in his 'Epistle Dedicatory' to his version of *The Merry Wives of Windsor* wrote: 'It hath pleased one of the greatest Queens that ever was in the world. This Comedy was written at her command and by her direction and she was so eager to see it Acted that she commanded it to be finished in fourteen days and was afterwards, as Tradition tells us, very well pleased at the Presentation.' Whence Dennis got the tradition is unknown, but it was repeated by Nicholas Rowe in the preface to his six-volume edition of the Works in 1709.

Rowe named his authority for his statement of facts about
Shakespeare's life. He was Thomas Betterton (1635–1710), who
established his eminence as an actor soon after the theatre
re-opened in 1660. He worked for D'Avenant who claimed to be
Shakespeare's illegitimate son. Downes, who had been a prompter
and wrote his 'Roscius Anglicanus or an Historical Review of the
Stage' in 1708, said that D'Avenant had seen John Taylor
Burbage's successor in Shakespeare's company, act 'Hamlet' and
so could instruct Betterton. Thus the tradition of Queen Elizabeth's demand came to Rowe from a good theatrical source.
Rowe added that the queen 'was so well pleased with the admirable character of Falstaff in the two parts of *Henry IV* that she
commanded him (Shakespeare) to continue it for one more play
and show him in love'.

There was a meeting with ceremonies and revels of the Knights
of the Garter at Windsor Castle on St George's Day, April 24,
1597, and one of the newly appointed knights was George Carey
Lord Hunsdon, who had just become Lord Chamberlain and so
the patron of Shakespeare's company. Something new of theirs
was an obvious need. The facts as well as the tradition support
the belief that *The Merry Wives of Windsor* was first produced then,
having been written at short notice at an imperious request.

The period of fourteen days has been doubted by Shakespearian scholars who have not lived their lives under journalistic
or theatrical pressure and do not know the speed of a ready
writer with a date to be met. They therefore argue that Shakespeare took the events from an existing play called *The Jealous
Comedy* which had been produced by the Admiral's and Strange's
Men and marked as 'newe' by Henslowe in 1593. But this would
be poaching from rivals and, though Shakespeare habitually
lifted matter for his plots from numerous sources, he surely
would not so far admit his lack of creative power as to steal
recent work from a company in opposition and less esteemed.
In any case, the job was promptly done, nearly all in prose, which
may have saved time, and with some lack of invention since there
is a somewhat fatigued repetition in the gullings of Falstaff. None
the less, according to Dennis, it greatly pleased. The royal

command had been met and the royal taste in laughter had been simply satisfied.

It was the habit of the queen to get what she wanted and get it quickly. It was the habit of Shakespeare to be speedy and prolific with his pen among the more exacting labours of learning and rehearsing parts and sharing the management of a company. We may, if we like, turn the fourteen days into twenty-one. The doubting professors seem to have forgotten the tribute of Heminge and Condell, 'His mind and hand went together and what he thought he uttered with that easiness we have scarce received from him a blot in his papers.' If we had Shakespeare's original manuscript of the hurried work we might discern some hasty penmanship and even a blot or two. What of that? He had carried out his order. That on this occasion the queen was as generous with her purse as with her tongue can be doubted. She was not known for lavishness. The command fee was ten pounds payable to the company for their complete performance which they thought not only complimentary but more profitable than a routine appearance in their theatre. Elizabeth's Scottish successor, King James, raised the fee to twenty.

Among the ladies attending the queen at Windsor would naturally be the Lady Elizabeth Carey. She was now Lady Hunsdon and the wife of the new Lord Chamberlain who was at the castle to receive the honour of the Garter. If not one of the Tudor paragons she was known for her devotion to poetry and her discerning and generous patronage of the writers. She was one of those to whom Spenser dedicated 'The Faerie Queene' and the sole dedicatee of another of his poems. To her, acclaimed as right worthy and vertuous', he had offered his 'Muiopotmos or the Fate of the Butterflie'.

In 1597 the company which took its name from the Lord Chamberlain was rising to its highest renown. Lord Hunsdon held the office until he died in the same year as Queen Elizabeth but at a much earlier age; he was only fifty-six. By 1603 the players for whom he was responsible at court and their chief playwright had produced the most charming of Shakespeare's comedies and one, the most famous, of the great tragedies. Lady

Hunsdon could share his pride in what the 'Lord Chamberlain, his Servants' had achieved. Her devoted Spenser had reached one kind of eminence; Shakespeare and his fellows won a much wider glory for the Carey family.

Mention of Mary Sidney, who became the Countess of Pembroke, has already been made. Her entertainment as well as her encouraging patronage of the poets, in which Shakespeare almost certainly had some share, was constant and cordial. She received a flow of dedications, but more important to her was the continuation of her brother Philip's work as guide and counsellor to writers. Fulke Greville, himself a poet, a patron, and one of Shakespeare's aristocratic neighbours in Warwickshire, wrote of Philip Sidney

'This I doe the more confidently affirm because it will be confessed by all men, that this one man's example, and personall respect, did not onely encourage Learning and Honour in the schools, but brought the affection, and true use thereof both into the Court, and Camp. Nay more, even many Gentlemen excellently learned amongst us will not deny but that they effected to row, and steer their course in his wake.'

Brother and sister had worked together on his 'Arcadia' in the Pembrokes' country estate of Wilton; after his death on the battlefield of Zutphen she edited his work including his sonnet sequence 'Astrophel and Stella' for which labour of love she was fully qualified in literacy as well as devotion.

John Aubrey in his 'Brief Lives' recorded that 'in her time Wilton House was like a College, there were so many learned and ingeniose persons. She was the greatest patronesse of witt and learning of any lady of her time.' She combined what are now called the two cultures; the sciences attracted her as much as the arts. As Aubrey put it: 'She kept for her laborator in the house Adrian Gilbert vulgarly called Dr Gilbert, halfe brother to Sir Walter Raleigh, who was a great chymist in those dayes.' Resident too were 'Mr Henry Sanford who was the earle's secretary, a good scholar and poet', and her physician Dr Thomas Moffett author of a book on Insects to whom she gave 'an

honourable yearly pension'. There was also on her staff 'one
Boston, a good chymist, a Salisbury man borne, who did undoe
himself by studying the philosopher's stone, and she would have
kept him but he would have all the gold to himself and so dyed,
I think, in goale.' That Boston ever manufactured gold is most
unlikely and that he so 'undid' himself is the kind of yarn that
Aubrey loved to recount.

That delightful but unscrupulous gossip did not sift the tattle
which came his way. In addition to his valuable curiosity he had
what is commonly known as a dirty mind. He alleged that
Lady Pembroke was 'very salacious', an adjective more fitted to
his own taste in anecdotage. He charged her with frequent
adultery and even recounted the absurd chatter of 'two old
gentlemen' that she committed incest with her brother. When
Aubrey said that 'the curious seate of Wilton and the adjacent
country is an Arcadian place and a paradise' he was telling the
truth. His gleeful traducing of the Eve in this Eden is insupport-
able nonsense. Sidney and his sister were keenly Protestant and
had the moral code of their creed.

'Vertue' was a constant attribute of her character. Mid-winter
presents were then made on New Year's Day, not at Christmas,
and men of letters sent their verses to their patrons on that
occasion. In 1590 William Smith sent to Wilton 'A Gifte made
upon certain Flowers' which are in turn likened to Lady Pembroke. Of the violet he wrote

> *The violet doth growe in grove or feeldes,*
> *In hedges, or in gardens, or high waies,*
> *But whereso'ere it growes, it pleasure yeeldes:*
> *So: where I come, I allwaies finde yor praise,*
> *Your name, and vertue too, all people heare*
> *and touch with wounder, everie common care.*

In his chapter on the countess in his book on 'Sir Philip Sidney
and the English Renaissance' John Buxton quotes this and
justly adds: 'I should like to know more of the poet who
devised so elegant a fancy and who was capable of the fine
simplicity of that last line.' The epitaph written by another

member of the Wilton paradise, William Browne, described as 'perfect' by Mr Buxton, has been made familiar by anthologists.

> *Underneath this sable herse*
> *Lies the subject of all verse:*
> *Sidney's sister, Pembroke's mother:*
> *Death, ere thou hast slain another,*
> *Fair, and learn'd, and good as she,*
> *Time shall throw a dart at thee.*

The Pembroke named as her son was the Lord William Herbert who has been thought by many of the best informed and most judicious Shakespearians, including Dr Dover Wilson, to be Mr W. H. of the Sonnets.

But before we come on to the Sonnet Puzzle, there is another connection between Shakespeare and the countess. In 1603, soon after the accession of King James, plague struck at London life and the court was rusticated. From October to December the king was in the region of Salisbury and a guest of the Pembrokes. At Wilton he hunted and he saw at least one play. With the theatres closed the King's Men were for a time at Mortlake where one of the Fellowship, Augustine Philips, lived. They were summoned to Wilton. It was a long journey to make on horseback and they were well rewarded with a fee of thirty pounds, received by John Hemings, for 'their pains and expenses in coming from Mortlake in the County of Surrey unto the Court aforesaid and there presenting before his Majesty one play'.

In 1865 the lady who was then Lady Pembroke told William Cory, a Fellow of King's College at Cambridge and a master at Eton, 'We have a letter, never printed, from Lady Pembroke to her son, telling him to bring James from Salisbury to see *As You Like It*', and adding, 'We have the man Shakespeare with us.' The letter has unfortunately disappeared, but Cory was a scholar and a poet not a gossip and there is no reason to discredit his account of the matter which was accepted by so careful an authority as Sir Edmund Chambers. Letters are easily lost or, if of literary interest, stolen.

The countess stayed mainly in the country. This Aubrey

maliciously and stupidly attributed to her husband's constraint and fear for her behaviour if she was exposed to the amorous gaieties of London to which her son William yielded at his cost. The obvious reason for her attachment to Wilton was its peaceful beauty and the company of the 'ingeniose persons' whom she assembled. Her early interest in the theatre had been academic. She was a skilled translator and in 1590, at the age of twenty-nine, had made an English version of a French tragedy, Robert Garnier's *Marc-Antoine,* which some think was used by Shakespeare when he came to write *Antony and Cleopatra.* When William, after leaving New College at Oxford, went to London at seventeen or eighteen he became theatre-minded and was later the patron of Shakespeare, Jonson, and Massinger. He and his younger brother Philip shared the supreme honour of the dedication of the First Folio whose editors mentioned but did not specify the favours given by their lordships to the author and his plays. William Herbert succeeded to the earldom in 1601 and was appointed Lord Chamberlain in 1615, the year before Shakespeare's death. He was made Chancellor of Oxford University in 1624 and the name of the college known as Broadgates Hall was altered to Pembroke in his honour. This would have been an honour dear to his mother but she had died three years earlier at the age of sixty.

What benefits Shakespeare derived from this patronage are unknown. William gave Ben Jonson twenty pounds a year for the purchase of books; that allowance was generous, equal to Ben's receipts for writing three or four plays and more than the annual salary of many a schoolmaster or vicar. After 1600 Shakespeare was not in need of money-gifts but, if they came his way, he was unlikely to refuse them. The patronage may have been shown in the way of personal friendship and invitations. The absence of the Earl of Southampton's name from the Folio dedication indicates a breach in the cordial relations existing early in the fifteen-nineties when 'Venus and Adonis' and 'Lucrece' were written. Evidently the new Earl of Pembroke took his place as patron.

If the young William Herbert was the recipient of the Sonnets to 'the lovely boy', a view which I share, it is extremely probable that the counsel to marry, which is so urgently repeated in the first seventeen of the sequence, was made at the request of the countess and her husband. He was ailing and wanted the future of his earldom and estates decided. The boy's future must be fixed. Marriages among the aristocracy were arranged as family bargains and it was customary for parents to regard heirdom to a title and lands as a valuable asset in the matrimonial market. His bride must be dowered in proportion. This procedure was naturally resented by the young men who had reasonable cravings for some years of bachelor freedom with a less restricted choice of partner.

The Earl of Southampton had jibbed at a proposed union with Lady Elizabeth Vere and was later forced into marrying Elizabeth Vernon when she was with child. The Pembrokes had had one of the Carey family in mind for William but he rebelled. He was only fifteen when this arrangement was being made over his head. Later there were negotiations for a wedding with Bridget Vere, a grand-daughter of the wealthy and powerful Lord Burghley. Again there was resistance. It could hardly be admitted in the dealings that William disliked the girl, but there could be complaint, sordid as we see it now but less impolite, about the sufficiency of the dowry. Romantic love flows with finery of language through the poetry of the period, but marriages were negotiated by realists. There was a strange lack of shame in their hagglings.

The Pembrokes knew that William, who had come to London in 1597, was acquainted with the poets and players. A mutual admiration of the now rising Shakespeare and their emotional, impetuous son would explain the eagerness of the countess to make Shakespeare use his influence in getting a suitable marriage settled. He was 'an ingeniose person'. He had William's ear. So the Marriage Sonnets were written and an exquisite compliment to the beauty of the mother as well as the son was included.

Look in thy glass, and tell the face thou viewest
Now is the time that face should form another;

Whose fresh repair if now thou not renewest,
Thou dost beguile the world, unbless some mother.
For where is she so fair whose unear'd womb
Disdains the tillage of thy husbandry?
Or who is he so fond will be the tomb
Of his self-love, to stop posterity?
Thou art thy mother's glass, and she in thee
Calls back the lovely April of her prime:
So thou through windows of thine age shalt see,
Despite of wrinkles, this thy golden time.
But if thou live, remember'd not to be,
Die single, and thine image dies with thee.

Aubrey, who was only three when the countess died, relied on report when he made his jottings about her. He wrote that 'She was a beautifull ladie and had an excellent witt and had the best breeding that the age could afford. She had a pritty sharpe-ovall face. Her haire was of a reddish yellowe.' He was kinder to her features than her morals which he grossly scandalised against all contemporary witness to her conduct.

John Buxton quotes a description by Nicholas Breton of 'the courtlike house of a right worthy honourable Lady'. Here, Breton wrote, were 'God daily served, religion truly preached, all quarrels avoided, peace carefully preserved, swearing not heard of, truth easilie believed, a table fully furnished, a house richly garnished, honour kindly entertained, vertue highly esteemed, service well rewarded, the poor blessedly relieved, and kindnesse was a companion in every corner of the house.' Wilton was not named, but Breton was writing in the countess's time and with knowledge of her. He had written an elegy on Philip Sidney and had sat at the 'table fully furnished'. Who else could it have been but the incomparable hostess?

Bernard Shaw in his Preface to *The Dark Lady of the Sonnets*, following Thomas Tyler who had staked an early claim for William Herbert as 'Mr W. H.', accepted the idea that Shakespeare had made 'Sidney's sister, Pembroke's mother' his model for the Countess of Rousillon in *All's Well That Ends Well*. In

Shaw's words this lady of Rousillon is 'the most charming of all Shakespeare's old women, indeed the most charming of all his women, young or old'. He held that Lady Pembroke had been remembered in the gracious mother of Bertram, another rebel against a commanded marriage and the status of a conscript husband. This delightful character, he added, 'has a certain individuality which suggests a portrait'.

However that may be, Lady Pembroke stands out among a rich assortment of tributary writing as an illustrious example of the great ladies of her time and the paragon of the Tudor Paragons. If she had 'the man Shakespeare' with her in her 'College' set in countryside which Aubrey described as 'romancy plaines and boscages' she herself was privileged. Hearing no doubt of his quality of a poet she could not be aware that added fame would come to her from being mentioned as his hostess. He too would feel the honour of acceptance and entertainment by the great lady who was to be remembered for her taste in letters instead of only for her title and her son.

Shakespeare had a richly contrasted experience of country houses during his upward journey from Mary Arden's Wilmcote to Mary Pembroke's Wilton. There is no proof in any writing that he was the guest of Sir Henry and Lady Rainsford at Clifford Chambers which he could reach by a short walk if he were ferried over the Avon. Their home was another hen-coop of the Muses. The lady of that house was the hostess of Michael Drayton and the Idea of his sonnets. She liked poets at her table. She may not have been in the paragon class of scholarship but she belonged to that fortunately numerous set of Elizabethan women who, like their queen, believed that the fine use of words and music was a necessary addition to the pleasures of a comfortable life.

CHAPTER X

High Fashion

No woman could earn a living with the professional players, but the greatest of the great ladies could take part in a masque which was performed at court or in a private mansion. The fashion for feminine miming as well as for dancing came to its height at the Jacobean court.

Royal participation had been enjoyed by Henry VIII. When Shakespeare, perhaps with Fletcher as colleague, wrote his play about that king he was drawing on an actual event when he included this stage-direction 'Enter King and Others as Masques, habited like shepherds.... They choose Ladies. The King chooses Anne Bullen.' When Henry is 'with dancing a little heated' Wolsey suggests a banquet in the 'fresher air in the next chamber' to which the king replies:

> *Lead in your ladies, every one. Sweet partner,*
> *I must not yet forsake you.*

The masquing women were as numerous as the men in this 'frisk' which had such momentous results for Church and State and such tragic consequences for two queens.

The Tudor masque was bi-sexual and the mixture of dance and charade remained so in subsequent reigns. At fairs and on festal days the girls joined in the roundel and the 'sportly hey-de-gay'. In London's high society they could dress up like stage-players and take the parts denied them in the public theatres. Francis Bacon in his Essay 'Of Masques and Triumphs' said that 'Double masques, one of men, another of ladies, addeth state and variety.' He also described the 'antimasques' which made a grotesque and comical contrast with the solemn graces of the masque proper.

In the former appeared 'fools, satyrs, baboons, wild-men, antics, beasts, sprites, witches, Ethiopes, pygmies, turquets, nymphs, rustics, cupids, statues moving, and the like'. The ladies might not care to be seen as witches, but they could happily appear as nymphs or in the *tableaux vivants* as statues coming into life and graceful motion.

Queen Elizabeth obviously enjoyed witnessing masques since they were lavishly organised wherever she went. She disapproved strongly of extravagance in court masques. Soon after her accession the Master of the Revels reported that the annual charges for making of masques had been cut down from at least four hundred pounds to rather over two hundred. She appreciated the vogue but liked it to be thriftily followed.

But, while she was watching her bills, others were ready to fling money about. The raree-show of a menagerie could be mingled with the graces of a masquerade. When the queen was expecting to meet Mary Queen of Scots at Nottingham in 1562 the 'Devices by waye of masquing at the Castell' were elaborate and contained some need for feminine courage as well for skill and extravagance in presentation. High fashion had its freakish side. The expected meeting of the monarchs did not after all take place, but the plans of the proposed display survive and reveal the trend in showmanship.

On the first night two ladies, representing Prudence and Temperance, riding on lions and attended by other women, were to lead the impersonators of Discord and False Report in chains. The two vices named were due, after some manœuvres, to be put in gaol by Jupiter. Then a revel was arranged in which the English ladies joined 'the nobility of strangers' and danced with the Scottish lords. On the second and third nights there were more zoological exhibits on order. Peace had to ride in a chariot drawn by an elephant with Friendship riding on its back. Later Disdain was to enter on a wild boar with Prepensed Malice in the likeness of a serpent. This time the English lords were to dance with the Scottish ladies while 'the conduits of the building ran with wine'.

Finally the combined parties were to sing a song 'as full of harmony as may be devised'. The moral of the intended masquing was excellent and the defeat of Discord and False Report would have provided a spectacle apt for a meeting of the United Nations in our time. The serpent was obviously a costumier's effect. The elephant must have been a real one and probably safe enough. What of the lions and boar? As dummies they would be absurd. If muzzled animals with claws cut they still were hazardous members of the cast.

This remarkable scheme had to be a non-event which may have saved much trepidation and possible casualties. That wild animals were introduced as a treat for special occasions is shown by a calamity which occurred later at Stirling Castle when Queen Mary's son James was the sixth king of his name in Scotland and not yet the first in England. Then the lions engaged caused a panic. News of the incident had evidently reached London and Shakespeare almost certainly alluded to it in *A Midsummer Night's Dream*. Bottom, demanding to take the lion's part in the workmen's play of Pyramus, is warned by Quince that his bellowing would make the ladies shriek and so promises to roar like any sucking dove since the mummers would certainly be hanged if the ladies were frightened out of their wits.

Queen Elizabeth liked to join in the dancing which followed a masque; of the main affair she preferred to be a spectator. Her successor, Queen Anne, the Danish wife of King James the First, was happy to participate in the revels of 'Let's Pretend'. She was a devotee of the professional theatre and made an appearance as an amateur in the court masques on which money was spent to a degree appalling to her careful predecessor. The Jacobean fashion left out the animals and brought in the artists.

The leading poets were engaged to write the librettos. Immediately after the Stuart accession Ben Jonson was employed to prepare an entertainment for the royal party on its way from Scotland to London. For them he composed a pastoral masque called *Satyr* which was played in the garden at Althorp. Henceforward the revels showed a steadily rising excellence in texts and decoration. In the autumn of 1603 Dudley Carleton recorded 'a play of Robin goode-fellow and a masque brought in by a magician of China'. The scenery was elaborate and after the miming the dancing was led by 'Queen Anne, the ladies of Derby, Harford, Suffolke, Bedford, Susan Vere, Southwell the elder, and Rich'. There was some confusion, doubtless hilarious, since Carleton reported that 'in the corantoes they ran over some other of the young ladies and so ended as they began with a song'. (The coranto was, as its name implies, a running dance or gallop.) If there were to be tumbles they were better with no lions or wild boars about. Among the gentlemen of the party was William Herbert, now the Earl of Pembroke, once obnoxious to Queen Elizabeth but after her death forgiven and established in high society by King James.

The summit of scenic beauty was reached by the recruitment of Inigo Jones who had brought back from Italy a mastery of Renaissance classicism in the Palladian style of building and adornment of the masquers' stages. He could spend freely and the themes which he decorated were specially suited to his taste since the characters often were those of the Olympian gods and goddesses and embodiments of the minor deities of Greece and Rome. Illustrious marriages were celebrated with masques to follow and the presiding presence of Hymen was familiar. The gay queen made frequent appearances as an Olympian and on one occasion astonished the court which was accustomed to seeing in a masque the long voluminous dresses of normal life. Carleton wrote of the Vision of the Twelve Goddesses, written by Samuel Daniel and not by Jonson, that the parade and intricate movements on the stair-way to the Temple of Peace 'presented with great majesty and art' provided the best presentation in his experience. In this the queen played Pallas Athene. She, like the other female divinities, was not burdened with a long part. Each had only four lines to speak. Those allotted to the queen were:

> *Next war-like Pallas in her helmet dressed,*
> *With lance of winning, target of defence;*
> *In whom both wit and courage are expressed*
> *To get with glory, hold with providence.*

They could hardly be feebler and may have been feebly spoken.
The texts of the masques were brief and the labour of learning

he roles was no imposition on the ladies. For this occasion Daniel
wrote just over four hundred lines, and that was a script of average
size. Her Majesty, as Pallas, was not the first speaker of the twelve,
which shows her modesty, but she had the satisfaction of pioneer-
ing a new fashion. This, if not so extreme in its curtailment as to
anticipate the mini-skirt of 1967, was at least surprising to the
spectators. Carleton commented that the queen 'had a trick by
herself for her clothes were not so much below the knee but that
we might see a woman had both feete and legs which I never
knew before'.

There was strife among the poets and artists. Ben Jonson,
easily provoked, admitted that he was 'at jealousies' with Daniel.
Nor could he tolerate the sovereign position of Inigo Jones in the
devising of the Jacobean revels. He grumbled that 'painting and
carpentry are the soul of masque'. He was a man of letters and a
playwright and would not have the text given a status inferior to
the spectacles which Bacon described as 'the petty wonderments'
of the masquing vogue. His fees for librettos were no doubt a
considerable compensation for wounded pride, but it was galling
to the professional men of the theatre to see the vast expenditure
on a single amateur entertainment in which their poetry, including
some delicate lyrics, was made pegs on which to hang a profuse
display of luxurious trimmings. No less exasperating was the
knowledge that the production costs of one court masque would
suffice for the staging and costumes of a dozen plays at the Globe
and half a dozen at the Blackfriars where the effects were an
important part of the attraction.

When the 'Masque of Flowers' was produced by the Gentlemen
of Gray's Inn at the Banqueting House in Whitehall on Twelfth
Night 1614 to celebrate the wedding of the king's favourite,
Robert Carr, Earl of Somerset, with Lady Frances Howard, Sir
Francis Bacon contributed two thousand pounds. This vast
endowment, worth at least twenty thousand pounds today, was
attributed to the belief that Somerset had procured for Bacon the
lucrative post of Attorney General. The morals of the Jacobean
court were squalid, but its taste in décor could be superb and was
supported with wild extravagance.

At Whitehall was the world of fashion and there the feminine influence was strong. As one of the dancers in a royal party Lucy Harington, who became the Countess of Bedford, has already been noted. She had married into the Russell family, one of the wealthiest of those newly enriched. She was a cousin of Philip Sidney and Lady Pembroke and a patroness of Michael Drayton who called her 'Great Ladie, essence of my chiefest good'. Ben Jonson was another whom she favoured and John Buxton quotes Ben's epigram, punning Lucy with lucent or bright,

> *Lucy, you brightnesse of our sphere, who are,*
> *Life of the Muses' day, their morning-starre!*
> *If workes (not th' authors) their owne grace should looke,*
> *Whose poemes would not wish to be your booke?*

He adds 'The pun permitted Jonson to address the Countess of Bedford as Lucy in his poems; we are not to conclude that he did so when they met in person.' She received dedications from John Dowland, the composer, and Florio, the lexicographer, in addition to Daniel and Jonson.

She had shown her shrewd anticipation of favours to come by joining a party which travelled north in order to escort Queen Anne from Scotland to England after the death of Queen Elizabeth. Well regarded at court she collected her 'ingeniose persons' in London and appointed favoured writers as Grooms of her Privy Chamber. Daniel and Florio were two of them and Donne attended what would later have been called her salon. But she did not apparently flaunt her social superiority in the company of writers. Jonson praised her for 'hating that solemne vice of greatnesse, pride'. Perhaps he did on festive occasions call her Lucy, but he took care to praise her virtue and her gifts of mind. To him she was

> *Faire and free and wise,*
> *Of greatest blood and yet more good than great.*

The peeresses who took part in masques or joined in the subsequent dances had to do so with ability and style when the company

was sober, which was not always the case. Shakespeare does not
appear as one of the Bedford group nor was he called in to write
librettos for the court or marriage masques. But he admired
dancing and mentioned many of its fashionable forms, the nimble
coranto, the lively galliard, the less volatile cinque-pace, and the
athletic capers of the high lavolt. A gentleman seeking distinction in the ballroom with feminine as well as royal approval
could not be a 'slouch'.

The first of the Stuart kings and queens could take the most
severe tragedy. *King Lear* was commanded for one of the Twelve
Days of Christmas in 1606. What Anne made of that we may
wonder. She had a great appetite for the 'wonderments', not to be
dismissed as petty when Inigo Jones was contriving them.
Masquing became a regular element at any royal celebration.
James enjoyed the pomps and dances laid on but he could be a
capricious spectator, and his temper was easily exasperated by
boredom. He broke into a rage on one high occasion when his
son Prince Charles was making his first appearance as chief
masquer. The entertainment was called 'Pleasure Reconciled to
Virtue', composed by Jonson and decorated by Inigo Jones. It
was seen by the Venetian Busino who left a long account of it
which is quoted in translation in Enid Welsford's history of 'The
Court Masque'.

When the dancers grew tired and flagged the king became
testy and shouted 'Why don't they dance? What did they make
me come here for? Devil take you all, dance!' The royal rage was
appeased by his favourite, the Marquis of Buckingham, who
immediately leaped with such grace and agility that he was
admired by all. The prince was out of breath but had cut some
very graceful capers. Busino said that he excelled in bowing,
being very formal in making his obeisance both to the King and
he lady with whom he danced'.

After their exhausting exercise, when the king had left them,
the jaded performers fell on the liquor, seasoned pasties and
sugar confections of their banquet with such greed that they
upset the table and sent glasses flying in a shower of broken glass.
Court manners of both sexes were a mixture of prescribed

courtesy and rough crudity. On one important occasion, when the King of Denmark was the guest in London of his son-in-law, the masquers, including the queen, were drunk before they began their masquing. They tottered rather than danced through an entertainment which became chaotic and squalid. Selden in his 'Table Talk' said that ballroom manners decayed. 'In King James's time things were pretty well. But in King Charles's time there has been nothing but Trenchmore and the Cushion Dance, Omnium gatherum, tolly polly, hoite come toite.'

One strange vagary of feminine taste was shown in a masque called 'Cupid's Banishment' presented before the queen in 1618 by 'the young gentlewomen of the Ladies' Hall in Deptford at Greenwich', a finishing school attended by two of the queen's god-children. After the gentlewomen had elegantly demonstrated that Hymen could bring about a chaste union of hearts among Diana's nymphs they offered an anti-masque 'all of Bacchus children' which exhibited 'the severall humours of drunkards and many pretty figures befitting that vaine'. There was already some 'hoite come toite' even in an academy nice for young gentlewomen.

It may seem surprising that Shakespeare never wrote any texts for the court masques. He was one of the specially favoured King's Men; he had been at once appointed a Groom of the Royal Bedchamber when the new reign began. If he was not yet generally regarded as first among the poets and playwrights he was undoubtedly known as one of the foremost. An invitation to contribute to the fashionable revels must have come his way. He had no objection to obliging titled persons. It is fair to suppose that he fought shy of this distraction. He did not now need the money. He had his reasons for evading service of the masquing craze and had no eagerness to aid the indulgence of the lords and ladies in their sumptuous exhibitionism.

Posterity may be thankful that he did not waste his time in turning out verses for the exalted amateurs to mouth and possibly mangle. They could pose and dance to their own satisfaction. But could they deliver a speech with the same efficiency? Such compositions of this kind as he inserted in his plays are not many and at least the miming would be done and the lines spoken by people who knew their job, could be properly rehearsed, and would not be half-tipsy on the night. As a member of the royal household he owed obedience to the masquing queen but, if others were eager to provide scripts for her probably inexpert diction, there was no necessity for him to do so. He had better voices and better themes to serve.

In the decade following the accession of King James he was continually and strenuously occupied. Those who write about Shakespeare's plays as the supreme glories of English literature and discuss at length the political and philosophic opinions deemed to be inherent in the treatment of his subjects often seem to visualise him as enjoying ample opportunities and leisure for wide reading and contemplation. In fact he was an intensely committed theatrical worker in all spheres of his profession. In 1603 he was at his summit as poet and playwright and yet continuing to act even in other men's plays such as Ben Jonson's *Sejanus*. He went on tour with long horse-back journeys when the London theatres were closed. More exacting still were his administrative tasks and worries as an actor-sharer and house-sharer with his company. After 1608 they had the Blackfriars as well as the Globe Theatre on their hands; both needed selection and training of new players. Why, if he could keep clear of the court's revels and wedding masques in noblemen's houses, should he be further burdened?

The elements of masquing in his plays indicate some aversion to the interruption of drama with modish diversions of this kind. Songs he could exquisitely write and dancing he liked and introduced within limits. But the parading of irrelevant gods and goddesses was made scantily; subsequently there had to be some concession as the taste for spectacle grew and the covered stage at Blackfriars offered chances for bizarre display.

There are two sorts of masquing in Shakespeare's work. In the simpler and earlier form characters in the plays mask their faces in order to provide misunderstandings through mistaken identities. In the long second scene of the fifth Act of *Love's Labour's Lost* the stage direction runs: 'The Ladies mask. Enter

Blackamoors with music; Moth with a speech; the King, Berowne, Longaville and Dumaine disguised as Russians.' And so on to the amorous exchanges while the men and women 'converse apart'. In *The Merchant of Venice* (Act II, scene v) Gratiano and Salarino come wearing masks to Shylock's door when Jessica is to elope with Lorenzo. A director can build this up if he chooses, but in fact there is no revel when Jessica has gone. Says Antonio firmly:

> *No masque to-night. The wind is come about.*
> *Bassanio presently will go aboard.*

and Gratiano replies:

> *I am glad on it. I desire no more delight*
> *Than to be under sail and gone to-night.*

A similar game of 'Let's Pretend' in *King Henry VIII*, with 'the king and others habited as shepherds' has already been mentioned.

The formal type of masque introducing gods and goddesses edges its way into the text of *As You Like It* (Act v, scene iv) when the various concluding marriages are being made. The stage direction is: 'Enter Hymen leading Rosalind in women's clothes and Celia. Still music.' The rhyming lines spoken by Hymen are doggerel

> *Peace ho! I bar confusion*
> *'Tis I must make conclusion*
> *Of these most strange events*
> *Here's eight that must take hands*
> *To join in Hymen's bands*
> *If truth holds true contents*

And so on. Hymen is given a song, but there are no words for it. Shakespeare was obviously bored with what he regarded as silly business.

The masque in *Cymbeline* (Act v, scene iv) may not have been inserted by Shakespeare himself. The writing of the play is dated between 1609 and 1611 and the manuscript may have been sent up from the country. A production was seen at the Globe in the latter year, but the masque was probably added for a production at the Blackfriars where spectacular effects were more easily contrived. The roof or 'heavens' of that house was painted to resemble marble and crystal; it had a trap and a winch for lowering and raising players through it. In this case there is an Apparition in which Posthumus' long-dead father and his two brothers 'with wounds as they died in the wars' protest to Jupiter about the wrongs suffered by the husband of Imogen. Then 'Jupiter descends in thunder and lightning, sitting upon an eagle. He throws a thunderbolt. The ghosts fall on their knees.' The appeal for justice to Posthumus succeeds and Jupiter is hauled up again. His parting lines are:

> *And so away: no further with your din*
> *Express impatience or you stir up mine.*
> *Mount, eagle, to my palace crystalline.*

This is on the level of the rhyming in Victorian pantomimes allotted to those members of the cast, Fairy Queen or Demon Rat, who were specified in the old programmes as Immortals. If the player of Jupiter did not enjoy himself, no doubt the audience, especially the women, who were not all intellectual Paragons and may have had enough Romano-British pseudo-history by now, were delighted with the gory spectres, the explosion, and the intrepid rider of the eagle. The piece was seen by King Charles the First on New Year's Day 1634 and 'well likte by the kinge'. Could the divine descent and ascension have been possible at Whitehall? That the lines were written by another is a reasonable guess. The Apparition is quite unnecessary except as a feat of show business. It met an expanding fashion in entertainment which the Blackfriars management was busily satisfying.

For the marriage and fertility masque in *The Tempest* (Act IV, scene i), described by Ferdinand as 'a most majestic vision and harmonious charmingly', three goddesses, Juno, Ceres, and Iris as well as 'certain reapers properly habited and nymphs in a graceful dance' are ordered by the dramatist. In this case the text is well written and many of its lines show Shakespeare's hand. The descriptions of landscape, the banks with 'pioned and twilled brims' which 'spongy April betrims' and the 'bosky acres and the unshrubbed down, rich scarf to my proud earth', are surely his. But *The Tempest*, if not first written for royal occasions, was used for them, being twice presented at court, once for the king in 1611 and again in 1613 for the wedding celebrations of the Princess Elizabeth and the Prince Palatine Elector. This time Shakespeare seems to have served the masquing vogue without reluctance as befitted one of the King's Men. But he put his spectacle into a play of rare quality to be produced by colleagues whom he trusted. He was not contributing to an amateurs' display.

A remark of Aubrey's notes him as no addict of party-going. One cannot imagine his being happy among the press of the fashionable masquers and the frowst created in a crowded room lit by numbers of candles and torches. Bacon counselled a spraying of 'sweet odours suddenly coming forth' as a pleasant refreshment 'in such a company as there is steam and heat'. Shakespeare with his sensitive nose might have agreed with that advice; he would also have concurred with Bacon's opening and finishing comment on masques 'These things are but toys.'

The masques, as Shakespeare knew, were play-things and much less than plays. Parade and panache were the essence. The audiences as well as the performers came in splendour and jewels blazed from the head even to a decorated shoe. Some of the great ladies had well-stored brains above their richly ruffed necks. All, paragons or light-wits, had finery above them. Whatever the excellence of their hair-dressing the 'crowning glory' was further crowned by inter-lacing with a tire. The tire-maker was one of a profession on whom they called to equip them for any splendid gathering. He had to be a craftsman as well as a salesman. The intricate contrivance of a glittering head-piece demanded an artist's hand.

The tires have a particular interest for us since they bring Shakespeare into this corner of the fashionable world. He stayed in several lodgings in London, in Bishopsgate and Southwark and later in Silver Street in Cripplegate ward. In the last we meet Madame Mountjoy, wife of Christopher Mountjoy, tire-maker to the royal family in the reign of King James. She is the only one of Shakespeare's landladies known to us by name and we hear of her since he became involved in her family affairs.

The Mountjoys were Huguenots and Christopher or his father had brought with him a profitable skill. In 1910 Professor Wallace of Nebraska University raked out of the records a fascinating discovery which is unique since it provides the only item in our knowledge of Shakespeare's private life in rented rooms. He was 'in digs' with the Mountjoys at least from 1602 to 1604. At the latter date he was working on *Othello* in one room while a wedding, with a dowry as usual in view, was being planned in another. Eight years afterwards he had to testify in a law-suit brought by Mountjoy's apprentice, Stephen Belott, who married Marie, the daughter of the house.

Belott claimed that his father-in-law had failed to produce the promised dowry of sixty pounds and had not included in his will a further verbal promise of a legacy of two hundred pounds. The Mountjoys were well enough off to keep a maid, Joan Johnson, who deposed in court that Mountjoy 'did send and perswade one Mr. Shakespeare that lay in the house to perswade the plaintiff (Belott) to the same marriage'. Shakespeare vouched for Belott's character in a kindly way, agreed that he had urged the marriage, but said that he had forgotten the details. Why not? This is no proof of failing memory. He was back in Stratford when the dispute came to court. That is shown in his deposition which begins 'William Shakespeare of Stratford-upon-Avon in the County of Warwicke gentleman of the age of XLVIII yeres or thereaboutes'.

Shakespeare presumably did know his own age, but the lawyer who drew up the document could not be precise because the signature might be made before April 24, while Shakespeare was still forty-seven. He must have been bored by this rather sordid squabble which was far away from his present home and had happened fairly long ago. As a result of his pardonable vagueness about the money involved the case was referred by the court to the leaders of the Huguenot church in London. By these arbiters Belott was awarded twenty nobles. Mountjoy failed to pay up and both men were found by the new judges of their own nation to be 'desbauchez'. Shakespeare's amiability in giving Belott a good character appears to have been misplaced, but there is no reason to suppose that the debauchery was noticeably flagrant when he was their lodger eight years earlier and that he had been living in a disreputable house. He had plenty to do and, if well looked after, was not worrying about niceties of conduct.

Of more interest than the quarrels in Mountjoy's home is the work which he and Belott did. In his volume of collected pieces called 'Shakespeare's Sonnets Dated' Dr Hotson closely examined the making of tires for the heads of fashionable women. He had been angered by the commonly made and erroneous suggestion that Mountjoy was a wig-maker; to be a specialist in tires put him well above that. The word tire may be a form of tiara whose modern meaning the Oxford English Dictionary gives as 'a jewelled or profusely decorated ornament worn by women above the forehead'. Shakespeare used the word tire both as a shortening of attire or dress and as the costly article produced by Mountjoy who added jewels to a hair-lace or coif made of gold thread. These tires were carefully designed and sumptuously wrought. They were not limited to the wealthy and titled ladies. Anne and Mary Fitton, daughters of a solid county family, stood for their portraits at the ages of eighteen and fifteen. Above their elaborate ruffs, huge sleeves, wasp waists, and voluminous sleeves are conspicuous tires.

Queen Elizabeth had a tire which was shaped like a ship and fashioned of mother-of-pearl and rubies. Examples of poetic praise are quoted. One song by Thomas Morley, Shakespeare's one-time neighbour and musical collaborator, ran:

> In nets of golden wires
> With pearl and ruby spangled,
> My heart entangled
> Cries out and help requires.

Falstaff, when he was flattering Mistress Ford to the top of his knavish bent, said that she had 'the right arched beauty of the brow that becomes the ship-tire, the tire valiant, or any tire of

Venetian admittance'. He did not say that she owned such a treasure, but only that she deserved it.

The fashion of the court was carried to the country fair. Autolycus peddled what he called 'golden quoifs' to the shepherds; he was probably lying about the genuine quality of the metal. He was not taking the road to be way-laid and robbed. He also offered to Mopsa and her kind

> *Any silk, any thread*
> *Any toys for your head*
> *Of the newest and finest?*

But Mopsa preferred ballads to bedizenment. There must have been tires at popular prices. If Mistress Ford did have one for special party-going it would be in the middle range.

Mountjoy was at work in 1594 and then failing, as he did with Belott, to be as good as his word. Dr Hotson quotes a letter of that date from an East Anglian gentleman, Philip Gawdy, in which he said that he had sent from London to his well-beloved sister what she wanted. Her needs were a farthingale of the best fashion, gold thread, a hair caul, and pumps. The only thing missing, he added, 'he should have had from Mr. Munjoye, but he fayled me very wrongfully according to his promyse; but it is coming'. A tire of the finest must have been expected. Did she ever get it?

Madame Mountjoy was not only a lodging-hostess with a maid to do the house-work. She shared in the tire-making and collected some of the proceeds. Dr Hotson unearthed from the royal accounts the information that King James's extravagant queen owed 'Marie Mountjoy, tyre-woman' fifty-nine pounds, a vast sum in those days. Anne was not prompt in payment. The bill was met by instalments. It is understandable that Madame, with her unreliable husband, should want to handle the business side.

In the same illuminating paper on feminine fashions it is pointed out that to speak of Mountjoy as a wig-maker, as several masculine scholars have done when discussing the stay in Silver Street, was insulting, since Shakespeare was repelled by false hair because it was often taken from the dead. Four passages are

quoted by Dr Hotson in which there is disgust with golden locks
and tresses removed from graves to 'live a second life on second
head' while 'the skull that bred them' is 'in the sepulchre'.

There was some audacity in writing thus of false hair since
Queen Elizabeth had many wigs. But one allusion is in the
Sonnets, which were not for her, and another in *Timon of Athens*
which was written well after her death. There is one mention of
the sepulchral origin of wigs in *The Merchant of Venice* which was
commanded at court by King James in 1605 but is described in
the First Quarto of 1601 as 'divers times acted by the Lord Cham-
berlaine, his Servants'. No performance requested by Queen
Elizabeth is known. If she did command that play Bassanio's
contemptuous remark about 'the dowry of a second head' snipped
from the skull of the deceased asked for tactful cutting of the text.

Shakespeare had his eye on the wardrobe of the fashionable
beauties. Margaret, Hero's maid in *Much Ado About Nothing*,
discusses the wedding garments of her mistress. The tire is
approved with a reservation about its matching with the hair
which would be better suited if the latter were 'a thought
browner'. The maid has seen the full splendour of a duchess 'in
full fig'.

Margaret. . . . your gown's a most rare fashion, i'faith. I saw the
Duchess of Milan's gown that they praise so.
Hero. O, that exceeds, they say.
Margaret. By my troth, 's but a night-gown in respect of yours,—
cloth-o'-gold, and cuts, and laced with silver, set with pearls,
down sleeves, side sleeves, and skirts round underborne with
a bluish tinsel: but for a fine, quaint, graceful, and excellent
fashion, yours is worth ten on't.

(*Much Ado About Nothing,* III.iv.12–22.)

Was the duchess's gown described in such surprising detail
immediately after Shakespeare had seen one of that richness worn
by one of the great ladies or the royal maids of honour at Whitehall? If so, he had been much impressed. Had he known one of
the maids to his rapture and with bitter disenchantment to follow?
She abides our question.

CHAPTER XI

A Pair of Black Eyes

THAT THERE was a Dark Lady in Shakespeare's life is scarcely disputable. The Sonnets evoked by her fascination and her transferred affections (affection to the Elizabethans meant a passion not a liking) are vibrant with a love-hate relationship which makes it impossible to regard them as a formal exercise in a fashionable type of writing. The Sonnets to the handsome man are also so charged with feeling aroused by admiration and resentment that they too cannot be taken as an elegant contribution to a literary vogue. With their mingling of raptures and revulsions the two sequences drive into the extremes of happiness and distress. Now serene, now savage, they are personal to the core.

The identity of the persons addressed has been and remains a matter of intense and intricate argument. There is no agreement and perhaps never will be. There are two favourite candidates for the honour of being the male recipient. (Though the unknown man lured away Shakespeare's pliable lady and is not a wholly admirable character it is surely an honour to have first inspired and then provoked some of the finest short poems in the English language.) The two earls of Southampton and Pembroke have recently been backed with much argument and not a little contention by Dr A. L. Rowse and Dr Dover Wilson. Dr Hotson recently came up with a third, a William Hatliffe who in youth enjoyed a flamboyant membership of Gray's Inn. The case for this new arrival is based mainly on the similarity of his initials to those of the 'Mr. W. H.' to whom Thorpe dedicated this edition of the Sonnets. There have in the past been a number of others including Oscar Wilde's entry, an imagined actor called

Will Hughes; there is some punning of Shakespeare's on 'A Man in hue, all "hues" in his controlling'. But puns are not proofs and no player of that name has ever been discovered in any of the theatrical records and cast-lists. Furthermore the man addressed is obviously a person of rank. The debate will continue.

It need not be joined here because the subjects of this book are feminine. To wonder who was the Dark Lady is surely natural since she too was honoured by the superb quality of most of the Sonnets sent to her. Neither Rowse nor Dover Wilson in their editions of the Sonnets names any woman. But curiosity in the case of this bewitching and tormenting creature can hardly be avoided by readers who are swept along on the waves of Shakespeare's impassioned surrenders to her sovereign charms and of his furious rebellions against her lascivious and treacherous behaviour. Inevitably she stirs surmise in normally inquisitive people. Some can shrug her off unconcerned, but many Shakespearians have not been content to be thus agnostic.

For some time Mistress Mary Fitton, known as Mall Fitton, held the field. She was a real person about whom quite a lot is known. She was a maid of honour to the queen and at the end of 1600 very much in the news, the talk of the town, and soon to be disgraced. She had become a gift to the Sneerwells and Backbites in the Whitehall school for scandal. Shakespeare must have known her and did in fact mention her in his play of that year, *Twelfth Night*, in whose third scene of the first act there is a reference to 'Mistress Mall's portrait'. When Sir Andrew Aguecheek boasts of his capacity for dancing, cutting a caper and doing 'the backtrick simply as strong as any man in Illyria' Sir Toby Belch replies, 'Wherefore are these things hid? Wherefore have they a curtain before them? Are they like to take dust like Mistress Mall's picture?' If, as Dr Hotson has convincingly argued in 'The First Night of Twelfth Night', the comedy was first played at court on that night in January, 1601, the condition of Mall Fitton must have been known.

She had been for some time intimate with William Herbert, was some seven or eight months pregnant, and gave birth to his illegitimate and short-lived son in February or March. Sir Toby's words are plausibly interpreted by Dr Hotson thus. 'Besmirching shame lay in wait for her all-admired face. She had therefore withdrawn it, like a curtained picture, from the vulgar gaze.' Here was a topical hit, good for a laugh or a snigger with an audience of knowing courtiers, but by no means as considerate or as chivalrous as one might expect from the well-mannered Shakespeare. However, if Mall was his Dark Lady who had gone from his bed to Herbert's, the Sonnets vehemently declare his distress. The agonised loser was in no mood to miss the chance of a score by keeping the sealed lips of a courteous gentleman. It is possible, however, that the cruel jest was an actor's gag which got into a playhouse script which was never edited by Shakespeare.

There is another reason for supposing that the name of Fitton was familiar to the players in general and to the Lord Chamberlain's Men in particular. William Kemp, named in the First Folio as one of the 'Principal Actors' in Shakespeare's plays, had taken the role of First Clown for some years before he left the company in 1599. It was a team of long-abiding colleagues. To walk out was exceptional. It is generally and reasonably supposed, on the evidence of Hamlet's acid remarks about clowning comedians, that Kemp, dissatisfied with the size of the parts written for him and discovering that an impromptu gag could set the house on a roar, had been disciplined and would not take the rebuff. In *Hamlet*, written a year or so later, the Prince in talking with the actors at Elsinore damned 'the pitiful condition' of the Fools who spoke 'more than is set down for them' and so won the laughter of 'some quantity of barren spectators'. This practice, complained Shakespeare, 'interrupted some necessary question of the play'. To that it could fairly be answered that, by dragging this Globe Theatre quarrel into the tragic story of Denmark long ago, the dramatist was himself undoubtedly interrupting the necessary questions of his own play.

Kemp later advertised his capacity for capering without stint and amused the public by dancing a morris for nine days on the roads from London to Anglia. He wrote and published an account of this antic, his Nine Days Wonder as he called it, with the title of 'Kemp's Morris to Norwich'. It would contain, he said in his opening words, 'many things, nothing hurtful'. But at the end he hit back with acrimony at his old colleagues and at Shakespeare under a derisive name. He denounced those 'rascalities' who 'fill the country with lies of his never done acts' and called these alleged rogues 'my notable Shakebags'. The row about gagging had rankled in the mind of the resentful clown. His book of self-reporting he dedicated to 'The truly ennobled lady and his bountiful mistress, Mistress Anne Fitton, Maid of Honour to the most sacred maid Royal Queen Elizabeth.'

Why was Anne Fitton made the recipient of Kemp's narrative? There is a serious mistake in the dedication. She was never a maid of honour. But before her marriage she was in London and probably accompanied her sister when Mall came up from Cheshire to take her place at court. During her stay Anne had obviously been good company and a social success if a letter sent to her at Arbery from the Strand in December 1596 is not mere flattery. The writer was Sir Henry Carey who was made Master of the Jewels seven years later by King James the First. His note from London ended 'No Newes here worthy you, all at this end of the towne are become melancholique for the want of your presens. I love you and ever will and so I betake you to your rest, being aboute to take my owne.'

In 1596 Kemp was with the Lord Chamberlain's Men. Mall had been appointed maid of honour in 1595 at the age of seventeen, and as such would be with the queen when plays were commanded. Anne may well have been one of an invited audience, delighted by the clowning, and ready to let the players know of her approval. But there must be an error one way or the other. Either Kemp mistook her rank when he composed his dedication three or four years after she had left London or he intended to dedicate the book to Mall and mistook her name. He may have been careless and confused when he took up his quill after his marathon morris. Or he may have been helped by another and fallible man in attempting authorship. The writing of it was quite a stylish as well as spirited affair and suggests one of the professional pamphleteers as a literary ghost. That other hand could have made the blunder which Kemp did not check since he is known to have danced out of England on a Continental tour about that time. Lady Newdigate-Newdegate, as editress of the 'Gossip from a Muniment Room', decided that 'Anne is plainly a misnomer for Mary'.

One thing is made certain by Kemp's dedication and the jest in *Twelfth Night*. Either Mall or Anne or both were known to Shakespeare's company. There may have been no more than the acquaintance of admiring play-goers with admired players and writers. But even so the hectic career of the younger daughter and the letters of her parents, her married sister, and the friends of the Fitton family contribute so much to our understanding of women's lives at the time of Shakespeare's rise to fame that they deserve some detailed attention.

Anne and Mary were the daughters, born in October 1574 and early in 1578, of Sir Edward Fitton of Gawsworth in Cheshire and Alice Holcroft, daughter of a Lancashire land-owner. The family was proud of its ancestry and position. If the Fittons were not to be classed with the high nobility they belonged to what is now called the Establishment. Their home was in a beautiful part of north-western England, sheltered from the east by the Derbyshire hills and moors and facing the rich grass-lands of the Cheshire levels. There were two sons, Edward who succeeded to the property and Richard who died unmarried in 1610.

Plenty is known about both the girls' lives. Their descendant, the lady who so usefully edited the voluminous papers found in the Muniment Room, relates that 'in accordance with the practice of the age Anne had a husband chosen for her while she was still a child and at twelve years of age was married in London to John Newdigate or Newdegate, aged sixteen, of Arbery in Warwick-shire'. The boy-and-girl wedding was a formality. The arrange-ment was a settlement. Anne did not leave home to join her husband in the Midlands until she was twenty or twenty-one. Her father-in-law had been a reckless spender and later died in a debtors' prison. But Sir Edward Fitton was no fool. He had not tied his daughter to a pauper. The Arbery lands were firmly settled on young John. It must seem to us a deplorable way of

determining the whole future of a small girl's life, but in this case
it led to a happy and fruitful marriage.

In 1595 Mary, for whom no such school-room union had been
fixed, was appointed a maid of honour to Queen Elizabeth at the
age of seventeen. In that year Anne joined her husband after
having been a wife in name for eight or nine years while Mary
went up to combine the mixture of palace ceremonial, official
decorum, masquing and dancing with the privy escapades and
amours of the queen's young ladies. Of those gaieties there was
royal ignorance and, when news leaked out, severe disapproval
with possible disgrace.

Mary's introduction to the queen had been arranged by an
influential friend of the family, Sir William Knollys, who was
indeed a personage and knew it. He was a first cousin once
removed of Her Majesty and the Controller of her Household.
He was also the uncle of the wayward Earl of Essex which eased
his position when his nephew was in great favour and proved
most harassing when the earl launched his scatter-brained and
futile rebellion in 1601. As controller, Sir William was in charge
of the staff and servants at Whitehall and had also to check the
palace expenditure, a ticklish task with a royal and choleric
mistress who liked to combine economy with splendour. He was
Malvolio on a grander scale, not Major but Maximus Domo and
he was a powerful friend at court.

He now had the further charge of Mistress Fitton's virtue,
another slippery article to have in hand. In a letter to her father,
written in the pompous style which he employed with gusto and
with a curious addiction to doubling the letter 'f'. he wrote:

'I will no ffayle to ffulffill you desyre in playing the Good Shepp-
erd & will to my power deffend the innocent lamb ffrom the
wolvyshe crueltye & fox-like subteltye of the tame bests off thys
place, wch when they seme to take bread at a man's hand will
byte beffore they bark, all theyr songs be Syrenlike, and theyr
kisses after Judas ffasshion, but ffrom such beastes delyver me
and my frends. I will wth my councill advyse your ffayre daughter,
with my true affection love hyr and with my sword deffend hyr
yff need be, hir inocency will deserve yt and hyr vertue will

chaleng yt at my hands and I will be as carffull off hyr weldoing as yff I wear hyr true ffather.'

The controller protested too much. He himself was captivated by the minx who was to be widely known as Mall. He made no secret of it in the many letters which he wrote to Anne who was now becoming a mother in the quietude and respectability of Arbery. He was her god-father or 'gossip' and to her he gossiped (in our sense) in his lengthy and florid effusions. He had married at fifty a wealthy widow, the Lady Chandos, who was older than himself. With astonishing candour he let Anne know that he would gladly be rid of her and passionately desired Mall to take her place. He may not have attempted to seduce his protégée; that would have been dangerous though seduction was plentiful at court outside the range of the queen's vigilance. But he eyed her as hungrily as any of the palace wolves whom he claimed to be warding off. All this, though he was a married man more than thirty years Mall's senior, he candidly admitted to Anne, even asking her to pray for his unseemly cause. In his eagerness to be 'delivered' from Lady Knollys he wrote, delighting in his laboured eloquence,

'. . . let me entreate your ffayre selffe to perce the heavens with your earnest and best prayers to the effecter & worker of all things for my delyverye, & that once I maye be so happye as to ffeele the pleasyng comffort off a delightful sumer wch I doubt not will yeald me the deserved frute off my constant desyres wch as yeat no sooner budd by the heat off the morning sonne but they are blasted by an untymelye ffrost, so as in the midst off my best comfforts I see nothing but dark despayre. I could complayne off ffortune wch ledd me blyndlye into this barren desert where I am readye to starve ffor want off my desyred ffoode. . . .'

At least the Controller was candid, but it is impossible to avoid the impression strongly implanted by his letters of a type now vulgarly known as 'a nasty old man'. Anne did not preserve copies of her replies. If, as one hopes, they were sharp they were not sharp enough to quench the flood of lamentation and self-pity.

Mall naturally would have none of this. In the sometimes

sparkling and sometimes muddy waters of Whitehall there were far more attractive fish than this repellent pike. (If the watery image seems coarse it is Shakespeare's. The jealous Leontes in *The Winter's Tale* envisages the cuckold who

> *holds his wife by th'arm*
> *That little thinks she has been sluiced*
> *By Sir Smile, his neighbour*.)

There were young and dashing trout for feminine anglers, such for example as the Lord William Herbert who came to London in 1598. Also, if the identification of Mistress Fitton with the Dark Lady be correct, there was a clever poet favoured by the queen and not too difficult to meet. The Controller might have had the sense to see that he had no chance.

The maids of honour were a trouble to Sir William. They were his near and noisy neighbours at the palace. His method of calling them to order was peculiar. Sir Nicholas Lestrange, who died in 1655, compiled a book of 'Merry Passages and Jests' which contained this anecdote.

'The Lord Knollys, in Queen Elizabeth's time, had his lodging at Court, where some of the Ladyes and Maydes of Honour us'd to friske and hey about in the next roome, to his extreame disquiete a nights, though he had often warned them of it; at last he getts one to bolt theire owne backe doore, when they were all in one night at their revells, stripps off to his shirt, and so with a payre of spectacles on his nose, and Aretine in his hand, comes marching in at a posterne doore of his owne chamber, reading very gravely, full upon the faces of them. Now let the reader judge what a sadd spectacle and pittiful sight these poor creatures endur'd, for he fac'd them and often traverst the roome in this posture above an houre.'

Mall would not be left out of any such frisking. Malvolio has been mentioned and here, as several have pointed out, is a strong indication that Shakespeare had heard of the absurd incident and used it for the scene in which the Major Domo rebukes the noisy revellers. Dr Hotson in 'The Twelfth Night of

Twelfth Night' has made out a strong case for believing that
Knollys was being baited in that play. He believes that the name
Malvoglio suggested Mall-voglio, 'I want Mall', to an audience
in the know. Olivia's steward is made amorous, consequential,
and fond of 'affection'd' speech. This trick of verbosity appears
continually in Anne's letters from her god-father. There is an
allusion to the white staff of office carried by the controller. 'He
holds Beelzebub at the stave's end.' Several other probable hits
at Knollys are brought in evidence.

Censorship of plays was strict in the matter of personalities.
The idea of a personal attack on a high official at the palace is only
tenable if the text had been marked as 'allowed' by Tilney, the
Master of the Revels, agreed to by Lord Hunsdon, the Lord
Chamberlain, and deemed inoffensive by the queen if she had
been consulted. It is very likely that Knollys had become un-
popular with all of them and that they enjoyed and permitted the
ridicule. No member of the audience would have been more
amused than Mistress Fitton, but, if the play was given in January
1601, she would not be there. Her picture, as Sir Toby put it, had
to be concealed.

Mall's levity and impudence are documented in a note by Sir
Robert Cecil.

'. . . in that tyme when that Mistress Fytton was in great fauour,
and one of her Majestie's maids of honour, and duringe the time
yt the Earle of Pembrooke fauord her she would put off her head
tire and tucke upp her clothes and take a large white cloake and
marche as though she had bene a man to meete the said Earle
out of the Courte.'

Pembroke was not the only man whom Mall could have met in
this way. In his short play *The Dark Lady of the Sonnets* Bernard
Shaw made her keep an assignation with Shakespeare. The time
and scene are 'Fin de siècle, 15–1600. Midsummer Night on the
terrace of the Palace at Whitehall.' Shaw had been asked in 1910
to contribute something for a fund-raising matinée on behalf of
the National Theatre. He did not mean his brief and lively
invention to be taken seriously, but he wrote a preface in which

he explained how he had come to be interested in the identification of Mall Fitton with the Dark Lady. An early champion of that idea had been Thomas Tyler, whom he had often met in the library of the British Museum and whose book on the subject he had reviewed in the 'Pall Mall Gazette' in 1886. He suggested that his review caught the eye of Frank Harris who took up the Fitton-Pembroke theory, wrote a play on it, and then developed it at length in his book 'The Man Shakespeare.'

In June 1600 the queen attended the wedding at Blackfriars of the Earl of Worcester's son and a lady of the court, Mistress Anne Russell. She was taken by water to Blackfriars in the royal barge and thence carried aloft on a lectica (a portable throne with canopy) by six knights. William Herbert was one who escorted the bride to the church. In letters to Sir Robert Sidney Rowland Whyte described the plan for a masque of eight ladies with 'a strange dance newly invented'. Mall was one of the team who each had 'a skirt of cloth of silver, a rich waistcoat wrought with silks and gold and silver, and a mantle of carnation cast under the arm; their hair loose about the shoulders curiously knotted and interlaced'. Whyte praised the beauty of the costumes and performance.

'Mrs Fitton leade, & after they had donne all their own ceremonies, these 8 ladys maskers choose 8 ladies more to dawnce the measures. Mrs Fitton went to the Queen & woed her to dawnce; her Majestie asked what she was; "Affection," she said. "Affection!" said the Queen, "Affection is false." Yet her Majestie rose and dawnced; . . .'

Affection, as has been noted, meant much more than the word does now; its emblem was a flaming heart. There exists a painting of the queen supported on her lectica. Beside her is a dark-haired girl with a flaming heart on her sleeve.

That was the climax of Mistress Fitton's career at court and of the favour shown to her. She had a way with her. The queen, then aged sixty-seven, did rise and dance at her 'wooing'. But the mention of 'affection' was tragically relevant and ominous. Her affair with William Herbert had begun and was to prove fatal. Whether she led him on or was seduced by him cannot of course be known. The historian Clarendon said that he was 'immoderately given to women'. If she was the Dark Lady of the Sonnets she was immoderately given to men. The discovery of her pregnancy brought her dismissal from the palace. He was sent for a term to the Fleet Prison. They could not say that they had not been warned.

It is a strange coincidence that both the men known to have been Shakespeare's patrons and canvassed as recipients of the Sonnets were guilty of the same offence and sent to gaol despite their rank. The Earl of Southampton had seduced a lady-in-waiting, Elizabeth Vernon, and had a short prison sentence. He accepted a forced marriage which in the end turned out to be a happy one. The queen had no mercy on courtiers who could not control their passions when they had finished performance of their duties.

Mall escaped punishment of that kind because of her physical condition. For her lying-in she was put in the care of a Lady Hawkins. It was a grievous time for both the lovers. To her birth-pains was added the loss of a boy. For him there was the loss of his father in the same year; the succession to the earldom of Pembroke came when he was under the darkest of clouds. On his release he was banned from the court. Southampton had accepted the obligation to marry. Herbert stubbornly refused it despite the pressure. If Mall had hoped to emerge from the scandal with a title she was defeated.

Herbert's conduct cannot be condoned. He had been having his fling with no thought of marriage and had taken Mall's easy virtue for granted. He did not lack money, but he wanted more, and the Fittons he could regard as not quite up to his class in rank and riches. Sir Edward Fitton wrote to Sir Robert Cecil in May of that year. 'My daughter is confident in her chance before God . . . but for myself I expect no good from hyme that in all this time hath not showed any kindness. I count my daughter as good a gentlewoman as my Lord.' He feared that she had been 'beguiled by the dignity of honour'. Honour of title the new earl possessed, but of honour in the other sense he at that time showed no sign.

After the queen's death he was restored to palace society by King James. He married the daughter and heiress of the wealthy Earl of Shrewsbury. There was money in the union, but misery too. Clarendon commented that his domestic life was most unhappy since 'he payed too much for his wife's fortune by taking her person into the bargain'. But that critic of his sensuality paid full tribute to his sense and sensibility as a patron of the arts and scholarship. In any volume of Shakespeare's collected works there is the dedication to 'the noble and incomparable pair of brethren' of whom one was 'William, Earl of Pembroke, Lord Chamberlain to the King's Most Excellent Majesty' who had 'prosecuted' both plays and playwright, 'with much favour'. At the end are the Sonnets in which the same man may, as many think, appear as the young light-of-love who robbed Shakespeare of his mistress.

Mall, when released from the care of Lady Hawkins, went back to Cheshire. If her father's persuasion had been successful and she had become the Countess of Pembroke it is difficult to be sure of her happiness with a reluctant husband and with Mary Pembroke remaining as the Dowager of Wilton and her mother-in-law for the next twenty years. Not that Mary was a tartar. She was as kind of heart as she was severe of moral code. There is a further implicit irony in the situation. If the Herbert-Fitton theory of the Sonnets be accepted it was from the countess at Wilton that the request to Shakespeare had come. He must plead for her son to beget a son. And this with Mall as partner the heir to the earldom had rapidly achieved. But the command to beget an heir was not obeyed as expected. Far from it.

When Mall left London Knollys, largely thanks to *Twelfth Night,* had evidently become a jest of the town and she too was a victim of the satirical rogues who wrote ballads on current affairs and sold them in the street. Shakespeare's Cleopatra, that matchless portrayal of a wanton, may have been based on memories of Mistress Fitton; Egypt's queen had the songsters in mind and made the menace of malicious doggerel one of the reasons for her readiness

> *To do the deed which ends all other deed,*
> *Which shackles accident and bolts up change.*

She would not live longer in times when

> *Saucy lictors*
> *Will catch at us like strumpets and scald rhymers*
> *Ballad us out o'tune; the quick comedians*
> *Extemporally will stage us.*

Dr Hotson quotes one of the scald (scurvy) rhymes of the year and also its topical interpretation.

> *Party beard, party beard . . .*
> *. . . the white hind was crossed:*
> *Brave Pembroke struck her down*
> *And took her from the clown*
> *Like a good woodman.*

A contemporary key leaves the identities in no doubt. The *white hind, crossed* or dislodged and *struck down* by the *good woodman* or practised lecher Lord Pembroke, is the

> *fair, white-clad 'Mris Fitton'; and* party beard *and*
> clown *are each glossed 'Sr Willm Knowles'.*

It is further pointed out that Sir Toby's remark about Malvolio being a Peg-a-Ramsey refers to a popular ditty sung to a tune of that name and containing the lines

> *When I was a bachelor I led a merry life;*
> *But now I am a married man, and troubled with a wife . . .*
> *Give me my yellow hose again, give me my yellow hose!*
> *For now my wife she watcheth me: see yonder where she goes!*

Feste also mocks Malvolio by singing, amid the latter's protesting cries of 'Fool',

> *My lady is unkind to me, perdy,*
> *She loves another.*

Mall's picture had been curtained over. But it was exposed again in the ridicule of the Controller. The quick comedian who had staged him and brought them both into target area of the rhymers was Shakespeare.

Lady Knollys obliged her husband by dying four years later. Mall had gone, but hope remained and opportunity appeared in the person of Lady Elizabeth Howard, daughter of the Earl of Suffolk. He was sixty-one and she was nineteen; they were married within two months of the funeral. The controller, despite his age, marched firmly up the ladder of awards and titles; he became a Knight of the Garter, Viscount Wallingford, and finally Earl of Banbury. Perhaps it was a happy marriage for both parties, but it is difficult to see it so.

Anne Fitton, now Lady Newdigate with a husband knighted, remained on good terms with her sister, but rustication did not mend Mall's ways. A Cheshire gentleman, Sir Peter Leycester, put it on record that she had two illegitimate daughters by a nautical friend of her family, Admiral Sir Richard Leveson. This may be a libel, but it is certain that another sailor, Captain Polwhele, married Mall in haste, just before or just after the birth of a son. Lady Fitton wrote to Anne that Polwhele was 'a very knave' and wished that she and her younger daughter had both died before she suffered 'such shame as never hade Chesshyre woman'. The new union was brief. Mall was a widow with two children in 1609. Her husband had owned a place at Perton in Staffordshire and she was left in funds. Later she married a Mr Lougher who had land in England and Wales. She was a widow again in 1639 and lived until 1647 when she died at the age of sixty-nine. She had out-lived Pembroke by seventeen years, the controller by fifteen, and Shakespeare by thirty-one. She had a number of grand-children, property to leave, and many memories.

The fact is inescapable that for some years in his life Shakespeare was enthralled and enraged by a dark beauty who led him on and threw him over. Her eyes in particular had a sovereign power. The word influence then meant something far stronger than it does now. When Milton wrote of 'ladies whose bright eyes rain influence' he was thinking of spell-binders. Shakespeare was under this species of dominion. The first of the second series of the Sonnets (number a hundred and twenty-seven) begins with a protest at the past and still prevailing admiration of fair and golden hair.

> *In the old age black was not counted fair,*
> *Or if it were, it bore not beauty's name;*
> *But now is black beauty's successive heir . . .*

The eyes of his mistress are 'raven black' and 'mourners seem'

> *Yet so they mourn, becoming of their woe,*
> *That every tongue says beauty should look so.*

That this universal alteration of opinion had occurred is doubtful while Queen Elizabeth was still alive. But one does not expect total accuracy in the poetry of ravishment and chagrin.

Again and again the eyes seem to be hovering over Shakespeare's hand.

> *Thine eyes I love, and they, as pitying me,*
> *Knowing thy heart torments me with disdain,*
> *Have put on black, and loving mourners be,*
> *Looking with pretty ruth upon my pain.*

This Sonnet, number one hundred and thirty-two, ends

> *Then will I swear Beauty herself is black,*
> *And all they foul that thy complexion lack.*

The other features of her who both pities and plagues are definitely stated. Her hair is as black as her eyes and her skin is notably white. She is musical and has nimble fingers expert at the keys of a virginal. This ebon beauty does not only exercise its sway, one might almost say its sorcery, in the Sonnets. It also appears unmistakably in some plays written between 1595 and 1599.

The remarkable point is the repetition of facial detail in this one instance. Shakespeare scarcely ever provided a definite portrait of his characters. The outlines are there. The men could be as fat as Falstaff or as thin as Romeo's apothecary to suit the actor who was naturally stout or able to carry capably a load of padding or one who was a natural skin-and-bones type. The play-goer

assumes that heroes are handsome and the villains ill-favoured.
We are not told of particular features. The admired women are
vaguely beautiful. Bassanio says that Portia's

> *sunny locks*
> *Hang on her temples like a golden fleece*
> *Which makes her seat of Belmont Colchis' strand*
> *And many Jasons come in quest of her.*

He himself has two kinds of gold in mind. Rosalind is taller than
Celia. Cordelia's voice is 'soft, gentle, and low'. That is scanty
information and even that much is uncommon. We are left to
imagine the looks of the heroines.

But the raven-black eyes stare at us with their power to subju-
gate in *Romeo and Juliet*, probably written in 1595. We are told
of them before Romeo has been overwhelmed by the loveliness
of Juliet with her

> *Beauty too rich for use, for earth too dear*

which 'shows a snowy dove trooping with crows'. Why mention
crows? There had been a raven, Rosaline, Romeo's first object of
adoration who never appears in the play. The impressionable son
of the house of Montague had been rapt by her and she is
described in a manner as coarse as vivid by Mercutio,

> *I conjure thee by Rosaline's bright eyes*
> *By her high forehead, and her scarlet lip,*
> *By her fine foot, straight leg, and quivering thigh*
> *And the demesnes that there adjacent lie.*

More grossness follows. Rosaline is no innocent as Mercutio
sees her. The picture of contrasted black and white is later
emphasised by him when he says of Romeo's first infatuation

> *Alas, that same pale-hearted wench, that Rosaline*
> *Torments him so that he will sure run mad*

and later adds, in prose,

> *Alas, poor Romeo, he is already dead, stabb'd with a*
> *white wench's black eye.*

It is the Sonnet lady to the life. There is no reason for this close portraiture. It is unlikely that Romeo's first choice would have been the wanton at whose sexual avidity Mercutio does more than hint. A theatrical excuse does not hold. There cannot have been a black-eyed boy-player available for casting as Rosaline since Rosaline is not in the play at all. Yet she is described from brow to foot in a way that Juliet, with her central and crucial part, never is. The only explanation is the dramatist's obsession. The idea of a lecherous beauty brings the image of one such actual woman bursting out of his subconscious self with the exactitude of colour photography. The play was written in the year that Mistress Fitton came to London. That proves nothing, but the coincidence is curious.

The same woman, again called Rosaline, does take the stage with a conspicuous role and is even more intimately described in *Love's Labour's Lost*. She is one of the three maids of honour or ladies in waiting who attend the Princess of France when she comes to visit the King of Navarre. They meet and attract the three young lords who have sworn to abstain from the society of women. Berowne, who often seems to be speaking about life with Shakespeare's own voice, is captivated by Rosaline. Yet with stinging words he denounces her as lecherous. Why should the princess be accompanied by girls who are sexually insatiable? Berowne accuses all three by indicating Rosaline as 'the worst of all' while he is succumbing to her charms. This time the black-and-white beauty and her conduct are pictured with even more physical detail and intensity of feeling.

> *A whitely wanton with a velvet brow,*
> *With two pich-balls stuck in her face for eyes;*
> *Ay, and, by heaven, one that will do the deed,*
> *Though Argus were her eunuch and her guard:*
> *And I to sigh for her! to watch for her!*
> *To pray for her! Go to; it is a plague*
> *That Cupid will impose for my neglect*
> *Of his almighty dreadful little might.*
> *Well, I will love, write, sigh, pray, sue, and groan:*
> *Some men must love my lady, and some Joan.*
>
> (*Love's Labour's Lost*, III.i.193–202.)

Later on Berowne, who like Shakespeare 'rimes', writes sonnets and includes one of his own in the play's dialogue, goes back to the imagery of pitch.

Berowne. The king he is hunting the deer; I am coursing myself; they have pitch'd a toil; I am toiling in a pitch,—pitch that defiles: defile! a foul word. Well, Set thee down, sorrow! for so they say the fool said, and so say I, and I the fool: well proved, wit! By the Lord, this love is as mad as Ajax: it kills sheep; it kills me, I a sheep: well proved again o' my side! I will not love: if I do, hang me; i'faith, I will not. O, but her eye,—by this light, but for her eye, I would not love her; yes, for her two eyes. Well, I do nothing in the world but lie, and lie in my throat. By heaven, I do love: and it hath taught me to rime, and to be mallicholy; and here is part of my rime, and here my mallicholy. Well, she hath one o'my sonnets already: the clown bore it, the fool sent it, and the lady hath it:
(*Love's Labour's Lost*, IV.ii.173–188.)

Furthermore, when he is talking to Boyet, one of the gentlemen attending the princess, he asks about Rosaline. 'Is she wed or no?' It is a natural query. Boyet replies 'To her will or so.' That is very strange and is only pertinent if there is a punning indication that she is intimate with a man called Will. There were two Wills in Mall Fitton's life, the young Lord Herbert and the poet-player. Boyet's answer must be taken in conjunction with the sonnet (number one hundred and thirty-five) which puns throughout on the word and name Will spelled with both a small and a capital 'w'. The two men's rivalry is explicit in the penultimate lines

> *So thou, being rich in* Will, *add to thy* Will
> *One will of mine, to make thy large* Will *more.*
> *Let no unkind, no fair beseechers kill;*
> *Think all but one, and me in that one* Will.

That there was an early version of this play is made certain by the statement in the title-page of the Quarto edition of 1598: 'A Pleasant Conceited Comedie called Love's Labor's Lost as it

was presented before her Highnes this last Christmas. . . . Newly
corrected and augmented by W. Shakespere.' The alterations and
additions had been made before the command performance
during the Twelve Days of Christmas celebrations in 1597. Mall
had been more than two years at court. It is not extravagant to
suppose that she would attend the queen and that some of the
recent 'augmentation' was intended for her ears by an author who
wrote in Sonnet number one hundred and forty-seven

> *My love is as a fever, longing still,*
> *For that which longer nurseth the disease*

and ended

> *For I have sworn thee fair, and thought thee bright,*
> *Who art as black as hell, as dark as night.*

There were times when Shakespeare had very black spots in front
of his own eyes.

Frank Harris in 'The Man Shakespeare' made a great point
of the allusions in these two plays to the whitely wanton who
infected her lover with fever and plague. I have found a further
remarkable appearance of the envisaged tormentor which Harris
had apparently failed to notice. That occurs in *As You Like It*
whose text was registered at Stationers' Hall on August 4th, 1600,
and must have been written during the previous year or months,
that is at the height of Mall Fitton's career and before her disgrace
and dismissal. The infatuation of the shepherd Corin with the
cruelly contemptuous shepherdess Phoebe is not an important
episode in the plot but it evokes from Rosalind a violent scolding
of the girl. This leads on to the well-known lines

> *Down on your knees*
> *And thank heaven fasting for a good man's love.*

Before that she has given a quite unnecessary description of
Phoebe's looks,

> *T'is not your inky brows, your black-silk hair,*
> *Your bugle eye-balls, nor your cheek of cream*
> *That can entame my spirits to your worship.*

A bugle was a black bead. So once more when a heartless man-tamer is being rebuked the familiar features are flashed before us. A shepherdess might be expected to be sun-burned and even weather-beaten, perhaps rubicund. But she is the Dark Lady again, white-faced, black-haired, and black-eyed. Why?

If the Sonnets were written to Southampton early in the fifteen-nineties, as Dr Rowse maintains with a vigorous confidence, there can be no place for Mistress Fitton in the triangular drama of two intense male friendships and one devastating feminine intervention. If we agree with Sir Edmund Chambers and Dr Dover Wilson that William Herbert was Shakespeare's admired patron and later his rival that does not certainly bring Mall into it. Neither of Herbert's champions nominates her. Since the future Earl of Pembroke was born in 1580 the Sonnets to a young man telling him that he ought to be married and a father by now must have been written in the last years of the century. Then the maid of honour was at the height of royal favour, pursued by Sir William Knollys, talked about for her reckless gaiety, and seduced by or seducing Herbert with the known calamitous results. Both the dates in the case and the events underlying the Sonnets make her a fair candidate for the questionable honour of being the Dark Lady, as Tyler and Harris insisted as though they were backing a certainty.

Harris carried his conviction to an absurd length when he said that 'Shakespeare owed the greatest part of his renown to Mary Fitton' and asserted in his final chapter that Shakespeare's intimacy with her lasted 'until his break-down in 1608' or thereabouts and was probably the chief cause of his infirmity and early death. If he had read 'Gossip from a Muniment Room', which appeared twelve years before his book, he would have known that Mall had to leave London in 1601, stayed at home in the country until she was in maternity trouble again, perhaps with the aid of Sir Richard Leveson and certainly with that of Captain Polwhele. Married to the latter she had two children and was the Lady of Perton Manor. That she haunted Shakespeare's memory is very likely; that he, then the busiest of men, went riding off to the North Midlands for an adulterous indulgence with a woman whom he had once come to detest is as unlikely as anything can be.

The editress of the Fitton papers which were found at Arbery dismissed the idea that Mall could be the Dark Lady. She was a good Victorian and thanked her good fortune for not living in the licentious reign of Queen Elizabeth. She obviously did not want an inky blot on the family records. In any case she could claim that the surviving portraits proved Mall to have had a fair complexion, brown hair, and grey eyes. Yet the book's reproductions of two portraits (not in colour) make her appear as extremely black-eyed and black-haired. Lady Newdegate-Newdigate showed an odd sense of colour when she wrote of 'the brunette described by Shakespeare'. There is nothing but raven-black and pitchy-black in the eyes and hair of which Shakespeare wrote. It is further stated that we have 'no hint in the letters that she (Mall) had any personal acquaintance with Shakespeare', but Kemp's dedication of his book to Anne as a maid of honour is accepted as a mistake for Mall and so invites the deduction that there was some familiarity with Shakespeare's colleagues. There was no reason for Mall to write home to her family about her relations with Shakespeare or Herbert. The talk of London was not for repetition in Cheshire. Only one of her letters survives. It is a declaration of continuing affection for Anne who, it seems, was never censorious. The grammar of this brief note can be criticised; its sentiments and some of its phrasing are charming.

Shaw said that he did not care a jot about the identity of the Dark Lady. 'She might have been Maria Tompkins.' But, loyal as ever to old friends, he said that he was sorry to see Tyler's case upset and made the half-jocular suggestion that Mall was so exasperated by the Sonnets that she dyed her hair to escape identification. There the case for the daughter of the house of Fitton rests, undoubtedly unproven. But any reader of the Muniment Gossip book confronted with the portraits as reproduced could swear that here is the Dark Lady 'as black as hell, as dark as night'.

New candidates appeared in 1964 when Dr Hotson published his book called 'Mr. W. H.' As the 'lovely boy' he proposed one

William Hatcliff, son of a Lincolnshire family who held high office in the revels at Gray's Inn. In order to suit Hatcliff's career at the Inn and with some ingenious arguments the Sonnets are dated back to the years 1588 and 1589. Since I am writing of Shakespeare and his women that contention can be left for others to evaluate. My interest is centred on the woman in the case.

G. B. Harrison was thanked for suggesting in a tentative way that a person known as Lucy Negro or Luce Morgan could be she. He thought that Mistress Morgan was an African. This Dr Hotson denies, holding that 'Black Luce was no more an Ethiop than the Black Prince' and that Negro was a nick-name. Black in the talk of the day could mean lustful. Dr Hotson delved into the records and drew on his own vast reading. He discovered that in the years 1579 to 1581 one of the queen's gentlewomen was called Luce Morgan and therefore would have the required attainments in music and dancing. She was on the receiving list for presents from the royal wardrobe for herself and also collected a tip of six shillings and eightpence for her servant on New Year's Day. Before long she must have committed one of the misdemeanours so frequent among the young ladies of the court and so was dropped with a thud.

Unlike Mall Fitton she had no country home to which she could retire. She had her living to earn, her body to sell, and no reluctance to be 'a daughter of the game'. She first became a prostitute and then set up in business as a bawd in Clerkenwell, rivalling the notorious Elizabeth Holland who kept a well-known brothel in Islington, was convicted for that offence in 1597, and was sent to Bridewell prison. She had suffered the horrible punishment of being 'carted' through the town with a paper fixed on her which proclaimed her commerce and invited jeers and stone-throwing. Lucy Negro was at one time married to a Mr Parker of whom no more has been discovered. Professionally known as Black Luce, Luce Morgan, or Old Lucilla she too was sent to Bridewell in January 1601. She apparently escaped the carting; perhaps, as Hotson says, she had influential friends. She was 'set to work' in gaol but not for long since a letter written by Philip Gawdy in December of that year says that 'Luce Morgan lives in reasonable discredit still' which suggests a return from gaol to more congenial employment.

She died before 1610. Her name had become one of the town jokes and appeared in plays and other writing of her time. An uncharitable epitaph said that she died of venereal disease. As far back as 1595 she had been mentioned as spreading the pox. She seems to have repented of her sins and was a Roman Catholic at the end. Hotson quotes much about her vices but nothing is there to justify his attribution of beauty to the dark visage of the woman rhymed by Davies of Hereford

> *Such a beginning, such an end. This Ile not applaud*
> *For Luce did like a whore begin, but ended like a bawd.*

The squalid life might have started at the Whitehall summit of the social ladder.

One of Dr Hotson's methods in seeking to prove his case is to extract from the Sonnets punning allusions to the names of Hatcliff and Morgan. To pick out a commonly used word such as 'more' and claim that its appearance is a pointer to the person of Luce Morgan does not greatly impress me. Nor can I believe that when the black eyes are called mourners there is a further indication of the owner's identity. The Sonnets were written to express strong and often passionate feelings and not as a nest of clues. Once this practice has been accepted there can be no end to the variety of meanings discovered. For example, those maintaining that Shakespeare's plays and poems were written by Edward Vere, the seventeenth Earl of Oxford, who signed himself E. Ver, have pounced on the appearances of the word ever as evidence of his authorship. That game can be played more and more and ever and ever.

It can be argued that Shakespeare brought brothel-keepers into his plays and that Mistress Overdone in *Measure for Measure* 'a bawd of eleven years continuance' and the loathsome character named Bawd in *Pericles* were drawn from memories of Luce in her later career. Dr Hotson might have noticed that the word 'more' occurs in the first words spoken by the keeper of the stew

in the latter play. It is also true that Shakespeare loathed the
hypocrisy of the London crowd who enjoyed watching prostitutes and bawds being flogged while they themselves were shame-
less fornicators. King Lear in his frenzy cries:

> *Thou rascal beadle, hold thy bloody hand!*
> *Why dost thou lash that whore? Strip thine own back;*
> *Thou hotly lusts to use her in that kind*
> *For which thou whipst her. . . .*

Two phrases in the Sonnets can be taken to indicate a married
woman who was promiscuous, which Mrs Luce Parker certainly
was. But the accusation that the Dark Lady was false to a bed-
vow does not certainly make her a wife. Mall Fitton could have
vowed that Shakespeare was her only bed-fellow and broken her
word when William Herbert was preferred. A betrayed and
infuriated lover can throw out the reckless charge of promiscuity
implied in 'the bay where all men ride' without indicting the
wanton woman with the professional prostitution and bawdry
practised by Luce Negro when she had gone downhill.

The name of the Dark Lady has been written off as an insoluble
problem by many scholars and further research and speculation
have been dismissed as a futile waste of time and trouble. She has
been called the Embarrassing Phantom. But still the ghost walks.
At a time when murder-mysteries have such a continuous appeal
for a vast army of readers and play-goers why should the fascination of a sex-mystery be ruled out? Those who delight in a clever
'who-dunnit' by Ngaio Marsh, herself an informed and devoted
Shakespearian, are not guilty of a contemptible curiosity if they
like to puzzle over the who-was-it of the Sonnets.

There are consolations for those baffled and likely to remain so.
Dr Hotson quotes Laurence Durrell's words that a solution would
'deprive us of one of our most enjoyable literary pastimes'. He
has done me the honour of quoting a sentence of mine

'If anybody can discover a new and effective key to the locked
rooms of these poems of strange provenance, abstruse meaning,
and ever-debated significance, what a number of unnecessary
books he will avert.'

The author of 'Mr. W. H.' believes that he has found the double answer and so made further books unnecessary. I am not so sanguine. But when yet another starts to probe the old puzzle set by the cryptic announcement of Thomas Thorpe, the Sonnets' first editor, I am ready to use his words and be a well-wisher to 'the adventurer setting forth'.

CHAPTER XII

Frailty of Women

THAT SHAKESPEARE had a serious illness, perhaps a nervous break-down, in his early forties was confidently stated by Frank Harris and the idea has had some cautious and qualified support from judicious authorities such as Sir Edmund Chambers and Dr Dover Wilson, neither of whom can be called fanciful. Harris went so far as to say that Shakespeare continued to be an invalid to the end of his life. Of that there is no indication. If he was exhausted when he had finished the great tragedies, he sufficiently recovered his energy to write a play a year, look after his property, and make journeys from Stratford to London. There is no evidence of a long illness during his retirement to Stratford. His end came quickly in the spring of 1616.

Harris thought that he never got over the intense excitements and exasperations which gave rise to the Sonnets and that Mall Fitton inflicted an incurable wound. Whoever the Dark Lady may have been, the effect cannot have been as lasting and as lethal as that. But there are many signs that feminine lechery and treachery were keenly remembered and so rankled in his mind that the idea of frailty and betrayal evoked speeches in the late plays of an astonishingly ferocious kind. In them a personal animosity seems to be burning. The writing has a peculiar vehemence with phrasing and imagery typical of the poet in his most powerful portrayals of passion and of jealousy.

The play on which Sir Edmund Chambers laid stress was *Timon of Athens*. In the section on this play in the first volume of his 'Shakespeare' he suggested as a possibly 'subjective view' that Timon's tragedy, rough and apparently unfinished, had been worked on 'under conditions of mental and physical stress which led to a breakdown'. Dr Dover Wilson in his chapter called 'The Razor's Edge' in his brief but memorable book called 'The Essential Shakespeare' sees the dramatist in the likeness of a climber who has reached with exacting effort a dangerous height. From it he has looked down into the clefts and gullies below and seen in them the menace of human stupidity and savagery, of cruelty without motive and of sufferings never deserved. *King Lear* is the peak of the tragic achievement; but the view which it offers to the mountaineer is so terrifying that he is on the point of losing his nerve and balance altogether. That was a disaster, it is suggested, which Shakespeare, perched on his razor's edge, only just escaped. He came down after a while to the green valleys below and the landing in Stratford's water-meadows was gentle. But there had been dangerous moments when the mind was whirling and all poise imperilled.

Also noted in this analysis of an acutely disturbed personality was 'the strain of sex-nausea which runs through almost everything he wrote after 1600'. The tyranny of lust could not be driven out of his thoughts. Never has the dilemma of impassioned man been more concisely or more movingly expressed than in the hundred and twenty-ninth Sonnet. It is deservedly well known but may be quoted again since its insistence on the conflict of love and ecstasy with lust and self-loathing is essential to the understanding of much that was to go into the plays written during the first decade of the new century.

> *The expense of spirit in a waste of shame*
> *Is lust in action; and till action, lust*
> *Is perjur'd, murd'rous, bloody, full of blame,*
> *Savage, extreme, rude, cruel, not to trust;*
> *Enjoy'd no sooner but despised straight;*
> *Past reason hunted; and no sooner had,*
> *Past reason hated, as a swallow'd bait,*
> *On purpose laid to make the taker mad:*
> *Mad in pursuit, and in possession so;*
> *Had, having, and in quest to have, extreme;*
> *A bliss in proof, and prov'd, a very woe;*

> *Before, a joy propos'd: behind, a dream.*
> *All this the world well knows; yet none knows well*
> *To shun the heaven that leads men to this hell.*

When that Sonnet was written nobody can certainly tell. Whatever its date its poignant cry of distress is apposite to the climber made giddy by the downward glance into the crevasse of human corruption. It is decided by Dr Dover Wilson that 'though the ravings of *Timon of Athens* show how near he came to plunging into the abyss' Shakespeare did keep his balance and pass on. In that play the sex-nausea is so predominant that some of Timon's speeches may be described as verbal vomiting. Accordingly it is worth some examination as possible evidence of the break-down which has been diagnosed. It carries the symptoms of extreme fatigue and incipient mental fever and even frenzy.

Its date is uncertain. Somewhere between 1606 and 1608 is a fair surmise. There is no sign that the King's Men ever produced it. There was no theatrical history until it was presented in a version rewritten by Thomas Shadwell of whom Dryden wrote:

> *The rest to some faint meaning make pretence,*
> *But Shadwell never deviates into sense.*

Called *Timon the Man-hater* this concoction was performed in 1678. It was not often given, but did to a small extent hold the stage, with the great benefit of Purcell's music added to it, for nearly a century. It is a travesty of Shakespeare's tragedy, in which the only speaking parts for women are the few lines given to two whores. By his time the public wanted actresses and actresses wanted parts. Shadwell gave Timon a fiancée who deserted him and a mistress who stood by him and committed suicide over his dead body.

There was no printing of Shakespeare's play in a Quarto edition. Heminge and Condell accepted it for the First Folio, possibly with some hesitation and to fill a gap. It must have reached the unfortunate printer in a messy and baffling condition. Prose and verse are confused. The writing swerves from the tremendous to the trivial. This has caused editors to suspect a feeble collaborator or the intermittent inclusion of Shakespeare's notes scribbled for re-writing when he had recovered his energy or his interest in a story which he was failing to handle as he wanted. In many passages Shakespeare's incomparable mastery of words is unquestionably there, especially in the raging anger of a misanthrope which comes near to mania when the two whores appear.

There are those who believe that Shakespeare was always a cool self-possessed impersonal dramatist who took his themes from the sins and sufferings of men as raw material for his consummately skilful service of his colleagues and the theatre. If that was so we are wrong to suppose that he allowed his private life to intrude and that he put his own joys and griefs into the work professionally supplied to a company for which new plays had continually to be found. In his carefully considered handling of *Timon of Athens* for the Arden series of editions Mr H. J. Oliver took this line and disputed my view of the play. He maintained that 'Timon's misanthropy, like everything else in Shakespeare's plays, is part of a dramatized situation and is in no sense a lyrical statement of the poet's own beliefs'. So the shattering poignancy of young Arthur's illness in *King John* must also be taken as completely detached from the death of Hamnet Shakespeare.

I cannot share this view of a wholly uncommitted poet and prefer Bernard Shaw's opinion that 'with the plays and sonnets in our hands we know more about Shakespeare than we do about Dickens or Thackeray'. The last two acts of *Timon of Athens* are a document in madness. The frenzied vehemence in Timon's outbursts as well as the failure to finish the play and put it in order do not prove madness in the author. But they compel me to find strong signs of extreme fatigue, of intense emotional strain, and of an agonised revulsion when sexual debauchery and its effects were bedevilling Shakespeare's mind.

At the end of Act III Timon has retired in a ferocious despair from his now detested Athens to the solitude of the woods. I cannot regard what follows as a normal example of play-writing in which the dramatist is portraying with efficiency but in detachment the pains of a distressed misanthrope. Timon's speeches are not a playwright's exercise. They are an explosion. The denunciation of mankind, womankind, and their sensuality is savage and searing; they out-range the outbursts even of the tormented and at last demented Lear. When sex is the theme the loathing of a foul world goes boiling into a fevered foulness of its own. Moreover the scalding speeches on this subject have nothing to do with Timon's case. That is a point of primary importance. They are as irrelevant to his ruin as they are exceptional in their rancour.

His tragedy is that of a rich Athenian who has poured out his wealth on fawning, flattering parasites. They call him Lord Timon and noble Timon while they batten on his bounty which comes near to lunacy in its reckless extravagance and spend-thrift exhibitionism. When he has squandered all his money he starts to borrow and at last to beg. He relies on some return for his previous charity. The contemptible beneficiaries will do nothing for him. The sycophants and cadgers are by no means poor and could easily save him from sinking in the financial morass of his own creation. But they have hearts of stone. Their ingratitude is as callous as his generosity has been profuse. In his destitution he turns vegetarian hermit, digging up roots to eat, finding gold which he now despises and gives away, and damning everything and everybody with the vigour of a well-fed, full-fleshed man primed with the strongest of liquor. His mind is failing but his tongue is not.

There have so far been no women in the story. No avaricious mistress has been his ruin. No harlot harpy fleeced him. No play could have been more sexless. When Timon arranges a masque for his guests the female dancers are Amazons, not nymphs of seductive beauty. Then another infuriated exile from Athens, Alcibiades, comes to the woods 'in warlike manner' purposing to sack the city which has wronged him. With him are two women of whom Timon takes, without reason, the worst view. Of one he says curtly

This fell whore of thine
Hath in her more destruction than thy sword,
For all her cherubin look.

He is accusing her of spreading syphilis and soon he is urging both the women to infect the whole city, including its 'rose-cheeked youth'. Her answer is short and pertinent. 'Thy lips rot off.' No more. That gives Timon his cue for his tirades against lechery and for inciting the two women to infect the whole of Athens with their pestilence. The subject of the pox, the name given in Shakespeare's time to both the chief forms of venereal disease, dominates Timon's mind which can hardly be called wandering since it is so much concentrated on harlotry and the physical plagues of the brothel. The symptoms of the afflictions are mentioned in detail, the agues, blains, ulcerous sores, the baldness and blindness, the collapse of the nose, the final impotence. All kinds of men are to be the victims of their lechery.

> Be whores still;
> And he whose pious breath seeks to convert you,
> Be strong in whore, allure him, burn him up;
> Let your close fire predominate his smoke,
> And be no turncoats . . .
> Whore still;
> Paint till a horse may mire upon your face
> A pox of wrinkles!

The harping on sex and the 'sugared game' with the melting down of youth in beds of lust continues when a churlish, cynical philosopher called Apemantus comes back into the play.

When Timon is denouncing the corrupting power of gold he is talking to the point. He has been ruined by the greed of those who feasted on his riches. His vice is of vanity. No 'daughter of the game', as far as we are told, has allured and burned him up. Yet the two women with Alcibiades, whom he at once addresses as whores and sluts, provoke such a torrent of sexual obsession that one would expect to be told that Timon has been brought to disaster by haunting the stews. Is it unreasonable to think that Shakespeare was on the razor's edge when he poured this concentration of venom into the great speeches of the play and could not bother or find the strength to complete the episodes which had not excited him?

Shakespeare had much to say on this gruesome subject. In his brothel-scenes and in the railings of Thersites in *Troilus and Cressida* there is a jocosity offensive to us though probably not to his play-going public. In Timon's case there is no searching for a coarse laugh. There is an appalling accuracy. As Dr R. M. Simpson put it in his book 'Shakespeare and Medicine': 'No more vivid clinical picture of the tertiary stage of syphilis has ever been written than when Timon addresses the two courtesans on how to take their revenge on men.' The detail is extended to the attempted cures as well as to the terrifying symptoms. Pistol had mentioned 'the powdering tub of infamy'. Timon refers to 'the tub-fast and the diet'. Part of the treatment, as Dr Simpson explains, was the use of 'a tub in which the patient was exposed to hot fumes from a powder of cinnabar'.

There has been the suggestion that Shakespeare himself had been infected by the Dark Lady. If he had remained familiar with Lucy Morgan he had abundant opportunity for being stricken with one pox or another. But this is a groundless supposition. As has been pointed out there is no indication of a long and physically destructive illness in his life. The break-down, if there was one, was psychopathic and did not last. Any citizen of Elizabethan London, especially if he lived and worked in Southwark, a district as well known for its prostitutes as for its players, could not escape seeing the human wreckage caused by reckless indulgence in 'the sugared game'. To be afflicted with sex-nausea was not remarkable in a sensitive observer of the Bankside population.

Shakespeare's repulsion did not vanish with the years. He calmed down, but there were things he could not forget. There lingered too, even in his supposedly tranquil maturity, an obsession with sexual jealousy and its virulence. In *Othello* he had not said the last word about that. The Moor's guilt is that of a man deemed noble but in fact so stupid that he will not sift the evidence of Desdemona's alleged infidelity. In the later plays the censure, almost hysterical in its violence, is directed by jealous husbands, not at particular women, but at the sex in general. When suspicion has been aroused in a single instance the con-

demnation is sweeping. The entire feminine sex is damned as
incurable in its licentiousness. When Posthumus has been
persuaded by Iachimo's lies of Imogen's infidelity he does not
merely condemn her. Out comes the usual indictment of the
entire sex,

> For there's no motion
> That tends to vice in man, but I affirm
> It is a woman's part: be it lying, note it,
> The woman's; flattering, hers; deceiving, hers;
> Lust and rank thoughts, hers, hers; revenges, hers;
> Ambitions, covetings, change of prides, disdain,
> Nice longing, slanders, mutability,
> All faults that may be nam'd, nay, that hell knows,
> Why, hers, in part or all; but rather, all;
> For even to vice
> They are not constant, but are changing stil
> One vice, but of a minute old, for one
> Not half so old as that. I'll write against them,
> Detest them, curse them:—yet 'tis greater skill
> In a true hate, to pray they have their will:
> The very devils cannot plague them better.
>
> (*Cymbeline*, II.v.22–37.)

Why does Posthumus talk of writing about the wickedness of
women? He was, we are told, 'put to all learnings' in his boyhood,
but he is not an author. Something slipped out while Shakespeare
was fuming over female viciousness. It is most revealing that
writing is more than once mentioned when that subject is in
mind. Berowne, scathing in his wholly unjustified condemnation
of Rosaline as promiscuous, writes sonnets: Ulysses, inveighing
against wanton women because Cressida is wanton, is made to
say:

> Fie, fie upon her!
> There's language in her eye, her cheek, her lip,
> Nay, her foot speaks; her wanton spirits look out
> At every joint and motive of her body.
> O, these encounterers, so glib of tongue,

> *That give a coasting welcome ere it comes,*
> *And wide unclasp the tables of their thoughts*
> *To every ticklish reader! set them down*
> *For sluttish spoils of opportunity*
> *And daughters of the game.*
>
> (*Troilus and Cressida*, IV.v.54–63.)

Setting down here intimates, if it does not expressly say, writing down. And it is they, the sex, not she, who is to be thus labelled.

Then there is Leontes, some of whose ugly remarks on treachery and seduction have been quoted in a previous chapter. He does not limit himself to traducing the innocent Hermione. Out comes the familiar generalisation,

>   *Should all despair*
> *That have revolted wives, the tenth of mankind*
> *Would hang themselves. Physic for't there's none.*
> *It is a bawdy planet, that will strike*
> *Where 'tis predominant; and 'tis powerful, think it,*
> *From east, west, north, and south: be it concluded,*
> *No barricado for a belly; know't;*
> *It will let in and out the enemy*
> *With bag and baggage: many thousand on's*
> *Have the disease, and feel't not.*
>
> (*The Winter's Tale*, I.ii.200–210.)

When Leontes continues to rave about 'meeting noses' and 'kissing with inside lips', these supposed preludes to adultery are not attributed only to Hermione. They are 'theirs, theirs only, that would unseen be wicked'.

In one late play and that of the finest there was a break with this revulsion against sex. The nausea has passed for a while. In the first scene of *Antony and Cleopatra* the Egyptian queen is immediately described as a strumpet and a lustful gipsy, but the sensual pair who gave all and let an empire tumble for their passion win Shakespeare's heart, rise to a kind of splendour in their ruin, and are transported to an afterworld in which, still sovereign and in death superb, they will 'make the ghosts gaze'.

Antony and Cleopatra contains the summit of Shakespeare's writing about love. He was well away from that razor edge. The scolding and cursing of women has ended for a while.

He may have written it away from London. Amid the crash of kingdoms and in a play whose imagery was repeatedly drawn from things immense, the sun and moon, the firmament, the terrestrial world and its oceans, there are sudden allusions to country matters possibly caused by some glimpse of the garden, the river Avon, or the farmyard. Cleopatra's desertion with her fleet and flight is very queerly compared to the running of a mare on heat and to a cow in a similar condition in June, while Antony, quitting the fight which she has left, is likened to a doting mallard which flies high in the mating season. Such metaphors are not so likely to sweep into the mind of a man working in the confinement of a city. Wherever he was he could for a while forget the sins of a whole sex and glorify the frailty of one member of it, the 'lass unparalleled'.

CHAPTER XIII

Home in the Evening

WHAT INSPIRED the magnificence of Antony and Cleopatra must be guess-work. It is no conjecture that Shakespeare went back to join and remain with his wife and daughters. He had been an unfaithful husband. It is well-nigh impossible to believe that the Sonnets were an abstract composition. There were other affairs too if we believe that tale of his anticipating Richard Burbage in keeping an amorous engagement. This may be what is called 'a smoking-room story' but it is contemporary and not one of the legends invented in the eighteenth century when anything, true or false, about Shakespeare was regarded as good and saleable news.

John Manningham, a law-student at the Middle Temple, kept a diary which has survived. To him we owe the information of a performance of *Twelfth Night* in the Middle Temple Hall in 1602 and also the anecdote about Shakespeare's speed in seizing an opportunity. He recounted that a woman play-goer 'grewe so farr in liking' with Richard Burbage when he played the part of Richard III that she arranged for him to come to her by night. 'Shakespeare overhearing their conclusion, went before, was intertained, and at his game ere Burbidge came. The message being brought that Richard the Third was at the dore, Shakespeare caused returne to be made that William the Conquerour was before *Richard the Third*. Shakespeare's name was William.' The first to quote that neat retort to a frustrated rival who was also a colleague would get a merited laugh at the Mermaid. True or not, Manningham's anecdote suggests that Shakespeare had no reputation for a secluded austerity in his London life.

The long absences from Stratford were at last over; he came

back to be a father to the daughters of whom he had seen so little for so long. Frank Harris suggested that with his memories of busy city days and glamorous nights he loathed the renewal of small-town and rural existence. That is most improbable. He had his boundless interest in the ways of all men and women and his searching eye for every quirk of character. He noted and enjoyed the minutiae as well as the major beauties of nature in the field and garden. His verbal flower-painting in the later plays is rich in detail and warm with delight. Men of his receptive kind are not bored. It is the dullard who finds the world dull. Nicholas Rowe, Shakespeare's editor and first biographer stated that: 'The latter part of his Life was spent, as all Men of Good Sense will wish their's to be, in Ease, Retirement, and the Conversation of his friends.' When the emotional storms had passed he did not, if this be a true report, yawn fretfully through the few years that were left. If there were fools about he could laugh. To those with a sense of humour life is always a satisfying meal, if not a perpetual feast.

His son-in-law was far from being a fool. Susanna had chosen well. Shakespeare was deeply interested in all kinds of illnesses and their cures. Close to him was Dr Hall's dispensary with the patients calling for consultation. It is significant that one of the last medical men to appear in the plays, Cerimon in *Pericles*, is highly praised and is portrayed as happy in his work.

> 'Tis known, I ever
> Have studied physic, through which secret art,
> By turning o'er authorities, I have—
> Together with my practice—made familiar
> To me and to my aid the blest infusions
> That dwell in vegetives, in metals, stones;
> And I can speak of the disturbances
> That nature works, and of her cures; which doth give me
> A more content in course of true delight
> Than to be thirsty after tottering honour,
> Or tie my treasure up in silken bags,
> To please the fool and death.

(Pericles, III.ii.24–35.)

This exactly fits in with Dr Hall's known skill in using minerals and giving 'vegetive infusions' for the relief of the prevailing scurvy and does more than hint at the personal portraiture of a well-regarded doctor who was content with the moderate rewards of his country practice. Cerimon is a thoroughly sympathetic character. To call on his daughter and son-in-law at Hall's Croft was not to be in tiresome or uncongenial company.

Dr Dover Wilson alludes to the view, without rejecting it, that Shakespeare was devoted to a Perdita of his own in Judith 'who was living in surroundings far more resembling those of the fourth act of *The Winter's Tale* than anything which could be found at court'. The heroines of the last comedies are charmers. When they were written Judith had not yet caused trouble over her choice of a husband. According to this estimate of her qualities she might be the model for Marina and Miranda too. But if she was so fascinating to her father, why were the marriageable men so little attracted and her wedding so long delayed? I do not see her as what the young men of today might call a 'honey'.

If we must look for family portraiture in the plays of Shakespeare's domestic retirement, what are we to make of Prospero? Many have seen in that aristocratic necromancer a 'portrait of the artist nearing fifty'. Prospero, it is true, is made the vehicle of exquisite poetry in which Shakespeare's hand is manifestly revealing some of his finest hours of writing. There is pessimism blended with the beauty of his speeches. Shakespeare was writing a comedy of romance with passages suited to the royal wedding of Princess Elizabeth, but he included the sad vision of a doomed world as perishable as ours will be when the hydrogen bombs are being scattered about the globe in plenty.

Prospero is a confused character, finally merciful to his old enemies and renouncing vengeance, but at other times grimly punitive. Sir John Gielgud's memorable performance did not let us forget that. When Ariel reasonably protests that his promised liberty is being withheld Prospero threatens him that he will rend an oak and peg him

in its knotty entrails till
Thou'st howl'd away three winters.

He calls the excellent young Ferdinand a liar unjustly, maltreats him with his magic powers and puts him to forced labour. Prospero is a famous part and many of our greatest actors have played it. But I have never felt that they were enjoying it. Also he is plainly depicted as a bore. When he is telling Miranda his life-story he three times accuses her of not listening and finally commands her to stop fidgeting with his sharp admonition to 'sit still and hear the last'. Shortly after that she dozes off. Prospero is so fond of his tale of old wrongs and of life on the island that he proposes to tell it all over again to his pardoned captives. He promises to make the narrative 'go quick away', but Miranda could have her doubts about that and doubtless preferred a stroll on the sands with Ferdinand.

If Shakespeare did see himself as Prospero, which I strongly doubt, he seems here to be ridiculing his own loquacity. Was he indeed becoming a talkative codger who wearied his wife and daughters with his reminiscences? Shakespeare has been charged with a number of faults by various biographers, including sensuality, snobbishness, and avarice. That Shakespeare was a bore is an astonishing accusation. Yet, if he saw himself as Prospero, it can be reasonably made. But I cannot believe that either his family or his neighbours ever began to regard him as the Nuisance of New Place.

If the warmly approved character of Cerimon was suggested by Susanna's husband there was no ill-feeling in that quarter. Undoubtedly Dr Hall was strongly Protestant and contentious in the affairs of the parish church. Susanna was described in her epitaph as 'wise to salvation'. Yet in the Sackville papers in which the misconduct of Judith's husband was discovered there is mention of Susanna as a recusant charged with failing to receive the sacrament. The Stratford 'act-book' records that on May 5, 1606 twenty-one persons were charged with this offence. Most of those named are known to have had Catholic sympathies. There was indignation all over the country at the activities of 'popishly affected' persons which culminated in the Gunpowder Plot. Those avoiding attendance at the church 'by law established' were noted as suspects and had to face local question-

ing. As one whose grand-mother was an Arden Susanna may
have been on the black list. On the other hand it is possible that
her absenteeism was caused by puritan sympathies. The recusants
were extremists of two kinds holding contrasted beliefs. If she
had retained a loyalty to 'the old religion' she abandoned it
promptly since she married John Hall a year later and he was
most unlikely to have taken a 'popishly affected' wife.

The matter is of interest for our understanding of Shakespeare's
relations with the Halls. The evidence shows that the doctor was
keenly Protestant, but it does not prove him to have been one of
the rigorous and bigoted puritans who regarded all sports and
entertainments as sinful and denounced the theatre as Satan's
workshop. If his views on the pleasures of life had been so narrow
there could have been a very sultry climate of opinion with
thunder in the air oppressing the two homes. But of this there is
no sign and Shakespeare's will proves his continuing friendship
with Dr Hall. Susanna was the chief beneficiary and there was no
Married Women's Property Act to protect her rights in the
legacy. To endow her was to endow her husband.

Yet there are some who think that Dr Hall was completely
intolerant of the play-house life and converted Susanna to his
acid puritanism. Why else, it is argued, did Shakespeare's papers
disappear after his death? It is alleged that when the Halls inherited
the manuscripts of Shakespeare's plays they destroyed them. The
answer is simple. These papers which, if somehow preserved,
would now be worth colossal sums of money, were not theirs to
keep because they were not there at all.

The dramatists had no rights in their own works when they
sold them to a company of actors. Shakespeare as a sharer among
the King's Men had his interest in all their takings. He did not
retain a property on what he wrote and he took no trouble to
ensure publication. To us with our appreciation of his unique
supremacy in his craft that seems an almost incredible modesty
or carelessness; but he did not think of his plays as immortal
and invaluable. It is wrong to visualise New Place in the likeness
of a modern author's home full of correspondence files, carbon
copies, and press cuttings. If he sent up the manuscripts of his

last plays to London they went away and stayed with the King's Men. It was the world's good fortune that they were still in the players' hands for Heminge and Condell to edit seven years after the playwright's death.

The company kept the original drafts, now somewhat impolitely known as the author's 'foul papers'. A fair copy had to be made for submission to the Master of the Revels who acted as censor with his eye most keenly directed to a play's political implications. If his 'allowance' was obtained it went to the company's book-keeper. Sometimes the copying was done by the dramatist himself, sometimes by the book-keeper, and sometimes it was handed to a professional scrivener who had to be paid. Extra copies were an extravagance. Accordingly the actors did not get the whole text for study and rehearsals. They were given their lines and cues on small sheets. The text of a play by Shakespeare may have been limited to his own 'foul papers', which according to Heminge and Condell did not at all deserve that adjective, and to one or two copies made by the scriveners. Certainly 'spares' would be very few, kept in London and carefully guarded by the book-keeper against the piracy of unauthorised printing and the risk of poaching by rival companies.

It is most unlikely that Shakespeare, when he wrote a play at Stratford, had a scrivener at hand. If he took the trouble to make his own fair copy needed for the censor and book-keeper in London it would have to be sent there by the carrier. The document was despatched and that was the end of that as far as the book-shelves and cupboards in New Place were concerned. Before it went he could have read his work to his family if they were interested. But it was not his to keep, nor was it Susanna's to inherit. His work in print found in the home could only be some of the better and approved Quartos and the two long poems published by his fellow-Stratfordian in London, Richard Field. The Halls inherited house, fields, and furniture, not manuscripts.

Thorpe's edition of the Sonnets, which did not appear till 1609, would, one might think, have met with a brisk sale. The author was in fashion. The vogue of the Sonnet had dwindled but it was by no means dead and here was rich reading for the gossips of the day eager to discuss the persons involved. But there was no further edition till 1640 and there were no immediate allusions in contemporary writing to indicate great interest in Thorpe's production. That is surprising. The usual and natural explanation is withdrawal or a ban on further printing imposed either by Shakespeare himself or by one of the earls concerned in the story, which was deemed better forgotten, however memorable the poetry.

It was not a book which Shakespeare would care to have about the house. A moderate literacy has been assumed in his wife and Judith. Susanna was more likely to be a comprehending reader if she had come across it. The Sonnets are cryptic and would have been very difficult as well as very unpleasant reading for Anne if she could grapple with them at all. Thorpe's Quarto would be kept out of sight. Probably, like the manuscripts of the plays, it was not on the premises at all.

Anne had had her satisfaction of the fine house and garden and of the accumulating property. There was none of the fretting about money in hand which had been inevitable in her early years of marriage. If she cared about her social ranking and the opinions of her neighbours, as is likely, she was the wife of William Shakespeare, Gentleman of Stratford. She might be concerned about the long delay in Judith's mating, but Susanna's marriage had been creditable and a happy one. The doctor's illness of body and ill-tempered quarrels with the council came long after Anne had gone. She must have been bewildered by all that had happened since the early years of hardship. When she died in 1623 she had known more than twenty-five years of the prosperity which had come to her from London. No doubt she scarcely understood what her man had in fact done and the full nature of his success. As the years of her widowhood mounted there would be stiffening of the limbs and possibly clouding of the mind. She could have echoed some words of Prospero's, if she had known them, 'Bear with my weakness. My old brain is troubled.' But she was the mother-in-law of an esteemed doctor and sharing her home with him and his wife. She had attention and security. There was no need to worry until Will was struck by that fatal but not cruelly protracted illness in the spring of 1616. There were seven years more. She had her right of dower, her kindred with her, and strange things to remember on the winding road from Shottery to New Place. She may have been looked up to; she was certainly looked after as she settled down to be Anne-Sit-By-The-Fire.

Principal books consulted

LIVES

Shakespeare. By Peter Alexander.
Shakespeare. By Sir Edmund Chambers. Two Vols.
Shakespeare of London. By Margaret Chute.
Shakespeare, Man and Artist. By Edward Fripp. Two Vols.
The Life of Shakespeare. By F. E. Halliday.
Shakespeare, The Poet and His Background. By Peter Quennell.
Shakespeare. By M. M. Reese.
Shakespeare. By A. L. Rowse.
Shakespeare's Southampton. By A. L. Rowse.
The Essential Shakespeare. By J. Dover Wilson.

GENERAL

In Shakespeare's Warwickshire. By Oliver Baker.
The Irresistible Theatre. By W. Bridges-Adams.
Sir Philip Sidney and the English Renaissance. By John Buxton.
A Book of Masques. Cambridge University Press.
Shakespeare in Warwickshire. By Mark Eccles.
English Girlhood at School. By Dorothy Gardiner.
Shakespeare's Audience. By Alfred Harbage.
The Man Shakespeare. By Frank Harris.
The Women of Shakespeare. By Frank Harris.
Shakespeare's Public. By Martin Holmes.
Shakespeare's Sonnets Dated. By Leslie Hotson.
The First Night of Twelfth Night. By Leslie Hotson.
Shakespeare's Motley. By Leslie Hotson.
Mr. W. H. By Leslie Hotson.
Elizabeth the Great. By Elizabeth Jenkins.
Shakespeare and His Circle. By C. Martin Mitchell.
Shakespeare's Legal and Political Background. By George W. Keeton.
Shakespeare's Sonnets. By A. L. Rowse.

The Dark Lady of the Sonnets, Short Play and Preface. By G. Bernard Shaw.
Shakespeare and Medicine. By Dr R. R. Simpson.
Shakespeare's Blackfriars Playhouse. By Irwin Smith.
Shakespeare's Family. By Mrs C. C. Stopes.
The Court Masque. By Enid Welsford.
Shakespeare's Sonnets. Edited by J. Dover Wilson.
Middle Class Culture in Elizabethan England. By Louis B. Wright.

ENCYCLOPAEDIAS

A Shakespeare Encyclopaedia. Edited by Oscar J. Campbell and Edward
    G. Quinn.
A Shakespeare Companion. By F. E. Halliday.

    Most useful help has also been given by Dr Levi Fox, Director of
the Shakespeare Centre, Stratford-upon-Avon.

INDEX